IMAGES
of America

BROCKWAY AND LITTLE TOBY VALLEY

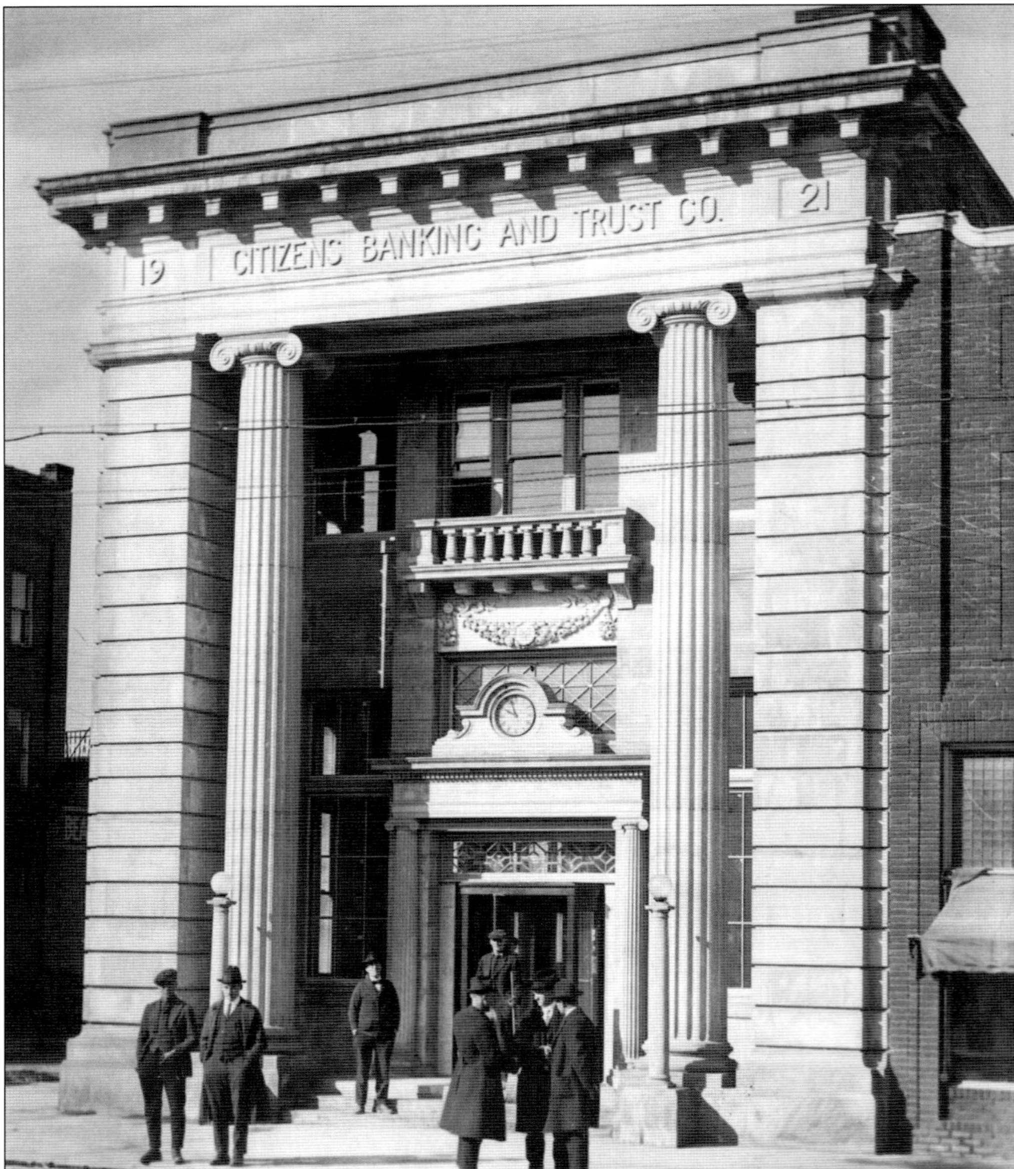

The Citizens Bank and Trust Company building was constructed in 1921. One of Brockway's landmark structures, it currently holds the Brockway Borough offices. The citizens take pride in the presentation of their town, especially during Brockway's Old-Fashioned Independence Day Celebration, during which thousands of visitors from across the region gather to participate in the festivities. (Taylor Memorial Museum of the Brockway Area Historical Society.)

On the Cover: The Buffalo, Rochester, and Pittsburgh Railway (BR&P) was constructed through Lower Toby Valley in 1883, with the last spike being driven in Brockwayville on February 24. The structure on the cover is the second BR&P depot, the first one being a wooden structure that was moved and eventually torn down. This new brick depot was constructed in 1913, and with recent additions is now being used as the "Brockwayville Depot" community center. (Brockway Area Historical Society.)

IMAGES
of America

BROCKWAY AND LITTLE TOBY VALLEY

John Keith

ARCADIA
PUBLISHING

ISBN 978-0-7385-7265-9

Published by Arcadia Publishing
Charleston SC, Chicago IL, Portsmouth NH, San Francisco CA

Printed in the United States of America

Library of Congress Control Number: 2009936363

For all general information contact Arcadia Publishing at:
Telephone 843-853-2070
Fax 843-853-0044
E-mail sales@arcadiapublishing.com
For customer service and orders:
Toll-Free 1-888-313-2665

Visit us on the Internet at www.arcadiapublishing.com

Dedicated to Wesley Alexander Keith, my son, with whom I hope to share all of the joys that the Little Toby Creek valley has shared with me

Contents

ACKNOWLEDGMENTS

A large portion of this book's text was sourced from Lew Reddinger's *Brockway Story*, published in 1986, and a thank-you is forwarded to him and the work of the Brockway Area Historical Society. The details Reddinger covers in his full narrative history are far too many to include in this book. The purpose of this book is to therefore enhance the story of Brockway through photographs that may not have been published in previous histories.

A big thank-you is expressed to editors Erin Vosgien and Tiffany Frary for answering all of the questions I sent them. A thank-you is sent to family and friends who hiked with me along the railroad grades and through the ghost towns of the valley. A huge thank-you is extended to my wife and baby boy for allowing me to spend hours and hours at local historical societies and in front of my computer scanning images and typing captions. I hope that the result is to their liking.

All images other than those noted are from the Taylor Memorial Museum of the Brockway Area Historical Society, founded in 1953 for the purpose of collecting historical data and artifacts to write a history of the town. Groundbreaking for a building occurred on April 7, 1972, and the museum opened on July 4, 1973. The Brockway Glass Company annex was added in 1992, and a second floor for storage was added in 2004. A small portion of the Brockway Glass Company annex was turned into a genealogy research center with hundreds of resources, copiers, microfilm readers, and computers. The entire Brockway(ville) Record that dates from 1887 is being digitized into a searchable format. Future plans for the museum include the rearranging of displays into a more chronological order, the creation of a "featured display" concept, the implementation of preservation of the thousands of photographs, documents and books, and the organization of a more extensive online research database. Anyone interested in joining the Brockway Area Historical Society to help accomplish these future plans should contact the society at (814) 265-8519 or at brockwayhistory@windstream.net.

Introduction

The origin of the Little Toby Creek valley follows that of many streams that drain northwestern Pennsylvania. As the great seas of hundreds of millions of years ago receded and returned, giant swamps full of tropic plants would become covered with sands and silts, grow again, and get covered again. These layers that formed during the Mississippian and Pennsylvanian periods of geologic time were responsible for the development of this region's rich coal deposits. The Appalachian Mountains, a chain of very old mountains that stretch along most of the East Coast, were formed when continental collisions forced the layers mentioned above to be pushed skyward and to fold, exposing layer after layer of sediment. It is speculated that the Appalachians reached the splendor of today's northern Rockies or Swiss Alps. Thousands of years of erosion by glaciers, freezing and melting of ice, rain and runoff has rounded the Appalachians to their current appearance.

Native American migration and inhabitance into western Pennsylvania occurred as early as 16,000 years ago, and most likely followed major rivers, allowing them to reach Little Toby Creek by means of the Ohio, Allegheny, and Clarion Rivers. Of the Five Nations of the Iroquois confederacy, it was the Seneca that roamed and scattered artifacts throughout Little Toby Valley. The first European in the area was Moravian missionary Rev. Christian Frederick Post, traveling from Clearfield, over Boone Mountain, and down Little Toby Creek to the Clarion River in 1758. Skirmishes between Seneca Indians, such as the famous Chief Cornplanter and the French and British, would continue from the 1750s until the American Revolution of 1776.

The late 1790s witnessed the first settlement in Jefferson County at Port Barnett, just southeast of Brookville. A General Wade and his Lieutenant Slade settled near the mouth of Little Toby Creek at about the same time. The War of 1812 forced settlers from the north into Elk County. The Reverend Dr. Jonathan Nichols of Connecticut, the first educated and cultured settler of the area, settled near present Brandy Camp. Philetus, Joel, and Asaph M. Clarke, three generations of the Clarke family of New York State, arrived with other families and settled the village of Kersey in 1819. The Clarkes would eventually move downstream to what would become Brockport and begin construction of the first sawmill on Little Toby Creek in 1821.

A gentleman by the name of John Smith Brockway, who amusingly had no Brockway family blood in him, purchased 640 acres of land at the Indiana County Courthouse in 1821 for "$3,245½." In 1822, John's "brothers" James and Alonzo Brockway moved in and built cabins along Little Toby Creek at the present Rocky Grill Restaurant and at the present Borough Building, respectfully. The area became known as the town of Brockwayville, situated in northeastern Snyder Township, Jefferson County. The third Brockway brother Chauncey Sr. purchased land in Brandy Camp from his father-in-law Jonathan Nichols. Soon to follow and establish lines of communication were the Shaffers, Walborns, Bennetts, Frosts, Walshs, Pendletons, Ingalls, and Fermans. The first post office along Little Toby Valley was established at Helen Mills in 1828 by Philetus Clarke. Alonzo Brockway established a post office in Brockwayville the following year, placing the Brockway name on the map for the first time.

With the expanding need for building supplies came the sound of the first water-powered sawmills to the Little Toby Creek valley. By 1829, three such sawmills powered by Little Toby were established. From here, the lumber would be floated on rafts to the Clarion and Allegheny Rivers, on to the city of Pittsburgh and beyond. The first of many thrilling rafting adventures that originated on Little Toby occurred during the spring flood of May 1830.

By 1836, Dr. Asaph Milton Clarke, now known as the "father of Brockway," took it upon himself to lay out the growing town of Brockwayville into organized plots. Over the next 25 years, many new settlers moved into the valley, most of which were lumbermen who wanted to make their living cutting the magnificent stands of white pine and Eastern hemlock. One of these was Norman B. Lane in 1857, for which the village of Lanes Mills is named, and whose beautiful house still stands over 150 years later at the southern end of Broad Street. Brockwayville produced several Civil War veterans, including Capt. Nichols M. Brockway. Son of Chauncey Brockway Sr., "Nick" Brockway also engaged in lumbering in 1878 after buying Peter Galusha's sawmill approximately 3 miles north of Brockwayville. Many lumber towns were established during the late stages of the rafting era of lumbering, and a majority of them lasted through the logging railroad era of lumbering. Small, versatile steam locomotives such as the Shays, Climaxes, and Heislers were used to haul cars of logs along steep, windy tracks from deep in the woods to the log ponds. Cars loaded with hemlock bark would be shipped to tanneries that popped up in several surrounding towns.

The people of Brockwayville and Little Toby Valley must have been absolutely ecstatic when the first steam locomotive rolled into town in 1883 along the newly completed Buffalo, Rochester, and Pittsburgh Railway (BR&P). Railroads established connections to the outside world, allowed the hard-to-reach stands of virgin timber to be cut, and also allowed the industry of coal mining to become the governing industry of the valley. Brockwayville would eventually have the BR&P Railway; the Ridgway and Clearfield (R&C) branch of the Pennsylvania Railroad; the Pittsburg, Shawmut, and Northern Railroad; the Pittsburg and Shawmut Railroad; and the Erie Railroad hauling lumber, coal, and passengers in and out of its once-rather-isolated valley. The earliest coal mines were established in and around Beechtree to the south and Kersey to the northeast. New coal mines popped up all over the hills surrounding Brockwayville and upstream along Little Toby Creek. The dawn of the 20th century saw clay industries moving into the Brockwayville area, including a clay tile plant at Drummond and a brick factory at Shawmut along Mead Run. The Brockway Clay Company would construct its clay tile facility to the northwest of town in 1926.

Another turn-of-the-century industry to be established in Brockwayville was the glass industry. The Brockwayville Glass Company opened in 1897 on the southeast side of town between the BR&P Railway and the R&C Railroad, but failed quickly due to poor glass-making ingredients. The next 10 years were up and down for the factory, as it was leased or sold to several different companies. It was not until a group of 12 businessmen put most of their life savings into the factory that the Brockway Machine Bottle Company produced its first glass jar on October 14, 1907. Through the efforts of the board of directors and the factory workers themselves, the company became incorporated as the Brockway Glass Company, had a second glass plant constructed in the village of Crenshaw, and eventually had glass plants built across the nation.

Many businesses sprung up along the streets of Brockwayville in the early 20th century. The name "Brockwayville" was shortened to "Brockway" in 1925. Photographs and descriptions of the businesses mentioned and many other establishments are found throughout the rest of this book.

One

Upper Toby Valley

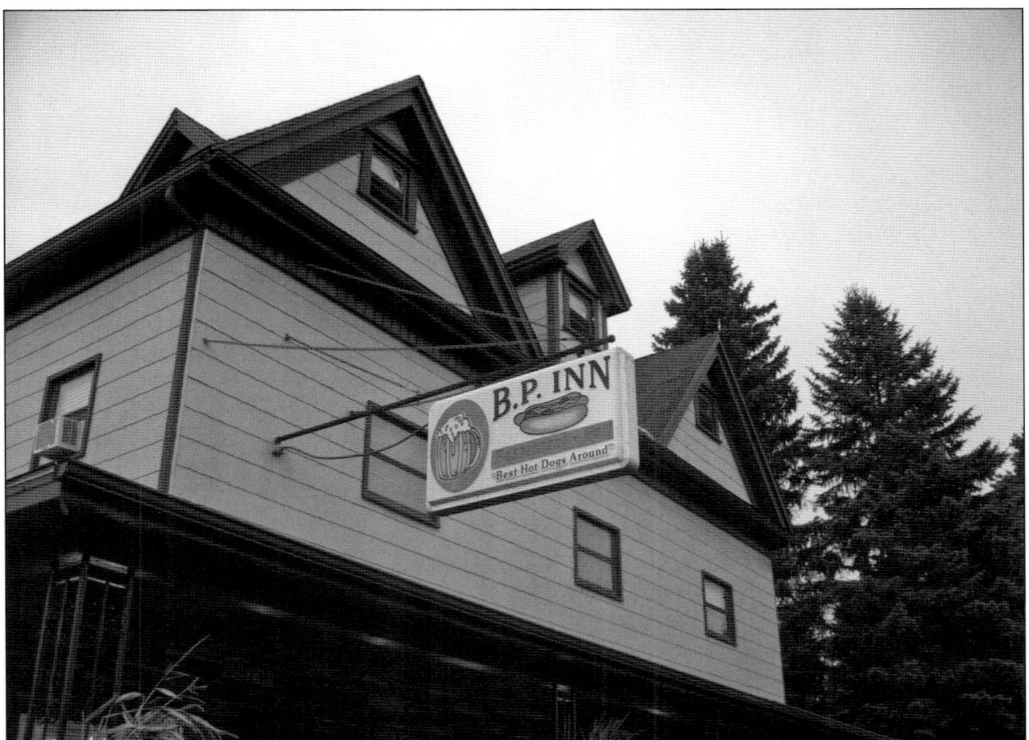

The Upper Toby Valley region stretches southwest from the headwaters of Little Toby Creek in Elk County to the line between Snyder Township, Jefferson County, and Brockway borough. This chapter also includes the settlements along Rattlesnake Creek south of Brockway. The image above is of the BP Inn, a favorite stop along U.S. Route 219 along the Elk–Jefferson County line.

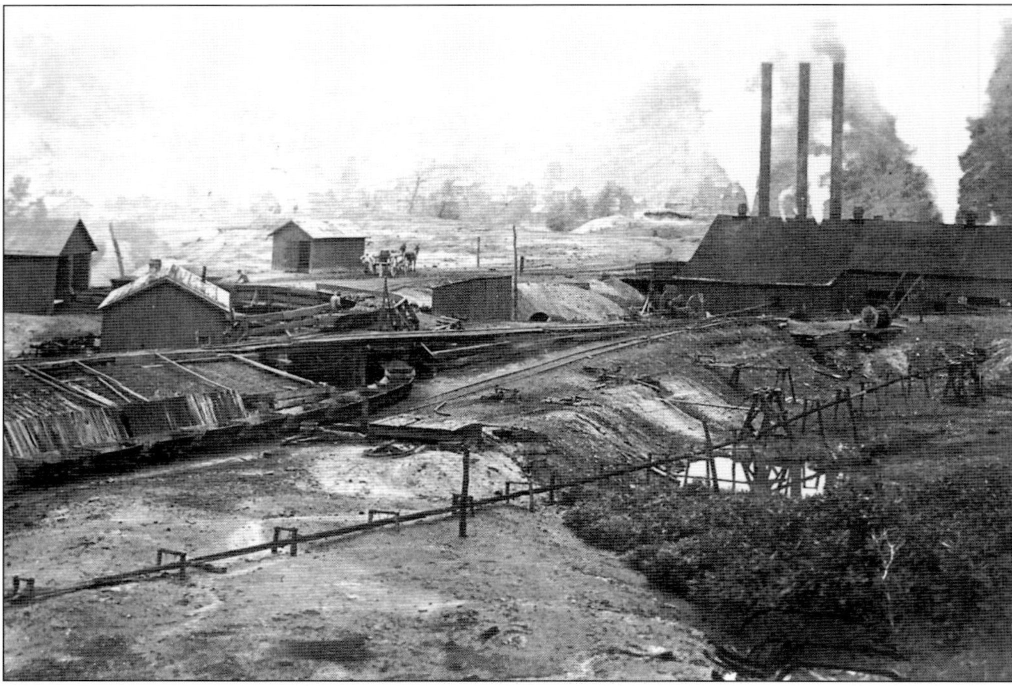

Coal mining has played a major role in the history of upper Little Toby Creek. This photograph shows the Coal Hollow mining complex, which was part of the Erie Railroad's 13,000-acre purchase of bituminous coal fields east of Brockwayville. The first mining in the area was by Dr. Charles R. Earley, who opened the Dagus Mines in 1848, less than a mile north of Coal Hollow. (Harriet Moyer.)

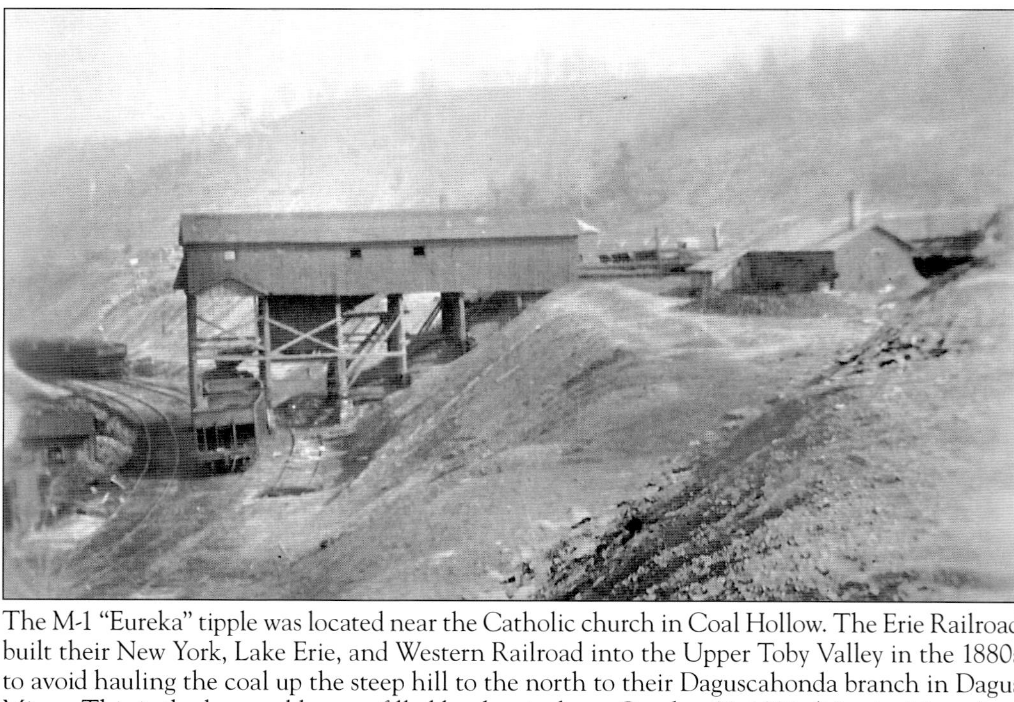

The M-1 "Eureka" tipple was located near the Catholic church in Coal Hollow. The Erie Railroad built their New York, Lake Erie, and Western Railroad into the Upper Toby Valley in the 1880s to avoid hauling the coal up the steep hill to the north to their Daguscahonda branch in Dagus Mines. This is the last coal hopper filled by the tipple on October 31, 1924. (Harriet Moyer.)

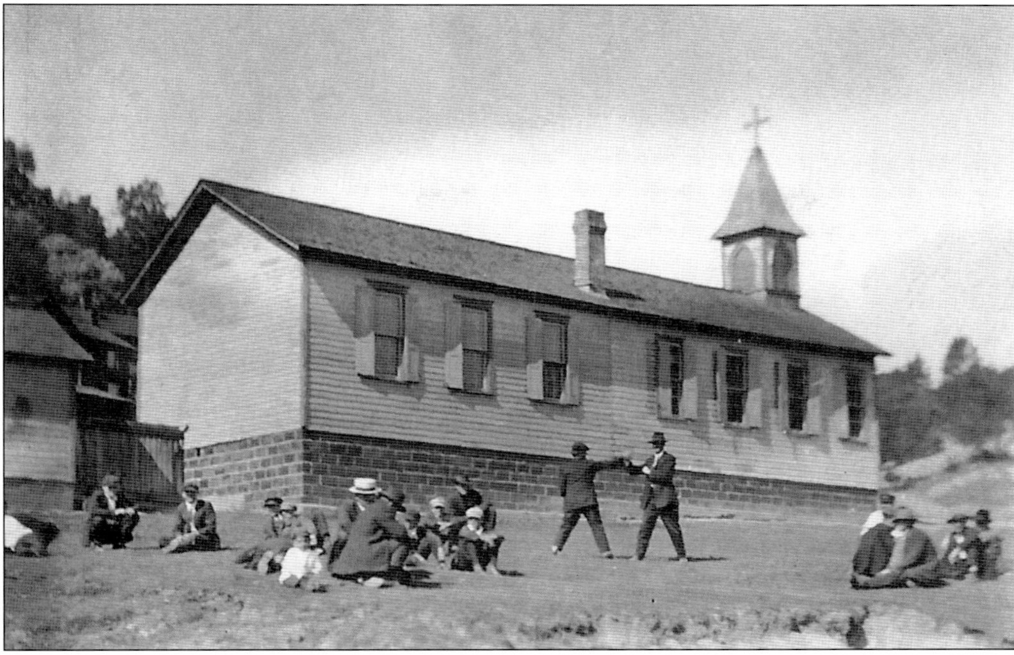

The Guardian Angel Roman Catholic Church sits high on a hill overlooking the small mining village of Coal Hollow. The structure still stands in its original position today, but is no longer used for worship. Of interest in this photograph is the boxing match that is occurring on the front lawn of the church. (Harriet Moyer.)

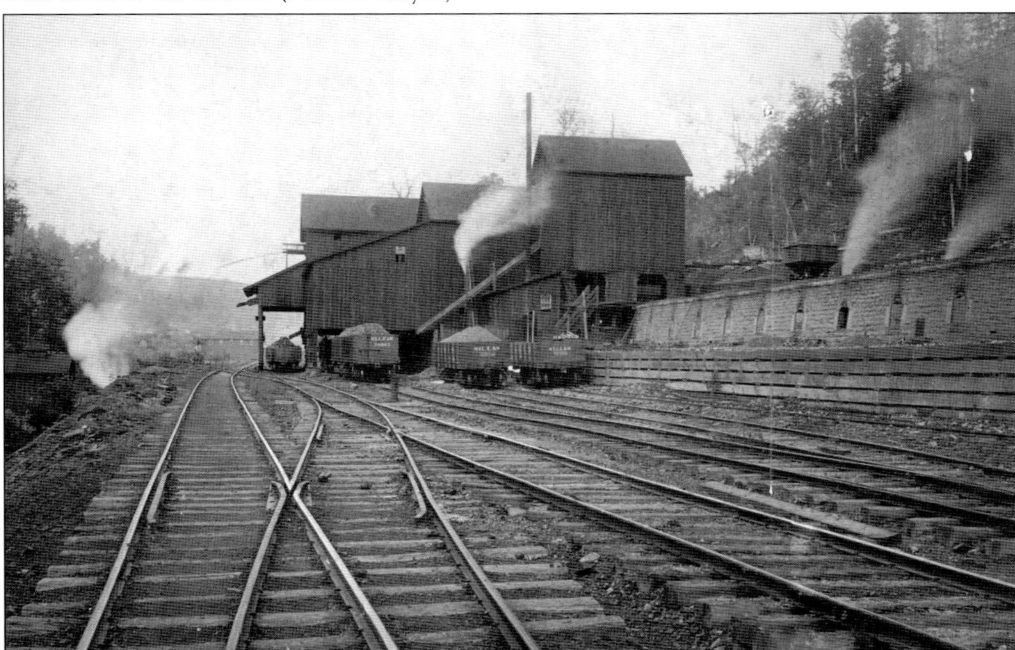

The coal in Upper Toby Valley was known for being good steam coal, but not always good coking coal. It looks like the Erie Railroad's mining subsidiary, the Northwest Mining and Exchange Company, found a rare patch of the right kind of coal to turn into coke. These coke ovens were built beside tipple No. 2 in the village of Toby in the 1890s.

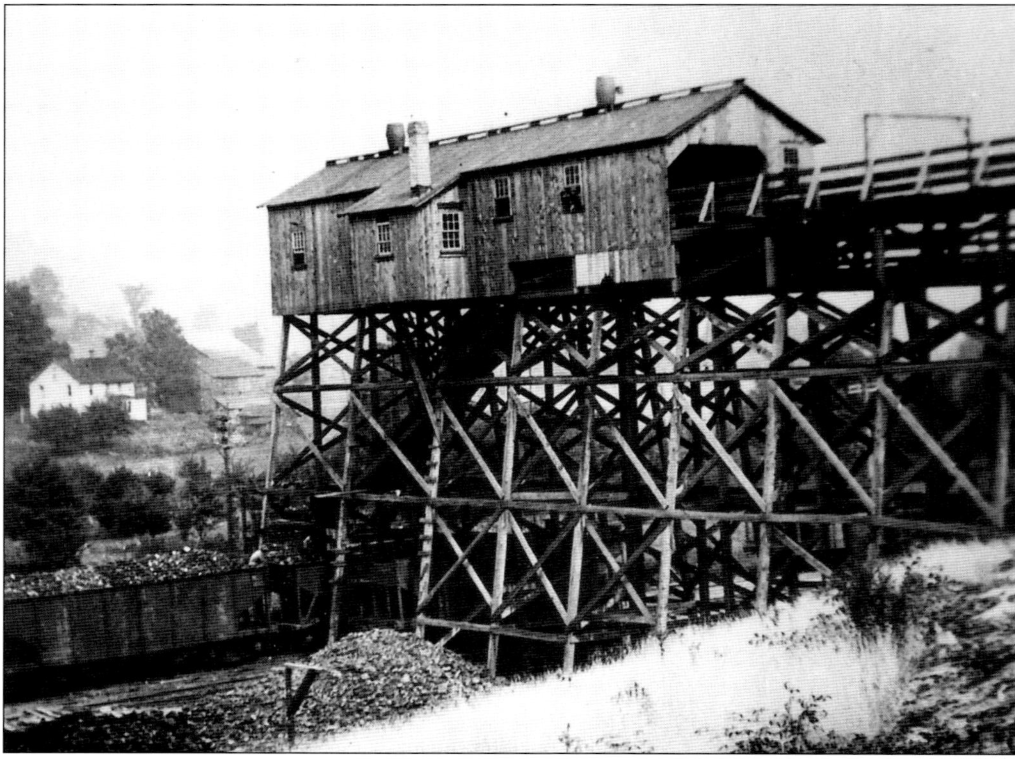

A second coal tipple in the village of Toby was the limestone tipple, located at the mouth of Limestone Run, a tributary of Little Toby Creek. Some of the coal was hauled to the tipple across a mine car track built upon a swinging bridge. The wood and steel cable bridge spanned the hillside with the mine opening and the spoil pile on which the tipple was constructed. (Harriet Moyer.)

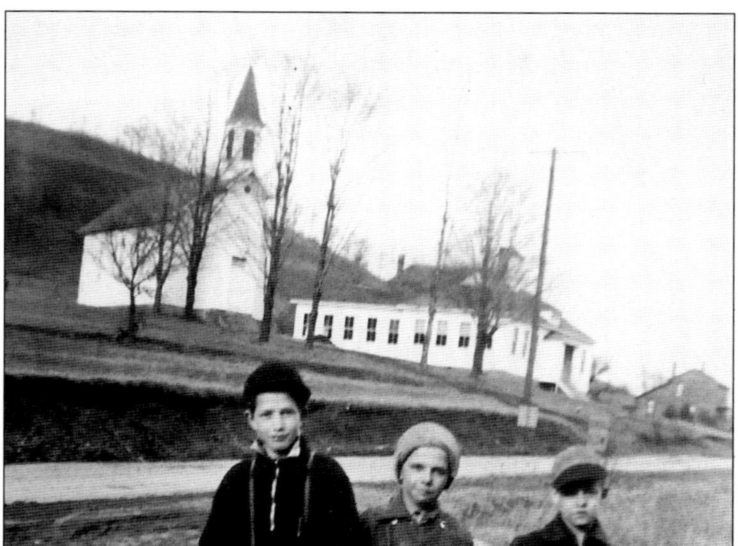

The Toby United Methodist Church and School was built during the mining heydays of the village. The church still holds services, but the schoolhouse no longer educates the children of the village. Miner's sons Leo Bilodeau, Raymond Smith, and Jack Moyer stand along Toby Road on Jack's eighth birthday, March 12, 1942. (Harriet Moyer.)

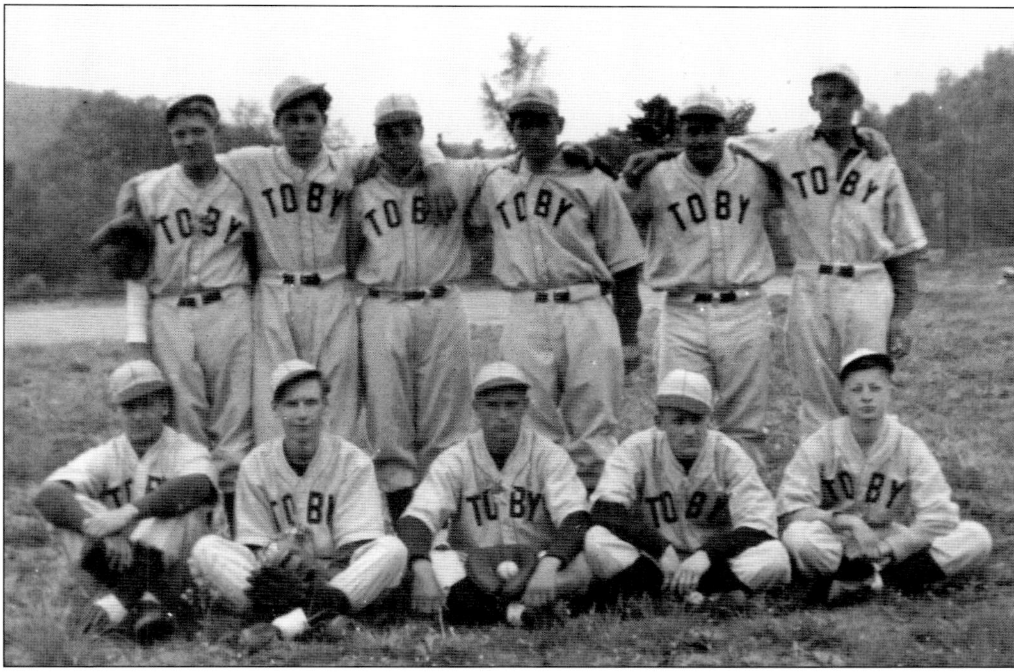

It seems as though every little coal patch village in the region had its own baseball team, and the village of Toby was no exception. A baseball field was built between Toby Road and the Toby Branch of the Erie Railroad. Fox Township still fields an all-star baseball team and competes within the local little league circuit. (Harriet Moyer.)

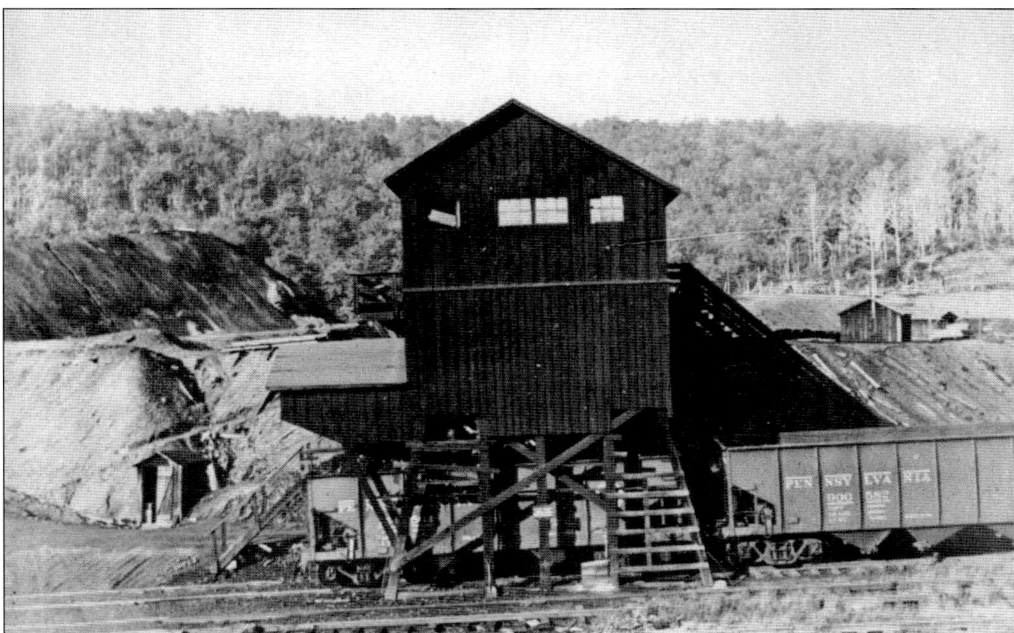

The Kyler mines were to the north of the village of Toby along Kyler Run. The Northwest Mining and Exchange Company built a branchline from Toby up the valley to the Kyler tipple, constructed in 1935. The photograph is of the tipple in the 1940s, and the tipple closed down in 1949. (Lawrence W. Kilmer.)

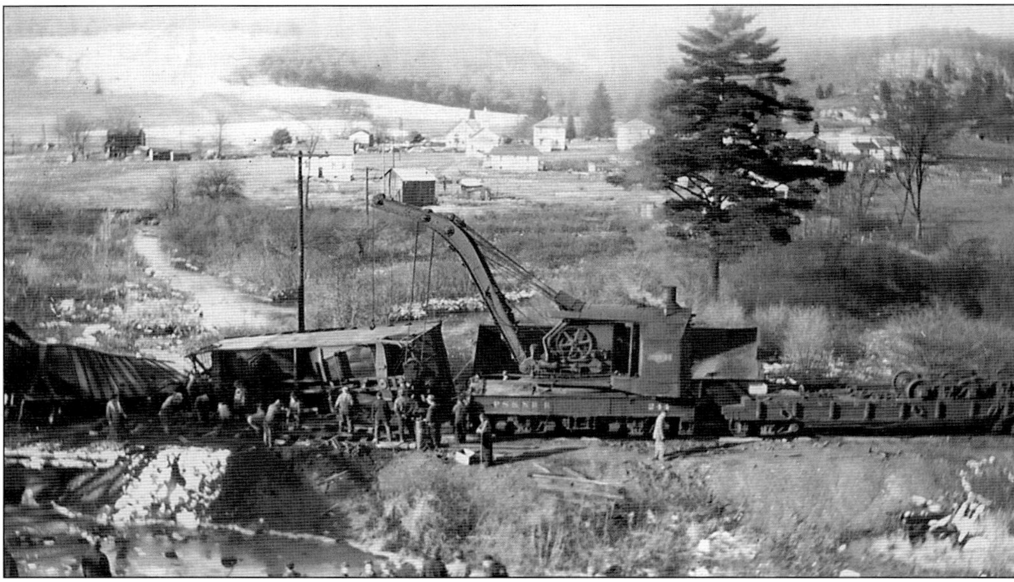

The other railroad built up the Little Toby Valley from Brockway was the Pittsburg, Shawmut, and Northern Railroad, otherwise known as the "Shawmut Line." The PS&N acquired trackage rights from the Erie Railroad to use their line from Brockway to Hydes. It then extended from the village of Hydes north through Brandy Camp, which is where this wreck occurred. (Bill Bauer.)

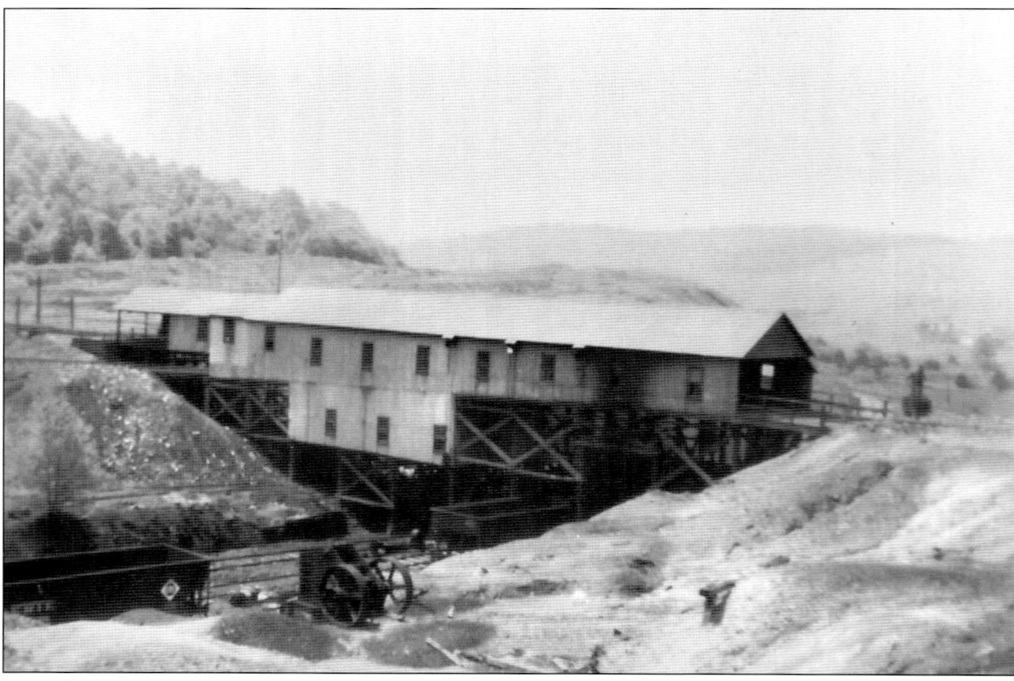

The Shawmut Mining Company No. 5 mine at Brandy Camp was constructed in 1895. It was one of the company's largest and longest-lived mines, employing about 600 men at peak production. The old tipple burned in the early 1930s, was replaced immediately, and upgraded again in 1937. It was abandoned after the Pennsylvania Railroad used it between 1947 and 1953, and it was torn down in 1984.

All of the buildings in Brandy Camp were at one point owned by the Shawmut Mining Company. It owned a church, two stores, a barn, a boardinghouse, and 91 company houses for the miners, all painted barn red. Brandy Camp has a United Methodist church and a Roman Catholic church, the original Holy Cross Roman Catholic Church being featured in this photograph.

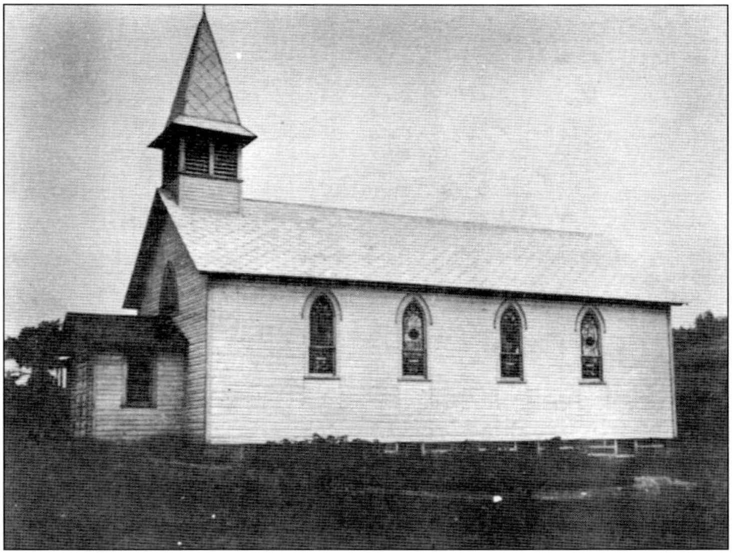

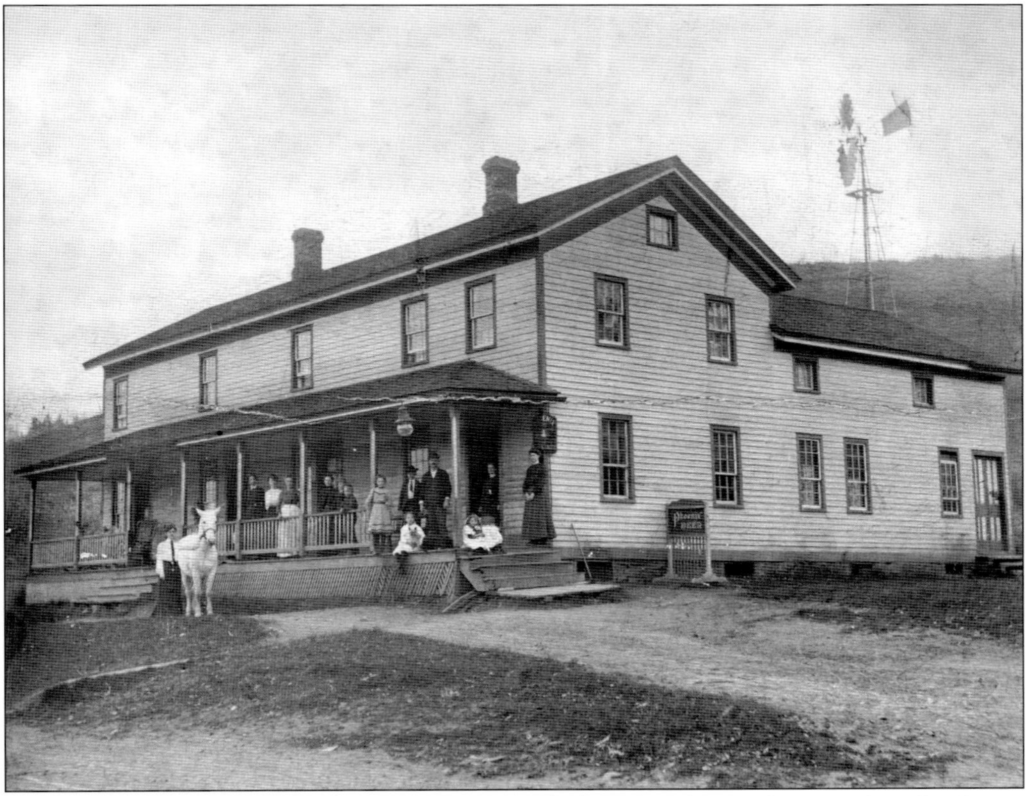

The Brandy Camp hotel was most likely the original Shawmut Mining Company boardinghouse on the southern end of Brandy Camp. It was probably a Shawmut miner's favorite hangout by the looks of the "Phoenix Beer" signs outside the building. The building still stands along U.S. Route 219 across from the Elbon United Mine Workers union hall. (Elk County Historical Society.)

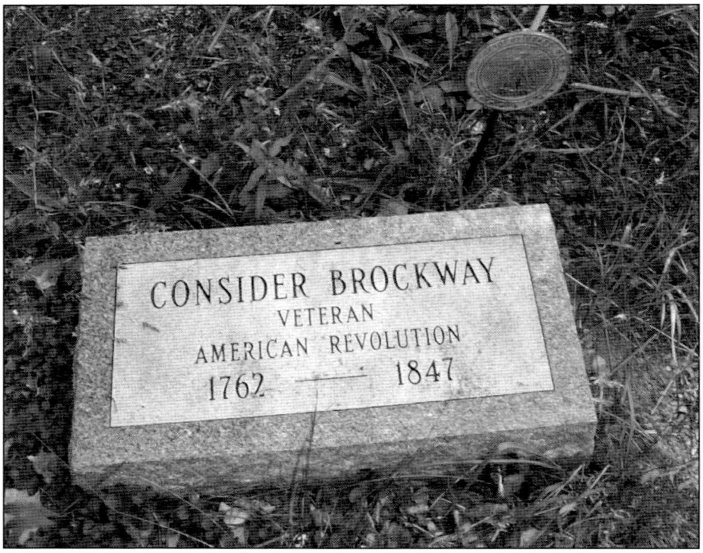

Consider Brockway and Jonathan Nichols Sr., two Revolutionary War veterans, remained in Brandy Camp when Consider's sons James and Alonzo moved south to settle in the wilderness of what would become Brockway. They both died in Brandy Camp, and were buried with their wives in an almost-forgotten burial plot. The Brockway and Elk County Historical Societies had new grave markers made and placed there in 1976.

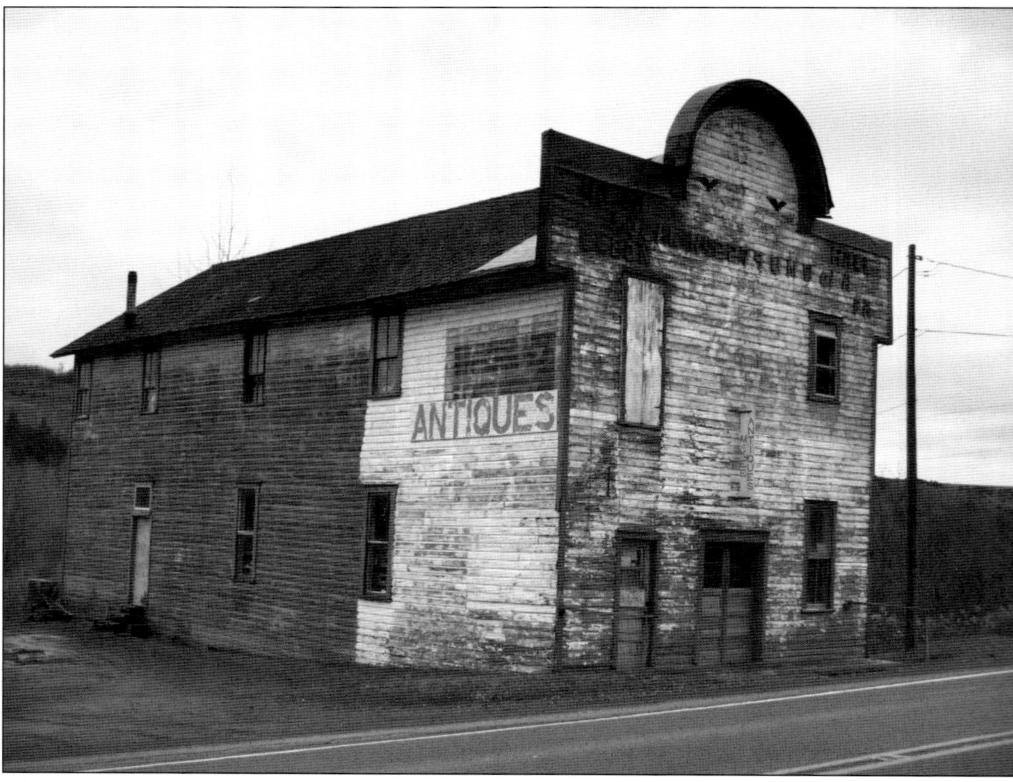

The union hall for the United Mine Workers of America Local No. 2279 at Elbon stands east across U.S. Route 219 from the Brandy Camp hotel. The working conditions of these early coal mines are almost beyond our current society's comprehension, except for the priceless stories that have been recorded from the miners themselves. As indicated in the photograph, the union hall is currently occupied by an antiques store.

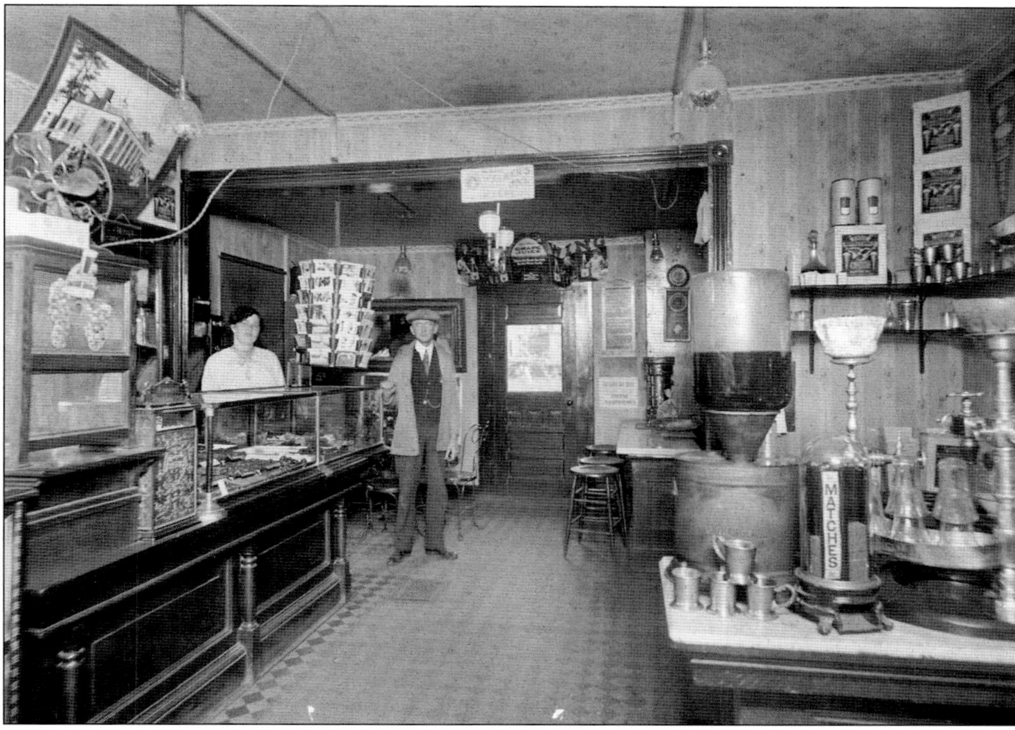

Shown here is the Shawmut Mining Company store interior at Elbon (Noble backwards). Burr Cartwright consolidated the Noble Coal Company into the Shawmut Mining Company. In 1891, he owned the entire land of Upper Toby Valley except for the land owned by the Northwest Mining and Exchange Company, and he was in charge of cutting their timber at his Horton City, Oyster, and Toby sawmills. (Elk County Historical Society.)

The post office at Elbon had a general store attached, and it too at one point was probably owned by Burr Cartwright. Unfortunately, the panic of 1893 hit Burr Cartwright after his huge Horton City sawmill operation burned. He was broke, and his lumbering, coal mining, clay tile and brick manufacturing, and railroading empire fell into the receivership hands of the Hydes, Halls, and Kauls of Ridgway and St. Marys.

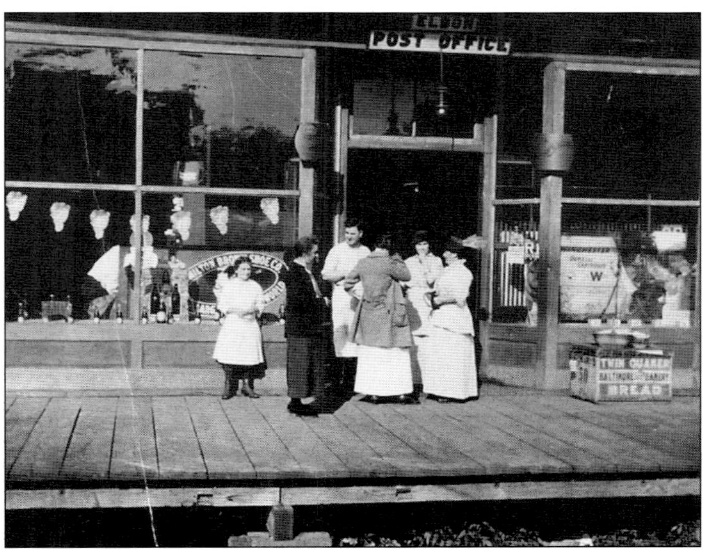

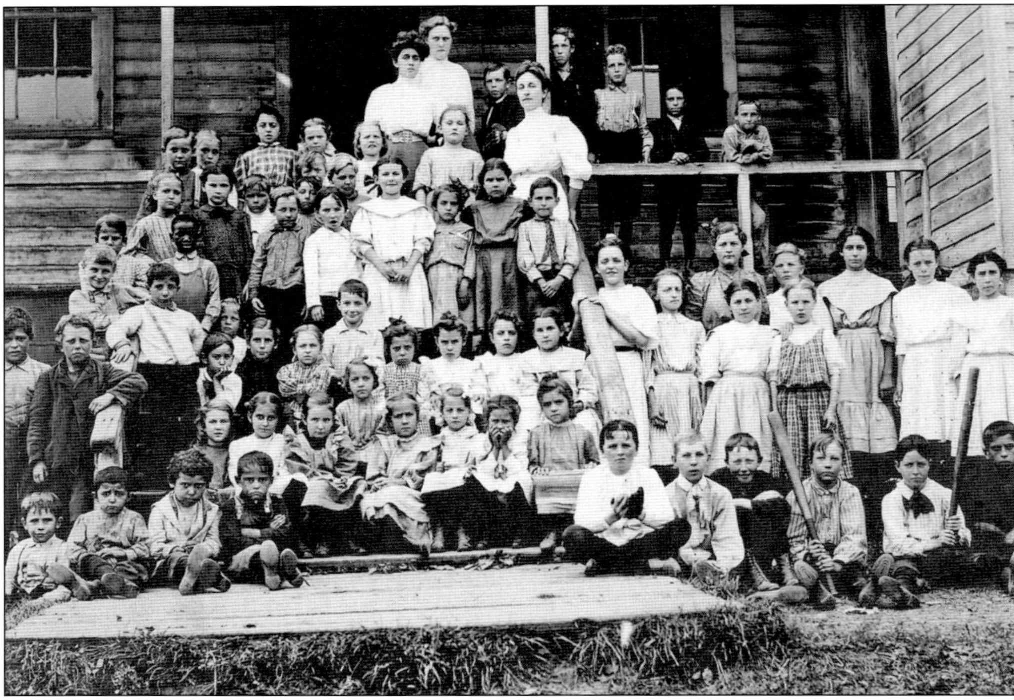

The classrooms of the Elbon School emptied onto the front porch of the building for a photograph. It looks like the school had three grade levels and a teacher for each grade. A topographic map surveyed in 1940 and 1941 indicates the existence of a schoolhouse across U.S. Route 219 from the Holy Cross Cemetery in Elbon. (Elk County Historical Society.)

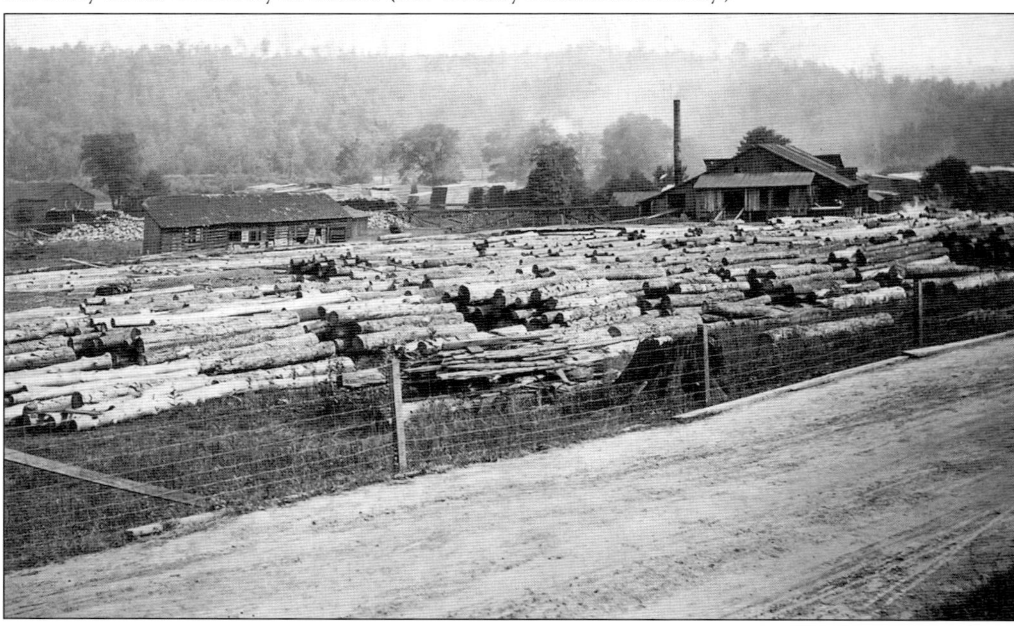

Joseph Smith Hyde, his son William H., and his partners Andrew Kaul and James K. P. Hall bought the financially troubled industries of Burr Cartwright, and at one point they owned almost all of the timberland between Little Toby Creek and Ridgway. The Hydes built this sawmill very near the mouth of Brandy Camp Creek along Little Toby Creek to cut their timberlands in that area.

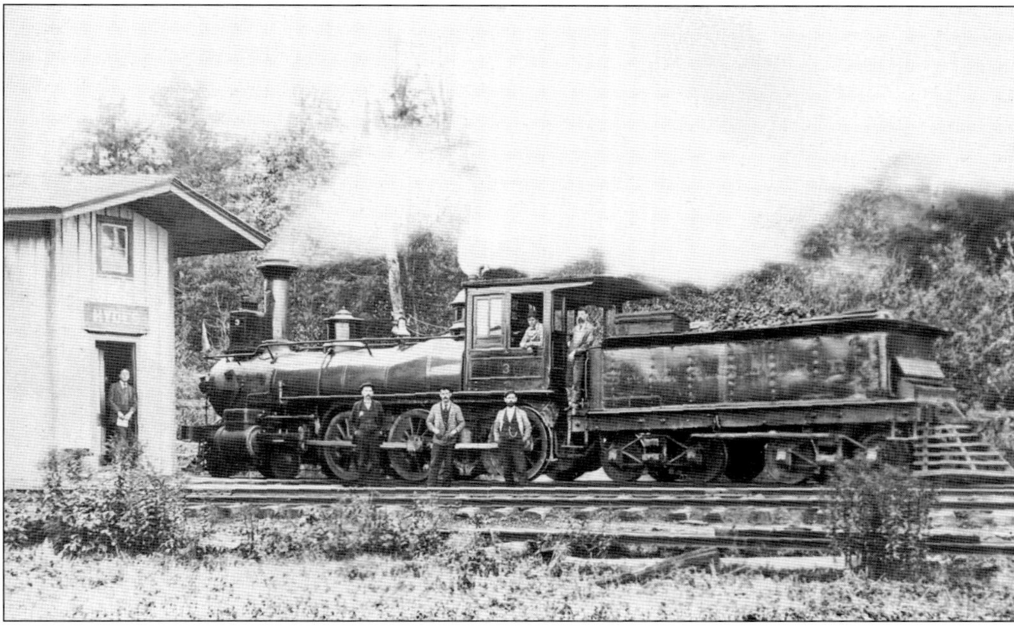

The St. Marys and Southwestern Railroad was originally Burr Cartwright's Ketner, Elbon, and Shawmut Railroad, a concept developed to connect his industries in Little Toby Valley with his industries in Glen Hazel. The Hydes, Halls, and Kauls agreed with his concept and built the railroad between the Hyde mill below Brandy Camp to St. Marys, which would become part of the Pittsburg, Shawmut, and Northern Railroad. (Elk County Historical Society.)

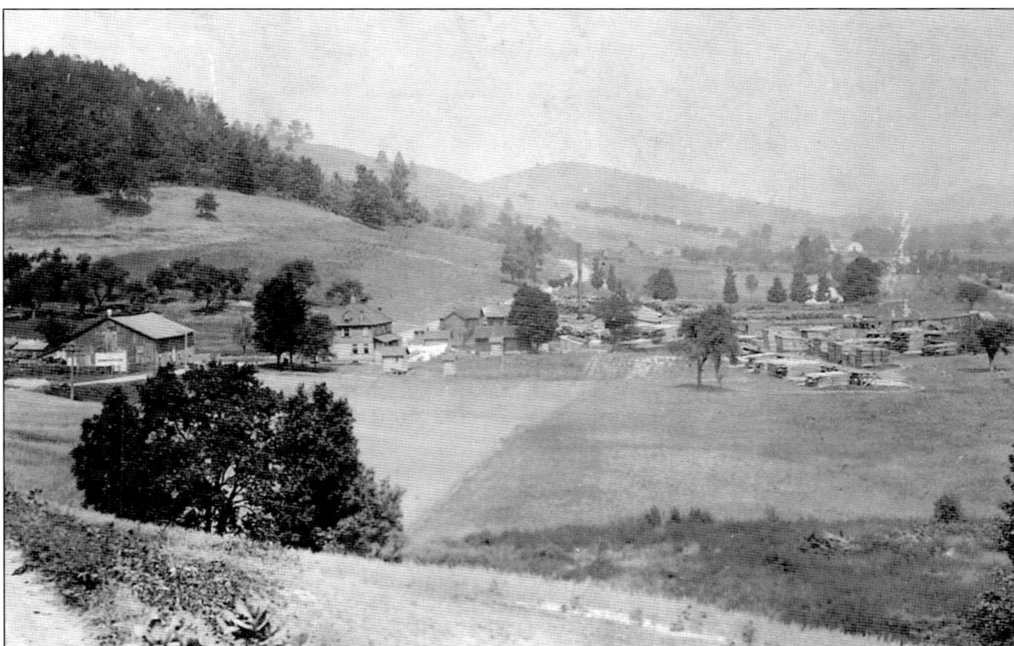

Burr Cartwright partnered with D. C. Oyster, Alfred Short, and Warren H. Horton between 1883 and 1885 to form the Ridgway Lumber Company. The company was contracted by the Northwest Mining and Exchange Company to cut the timber along Oyster Run for their coal mines. This sawmill was constructed at Helen Mills at the end of the old horse racetrack.

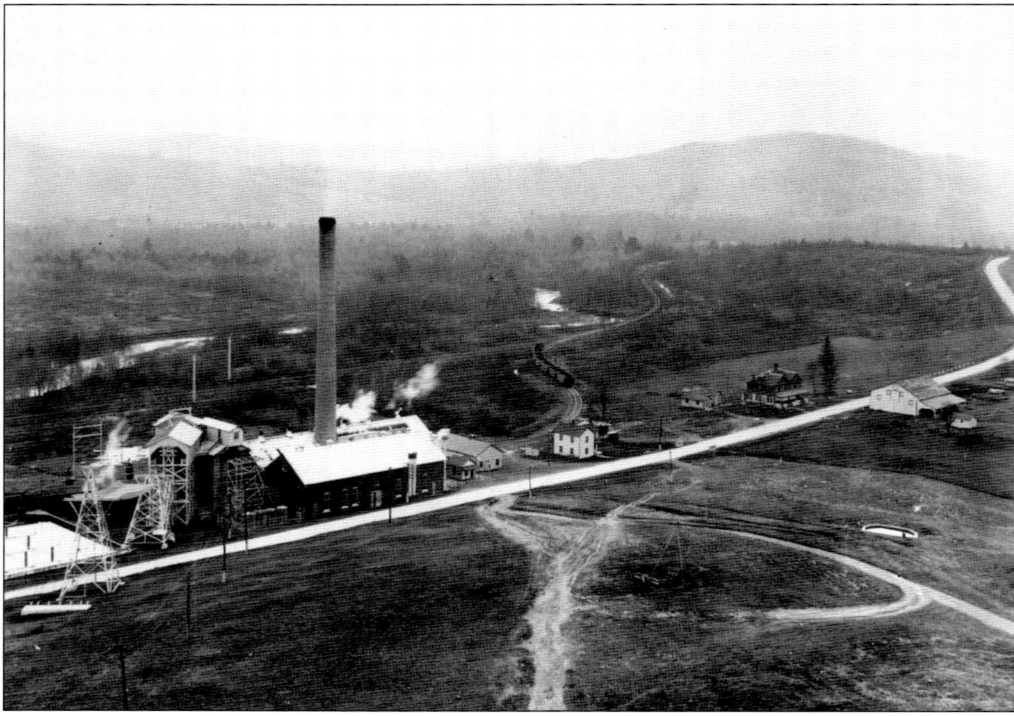

The Oyster mine power plant at Helen Mills was built to provide power to several of the mining operations belonging to the Northwest Mining and Exchange Company. Coal was removed from the Oyster Run Mine to serve the power plant, and to ship via the Toby Branch of the Erie Railroad. It was transported from the mine high on the hill via cable car to the plant.

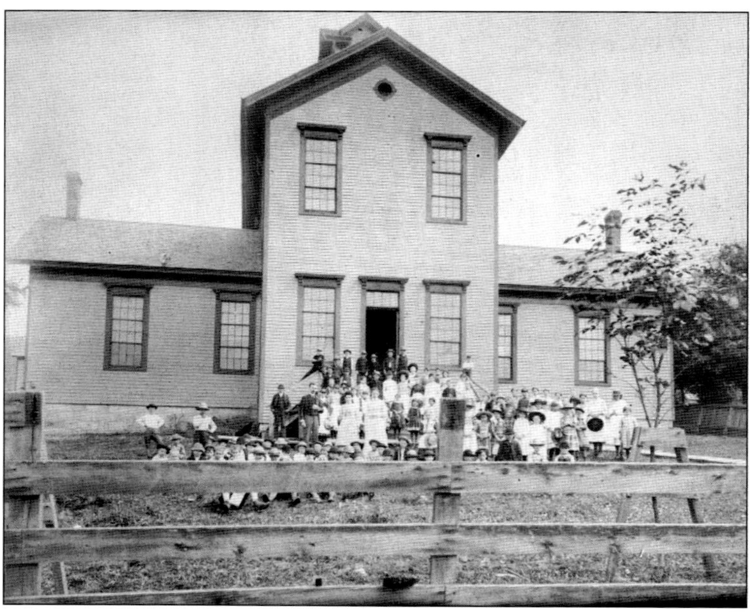

The village of Helen Mills predates the large-scale lumbering and mining operations of upper Little Toby Valley. A schoolhouse was constructed at Helen Mills to provide basic education to the children of the miners, lumbermen, and farmers of the area. The unique layout of the schoolhouse is the interesting feature of this photograph. (Elk County Historical Society.)

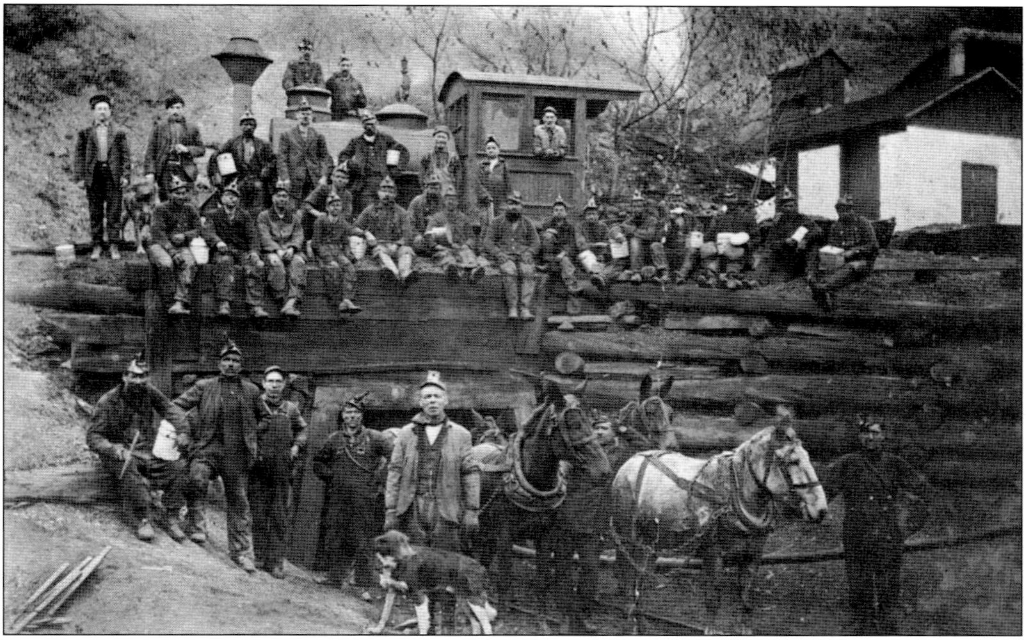

The earliest mine of the Shawmut Mining Company was established at the head of Mead Run in a village called Drummond in 1867. It was later numbered mine No. 7 and would have looked similar to the one shown in this photograph. The presence of the small steam locomotive at this Mead Run Valley Mine pushes this mine's date into the late 1800s.

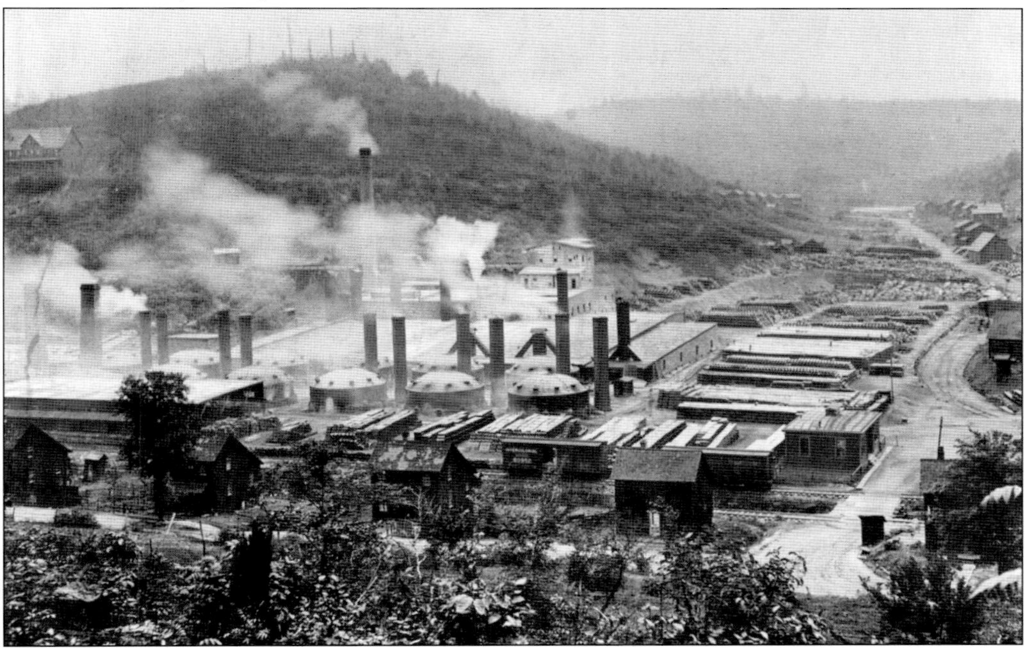

In addition to mining the Lower Kittanning coal seam, the Shawmut Mining Company also mined the fire clay that surrounded the coal seam. The Shawmut Clay Manufacturing Company at Drummond used this fire clay to make a variety of clay tile products. The mansion on the hill to the back left was built for the overseer of the operation, and the company houses for the miners surrounded the plant.

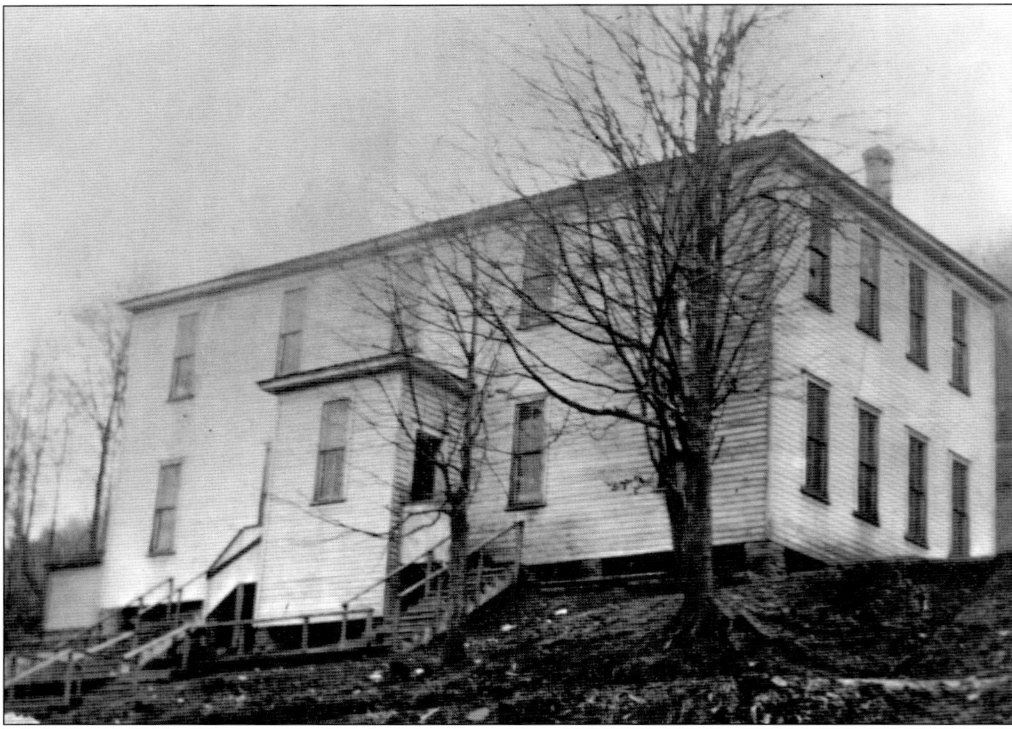

The Drummond School was built in 1905 high on the bank above the road that weaved its way up the valley from Horton City. The school was part of the Horton Township school district, but it closed in 1941 due to a dwindling population because of the shutdown of the Shawmut Clay Manufacturing Company tile plant. (Elk County Historical Society.)

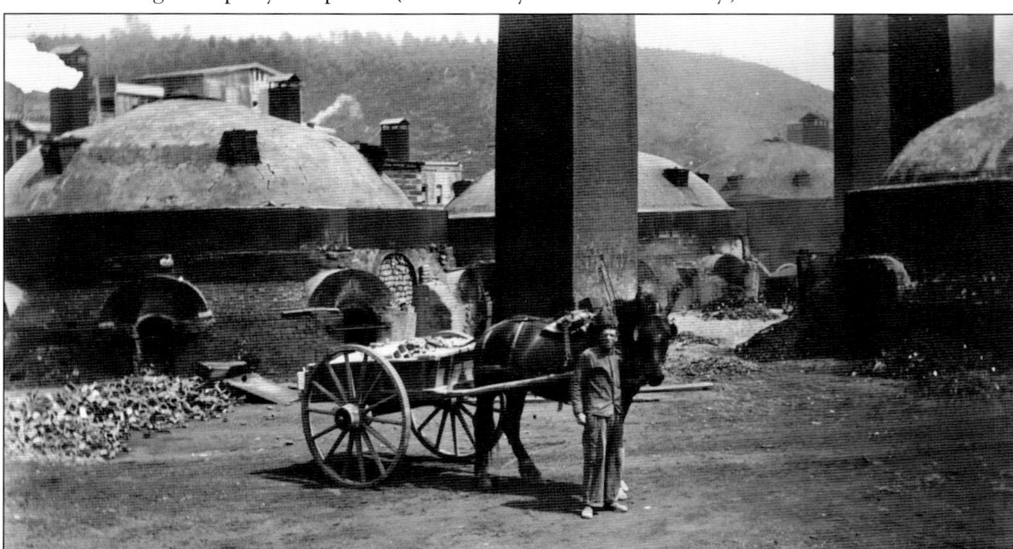

A man and a mule hauling a cart of broken clay pipe pause for a photographer in front of the kilns of the Shawmut Clay Manufacturing Company factory at Drummond. The proximity of the photograph to the kilns really brings into perspective the size of the kilns, therefore the size of the operation. There were at least 15 beehive-style kilns and several other types of ovens at the manufactory.

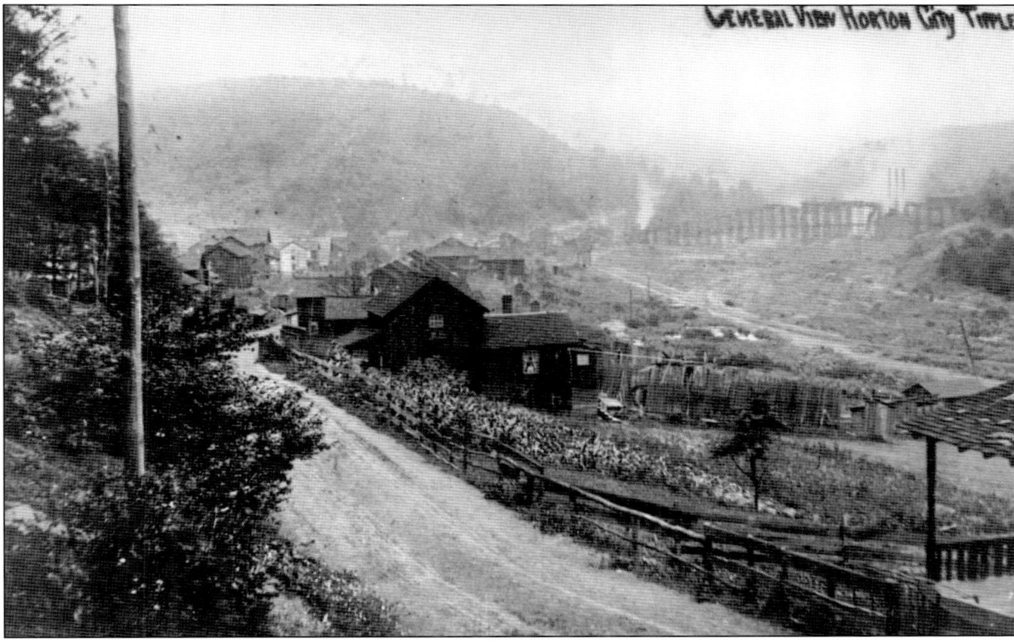

The Shawmut Mining Company opened mine No. 6 at the northern end of Horton City in 1899. In 1906, the mine met the No. 8 mine at Drummond underground. The No. 6 mine was abandoned in 1910, but coal was still being removed from the No. 8 mine until 1926. The No. 8 mine used mules to haul the coal out until 1925.

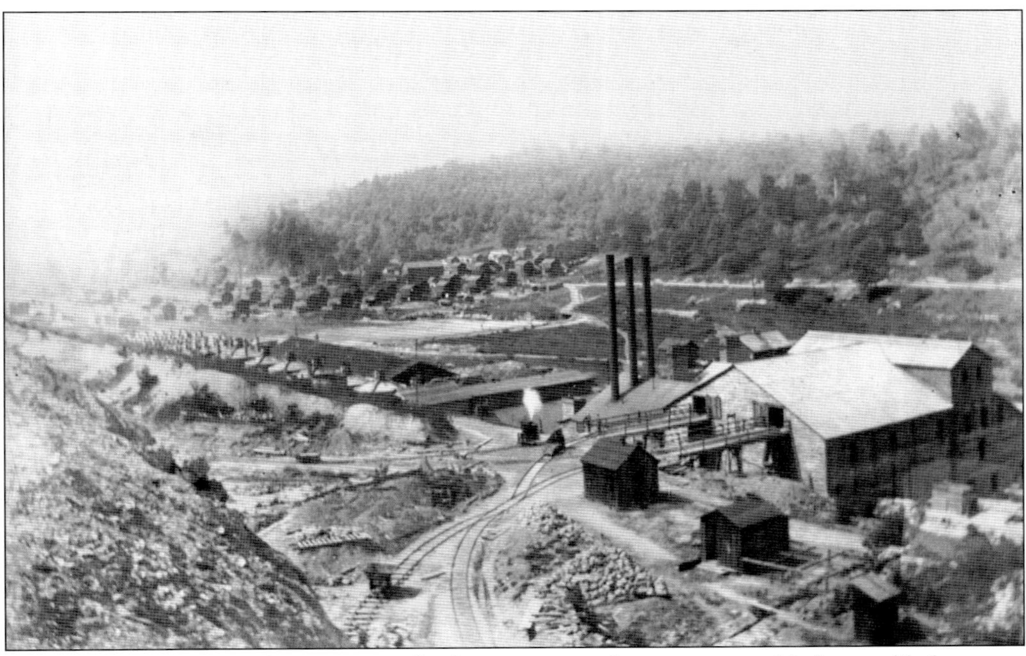

Anyone who has taken the time to walk ghost towns in the region most likely stumbled across a brick stamped "SHAWMUT" among the foundations. The Shawmut Brick Works was constructed across the valley from the business portion of the village of Shawmut. Its bricks were used locally to pave streets, but were also shipped nationwide. Bricks stamped "SHAWMUT, PA" can be found on Borden Avenue in Queens, New York.

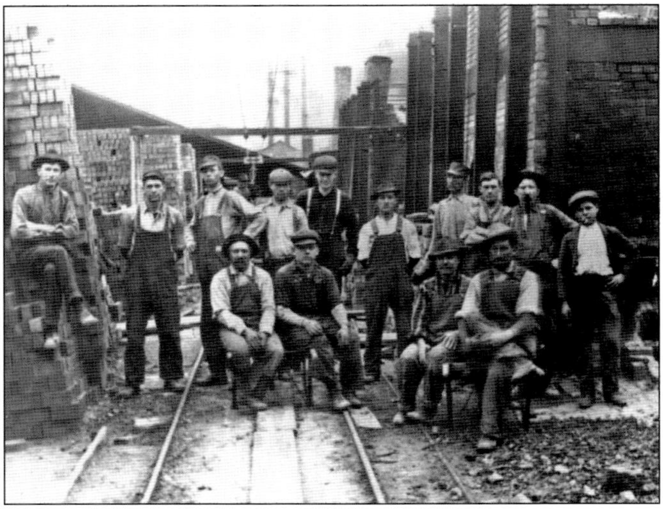

Brick masons at the Shawmut Brick Works pause during a busy workday for a local photographer. The Shawmut branch of the Pittsburg, Shawmut, and Northern Railroad ran immediately beside the plant on its way to the mines in Horton City and Drummond and the Shawmut Clay Manufacturing Company tile plant in Drummond. Several walls of the brick plant are still standing, and the area is littered with "SHAWMUT" bricks.

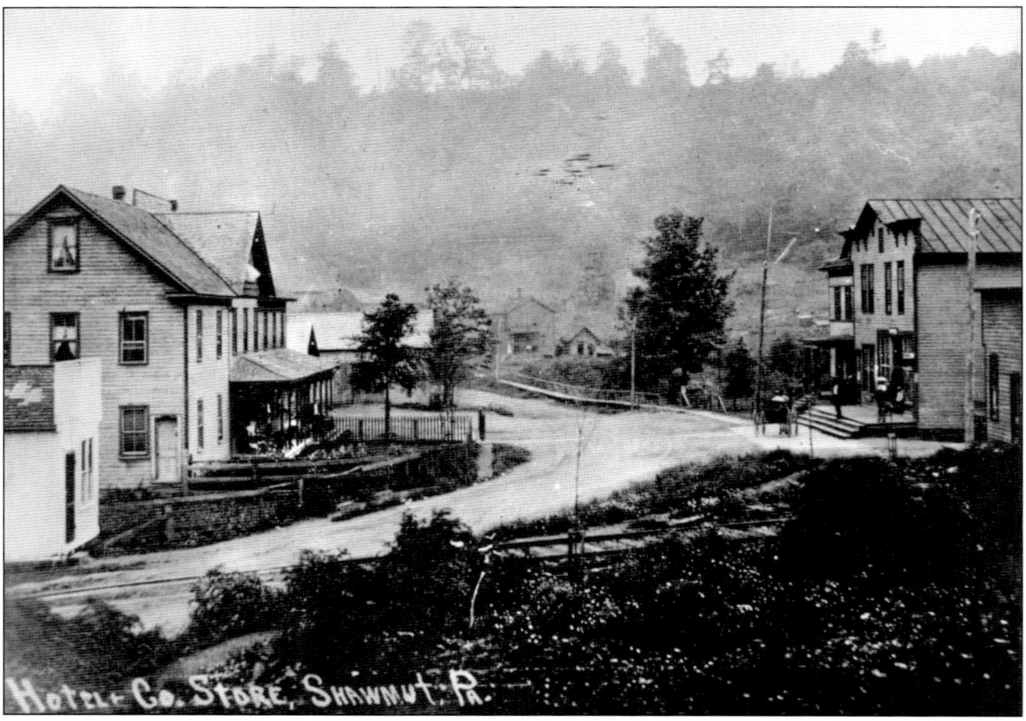

This is Main Street of Shawmut, Pennsylvania, looking south toward Cartwright and Brockport. The Shawmut Hotel is on the left, and the Shawmut Commercial Company store and post office on the right. The Shawmut Mining Company office is barely visible behind the store. The railroad spur in the foreground leads to mines and a battery of coke ovens back the valley to the right (northwest).

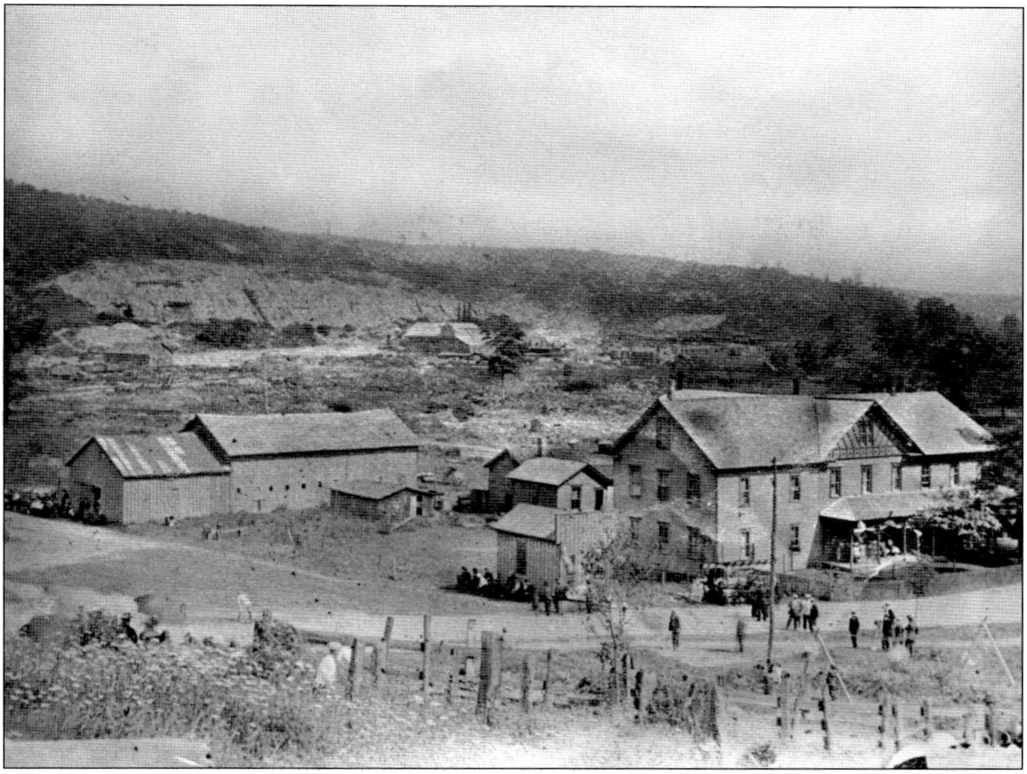

This is a great view of the Shawmut Hotel and stables. Careful study of the lower left of the photograph will reveal a baseball field. Another source of entertainment in Shawmut was the Motion Picture and Vaudeville Theatre. In the distance on the left can be seen buildings associated with a coal mine, and in the center, the Shawmut Brick Works plant against the base of the distant hillside.

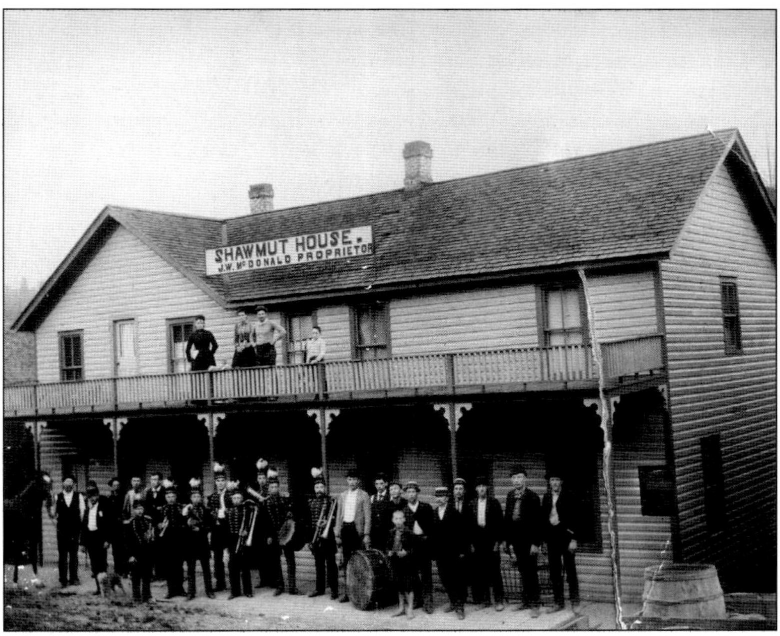

The Shawmut House owned by J. W. McDonald was a smaller boarding establishment compared to the Shawmut Hotel in the previous photograph. The interesting feature of this photograph is the brass band in front of the boardinghouse. A sign on the right of the porch reads "Rochester Lager Beer." (Elk County Historical Society.)

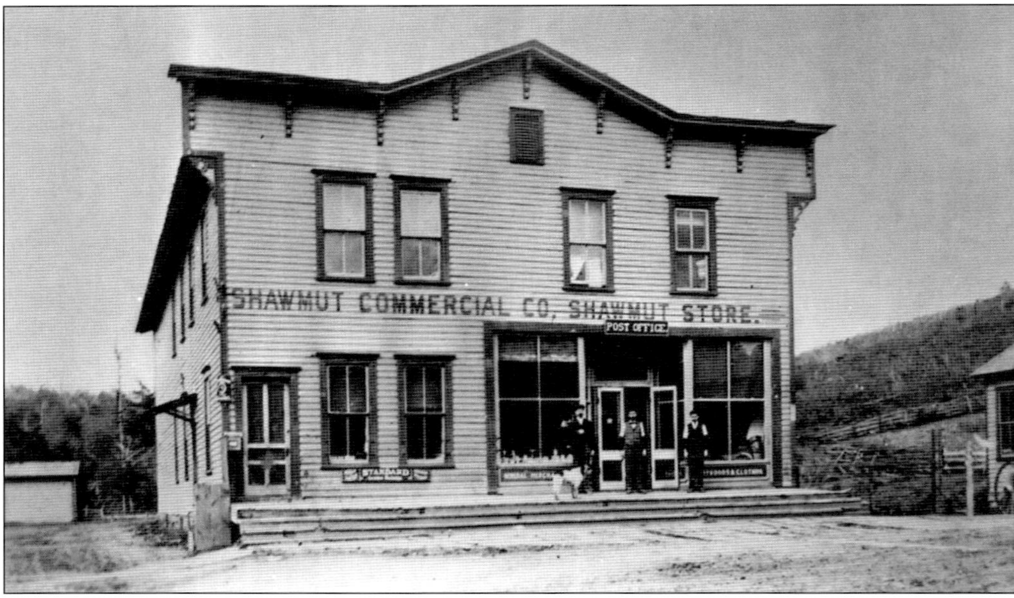

The Shawmut Commercial Company store and post office shared a large building on the west side of Main Street along the business portion of Shawmut. The Shawmut Commercial Company was formed to handle the construction of company stores, houses, boardinghouses, and stables at locations deemed appropriate by the Shawmut Mining Company. Similar stores were built in the coal towns of Brandy Camp and Elbon.

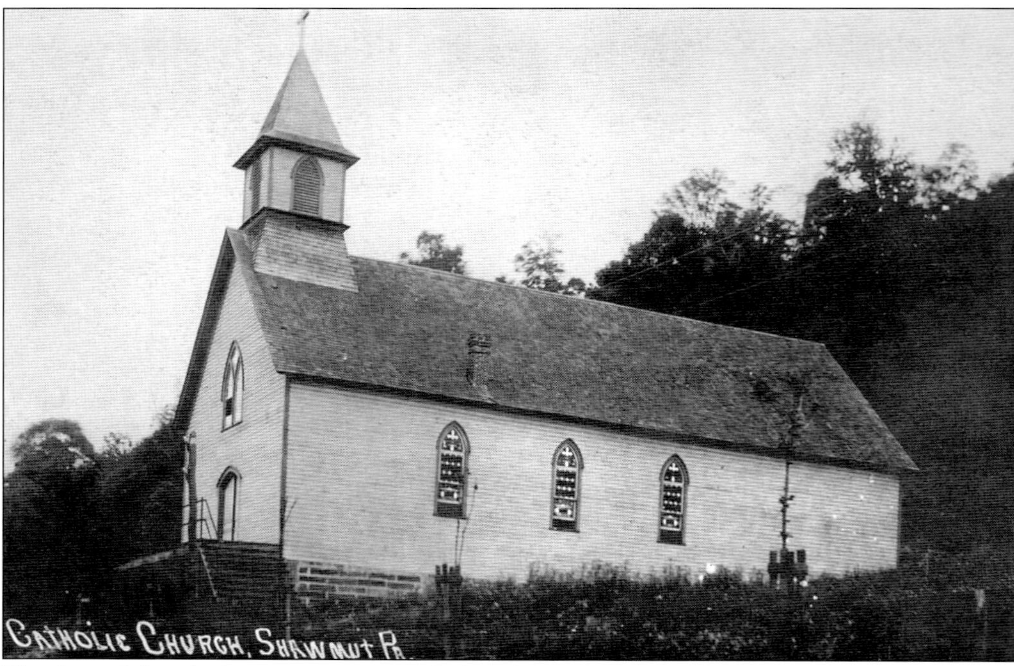

The Saint John the Baptist Roman Catholic Church in Shawmut was on the southern end of town, on the west side of the road and built up on a knoll. Fr. Anthony Orlando was the pastor, but gained the additional responsibility of the congregation at the Holy Cross Roman Catholic Church in Brandy Camp in 1901. The church was eventually removed sometime after the mines closed and the population dropped.

The Shawmut school was located to the southeast of the Roman Catholic church on the east side of the road. This photograph was taken during the 1904–1905 school year, while Oleta Fox was the teacher. Originally thought to be another photograph of the Drummond school, it was noticed that the Drummond school sat above the road, while the Shawmut school sat below the road.

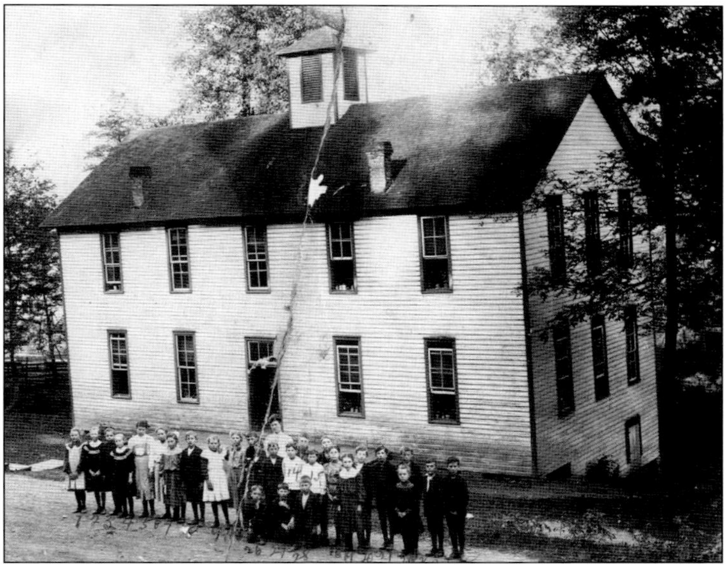

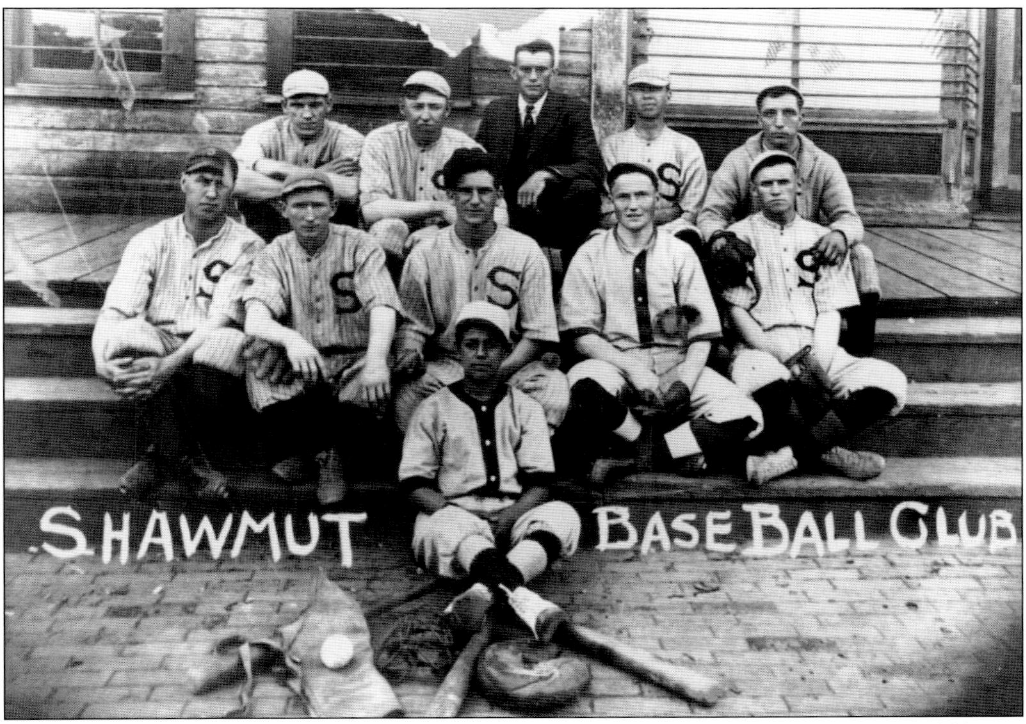

Almost all coal towns along Little Toby Creek had a baseball team, and Shawmut would be no exception. Other towns known to have ball teams and fields include Dagus Mines, Kersey, Toby, Coal Glen, and Brockwayville. From left to right are (first row) Leo Falcone; (second row) Ray Butz, Paddy Martin, Fred Himes, John Martin, Harve Moline; (third row) Walford Moline, Archie Chestnut, Ed Bilquist (manager), Frank Taylor, and Wal Faulkner.

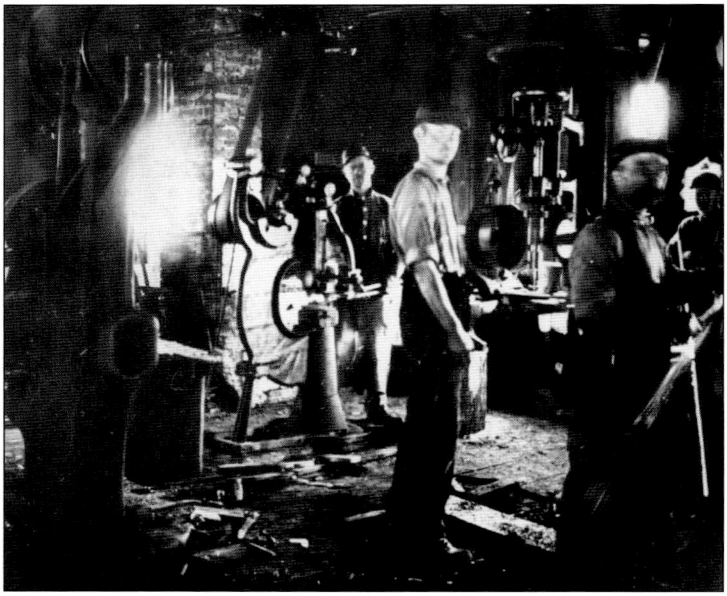

Little is recorded about the village of Cartwright, but its proximity to Brockport suggests that the two villages operated as one. One Cartwright industry has been preserved in photography, the Niels Youngdahl Blacksmith Shop. Within the shop are Niels, William, Harry, and Arthur Youngdahl, and Lours Larson. The shop likely produced mining tools for the Shawmut Mining Company and other various ironworks for the locals.

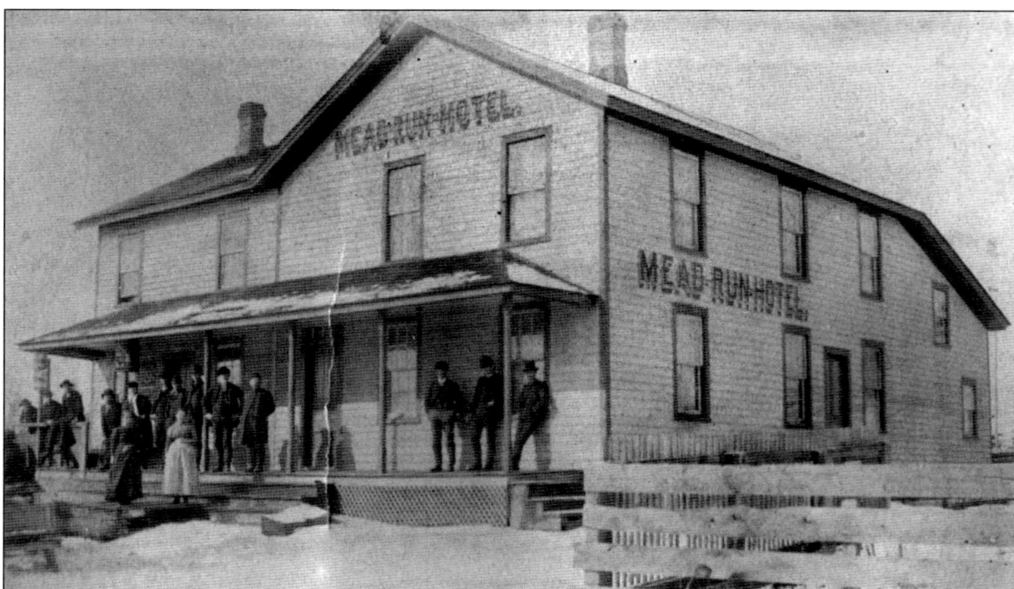

The location of the Mead Run Hotel remains a mystery. Mead Run flows from Drummond south through Horton City, Shawmut, Cartwright, and into Little Toby Creek in Brockport, so it could have been in any one of these villages. It is speculated that it was located in Brockport on the north side of the Erie Railroad tracks behind the Brockport Methodist Church.

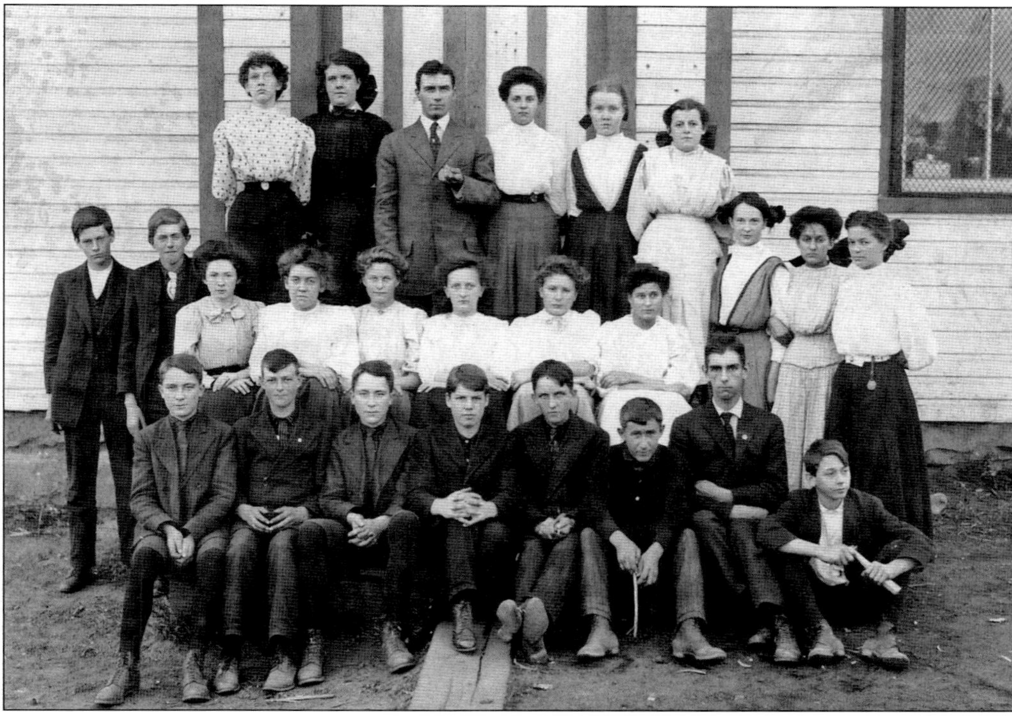

The Brockport high school was enlarged to four rooms and had a two-year course in 1907, but progressively changed to a four-year course by 1923. The teachers stand in the center of the back row, and the girls and boys remain segregated. The photographer commanded everyone's attention except for the boy in the lower right, whose disinterested look tells the classic story of boredom. (Elk County Historical Society.)

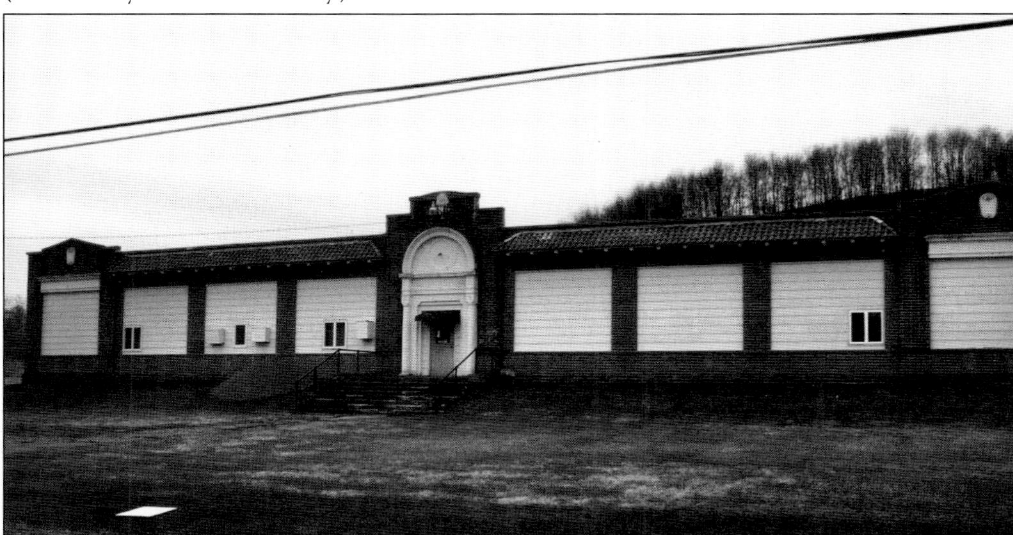

The elementary and high schools of Brockport were consolidated in the new Horton Township School, built in 1924. Classes remained in the Horton Township school building for about 50 years, until students in northern Horton Township were sent to Ridgway, and students in southern Horton Township were sent to Brockway. The structure still stands on the left side of Shawmut Road just above Brockport.

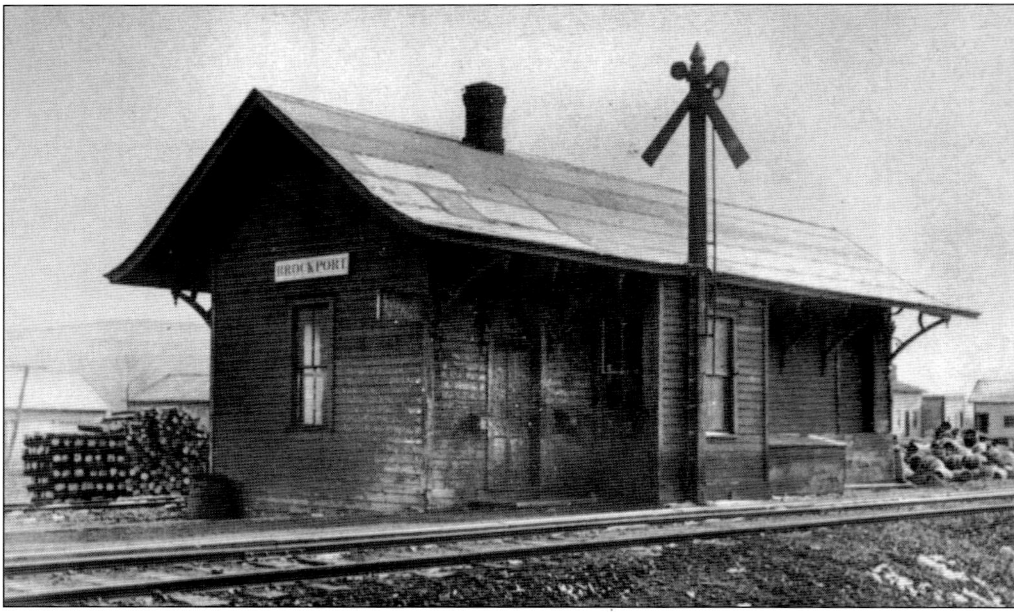

The Erie Railroad built this small station in Brockport in the late 1800s. The mines up the Mead Run Valley to the north and Little Toby Valley to the northeast provided an incredible amount of coal traffic through the village. Passenger service was also provided by the Erie and the Pittsburg, Shawmut and Northern Railroads. A Hoodlebug ran the rails to bring students to the Brockport high school.

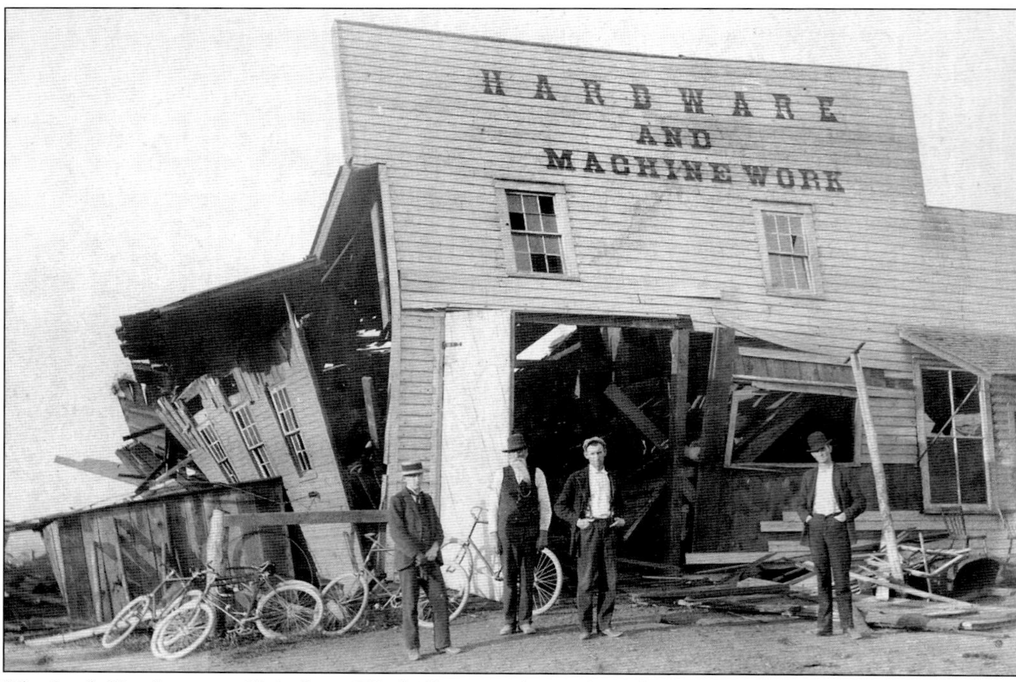

The Leck Hardware and Machine Work Shop was located on the southeast corner of the Boggy Run Road Bridge over Little Toby Creek. On June 25, 1897, the steam boiler exploded, instantly killing Adam Leck and his son William. Son Frank survived and rebuilt a smaller machine shop. Chauncey Brockway Jr. stands second from the left. He ran his gunsmith business out of the shop.

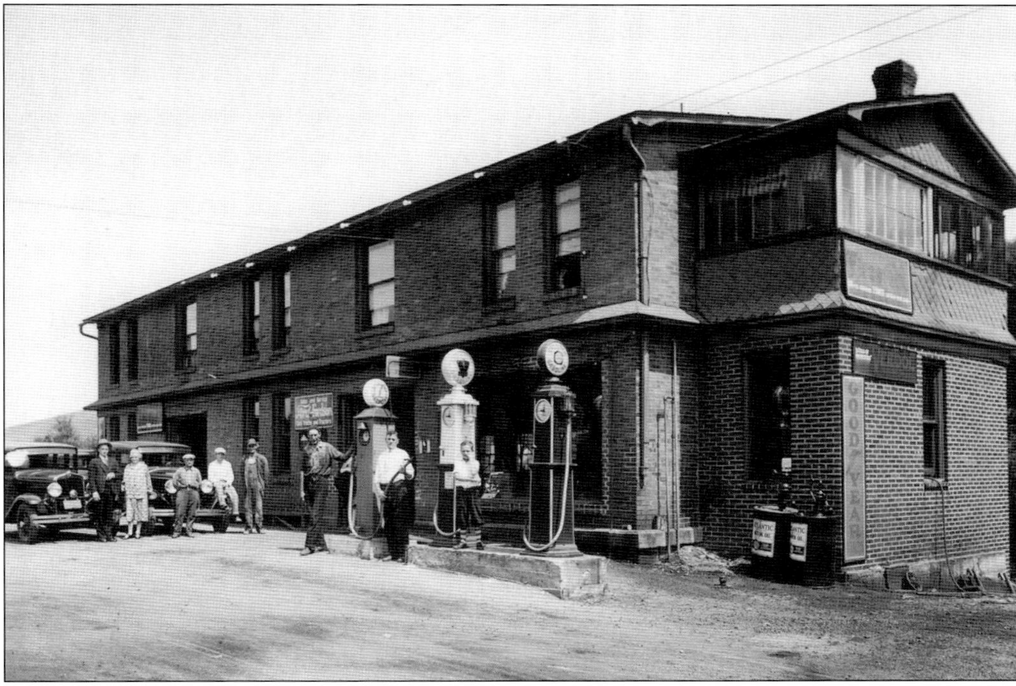

The invention of the automobile introduced the need for service stations along major roads. Johnson's Atlantic Garage was along U.S. Route 219 in Brockport and provided only the finest in automobile service. Advertisements for Goodyear and Firestone tires, Veedol motor oil, and Ford-Fordson cars, trucks, and tractors hang on the exterior walls of the garage.

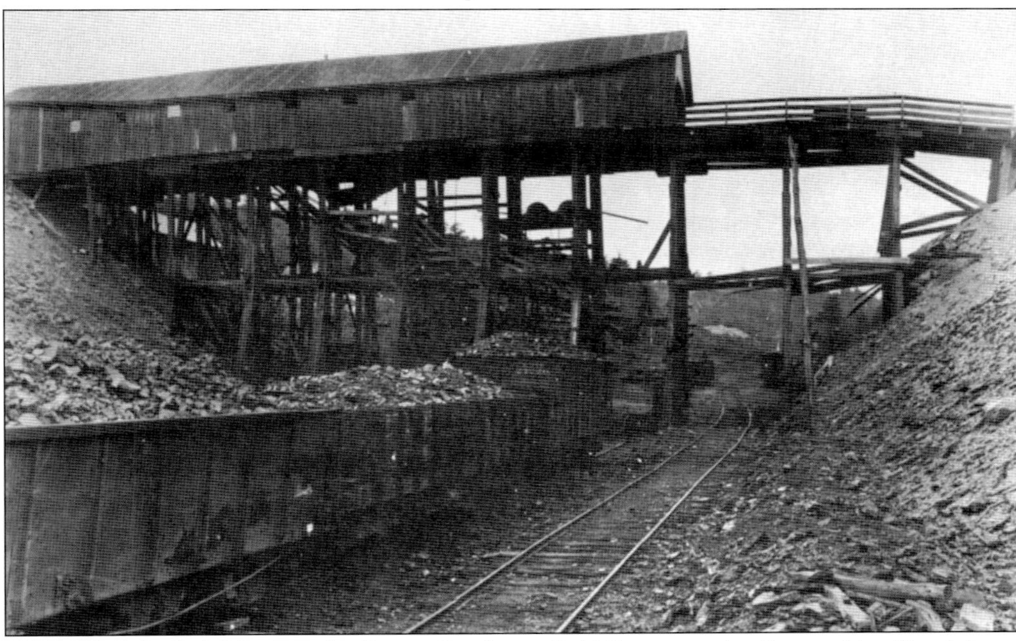

The tee box for hole No. 1 at the Owens-Brockway Golf Course up the County Line Road sits on the Erie Railroad branch that served the Northwest Mining and Exchange Company's Clarion No. 4 mine up the valley. It was opened in 1895 and called the County Line Mine. The mine was operated from Crenshaw, and the miners were taken by train to the mines in five passenger coaches.

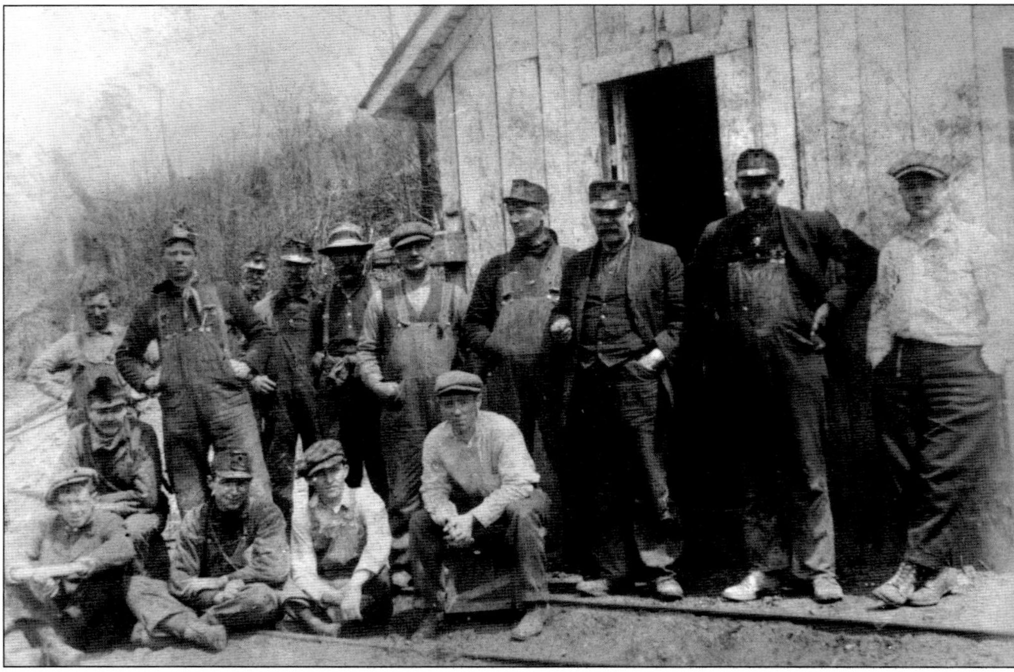

A group of workers at the County Line Mines pose for a photograph. The mine set a local production record by mining and loading 1,600 tons of coal in a 10-hour period. The late 1920s introduced serious fear when the Northwest Mining and Exchange Company purchased coal lands outside of Little Toby Valley. The shift in production caused the closing of the County Line Mine on April 1, 1927.

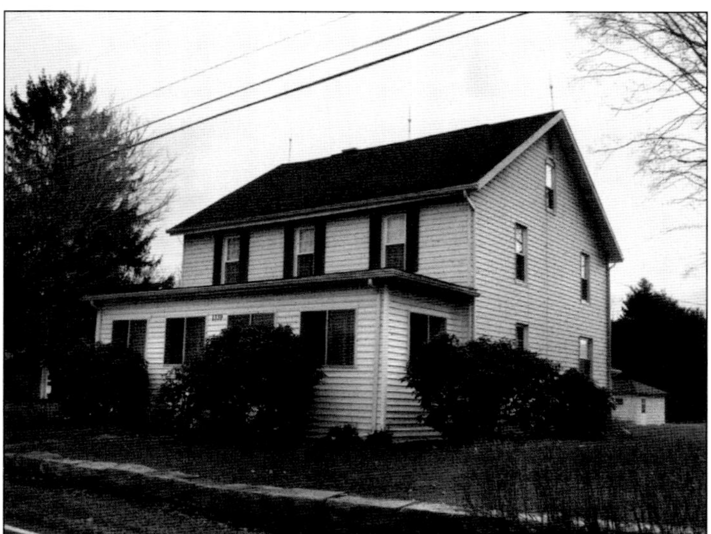

Chauncey Brockway Sr. and partners built a sawmill on Little Toby Creek in 1827. The Brockways built a house and operated a farm near the mill for many years. They sold the farm to William Youngdahl who turned the farm into one of the most successful dairy farms in the valley. William's son Raymond continued to operate the dairy farm, and his wife, Betty, still lives in the farmhouse today.

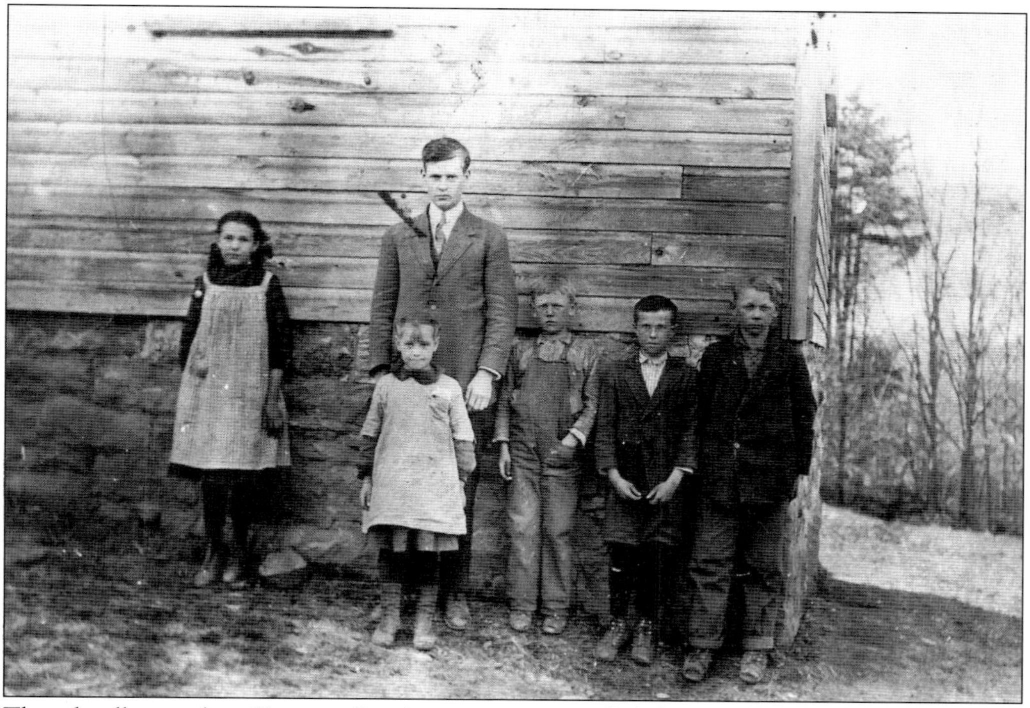

The schoolhouse along Keystone Road was sometimes called the Keystone school and sometimes called the Whetstone school, and was taught by Merrill Brockway in 1913. Whetstone is the name of the stream that flows into Little Toby Creek at Keystone. The reservoirs that serve as the source of water for the Brockway Crystal Water Company are at the headwaters of Whetstone Run. (Elk County Historical Society.)

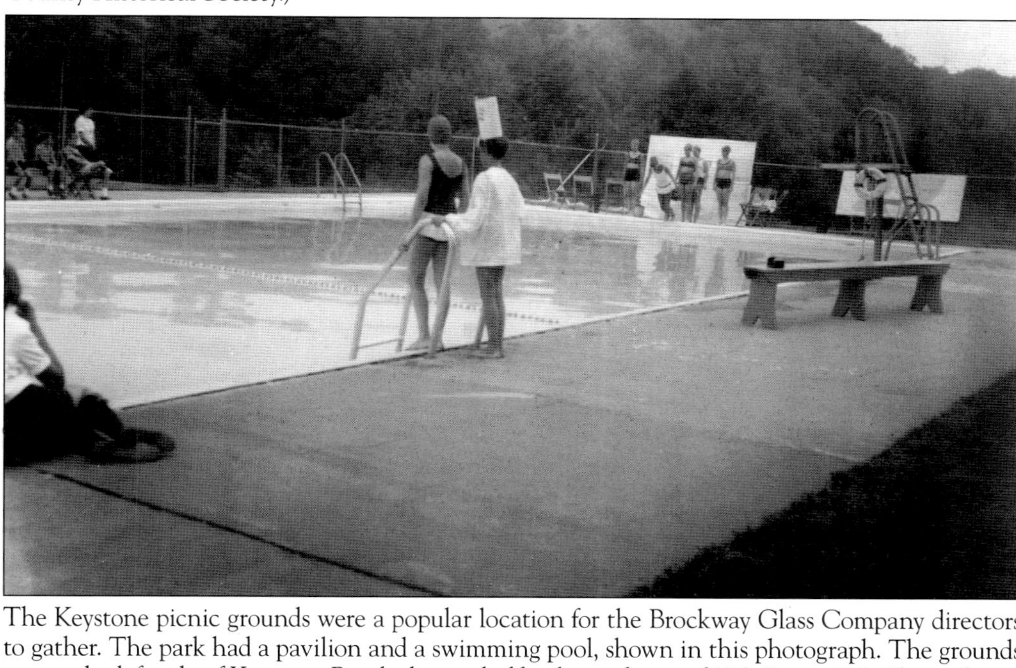

The Keystone picnic grounds were a popular location for the Brockway Glass Company directors to gather. The park had a pavilion and a swimming pool, shown in this photograph. The grounds are on the left side of Keystone Road, about a half mile southeast of U.S. Route 219. The park was abandoned and the pool filled in, but the concrete pier that held the sliding board still remains.

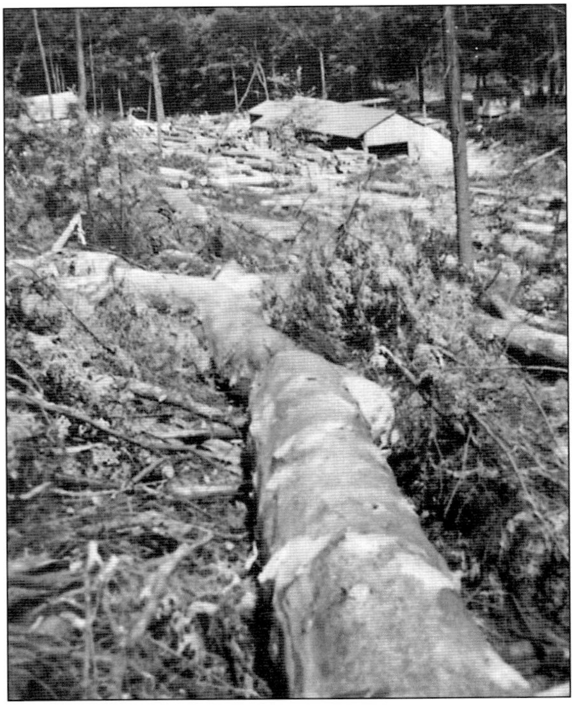

Most of Pennsylvania's virgin timber tracts in existence after the 1920s turned into state parks or forests. This mill was built in the late 1930s by Joseph B. Kosco of Brockway to cut the "McClelland tract," one last tract of virgin hemlock and white pine along the Whetstone Branch of Little Toby Creek at the foot of Boone Mountain. The tract apparently produced millions of board feet of high-quality lumber.

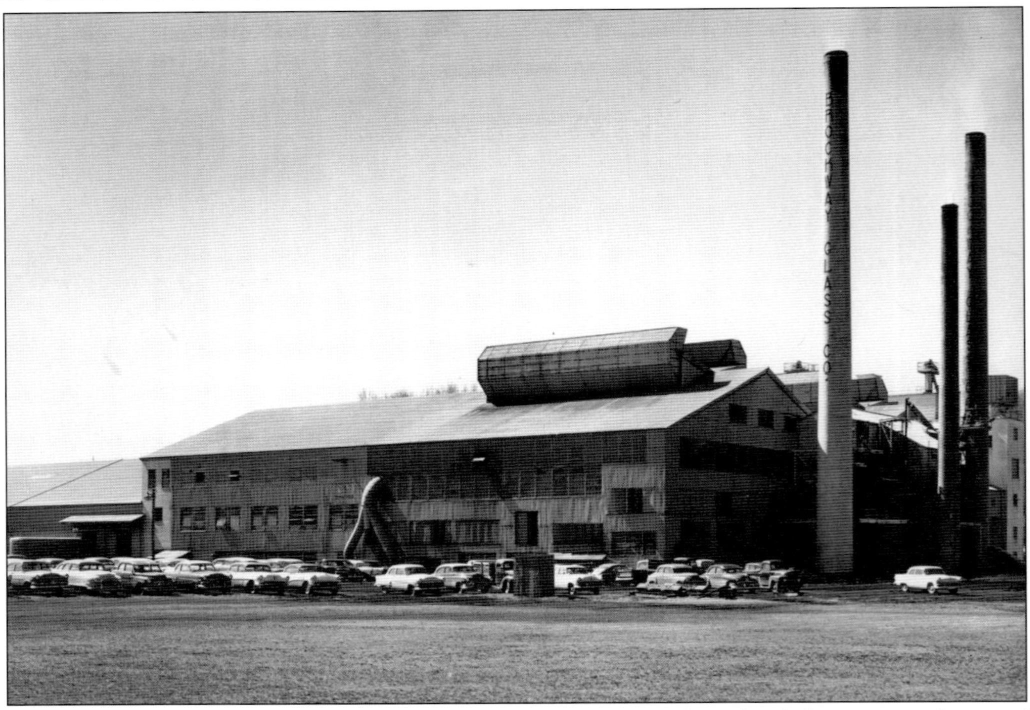

The Brockway Glass Company purchased the William Moore farm, land that was southwest of the Brockway-Youngdahl farm at Keystone. The site was very spacious for expansion purposes and had access to the Erie Railroad Toby Branch and U.S. Route 219 for shipping purposes. Groundbreaking for the second glass plant started in 1940. An engineering and research facility was later constructed adjacent to plant No. 2.

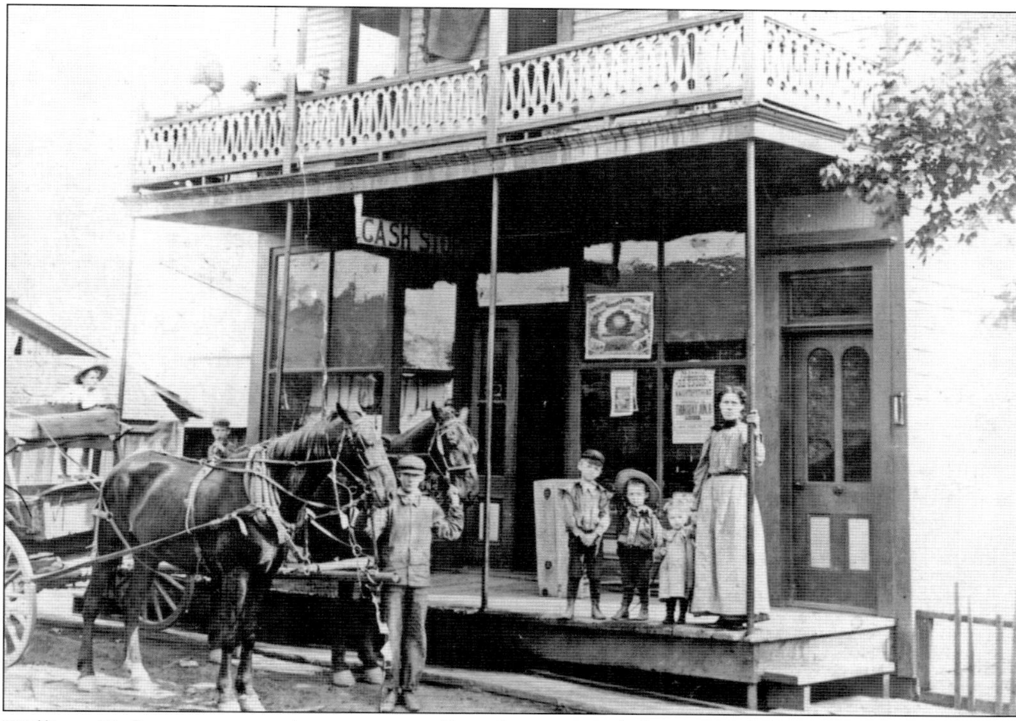

William Hafner ran a merchant store in Crenshaw around the turn of the 19th century for over 10 years. The Hafners were prominent farmers and sold dry goods, groceries, meats, and other staples of the era. William's wife, Etta, was a descendant of Joel Clarke Sr., a Revolutionary War veteran, who is buried in the Shaffer cemetery at the eastern end of Bond Street in Brockwayville.

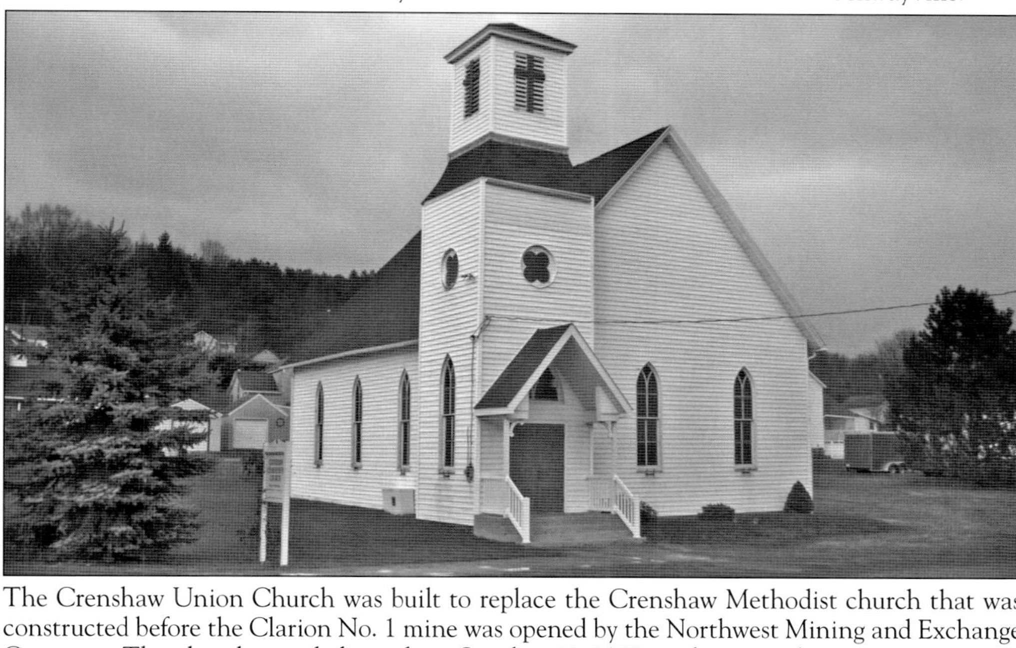

The Crenshaw Union Church was built to replace the Crenshaw Methodist church that was constructed before the Clarion No. 1 mine was opened by the Northwest Mining and Exchange Company. The church was dedicated on October 11, 1903, with a mixed congregation and a Swedish orchestra and choir from DuBois that provided special music. The church received a much-needed revitalization and renovation in the 1950s.

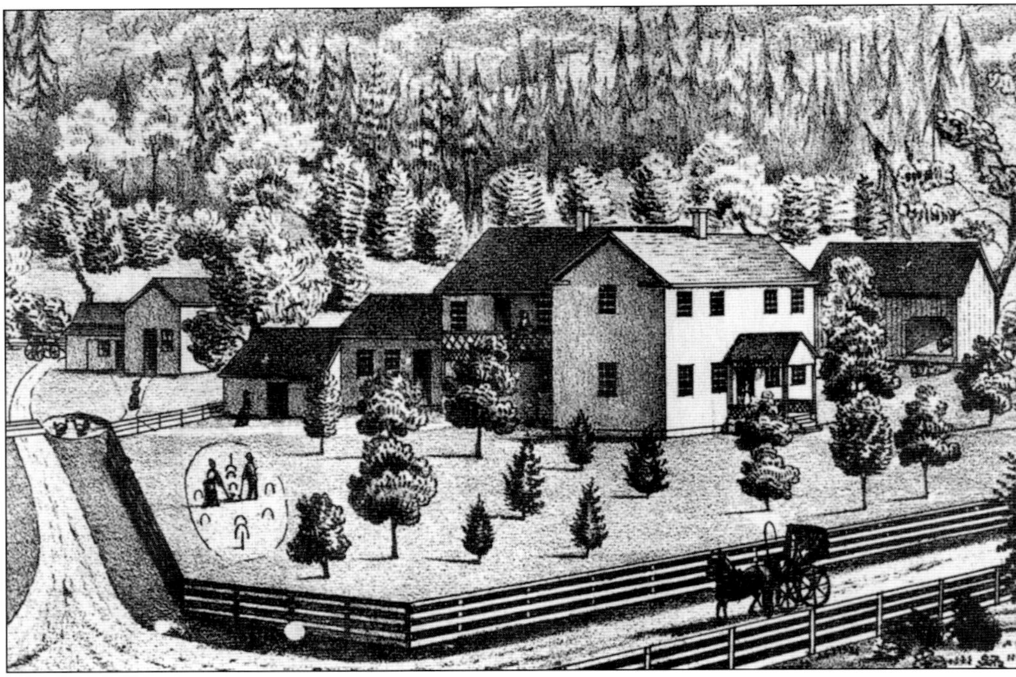

The firm Hoyt and Wilson built a sawmill in Little Toby Creek about a half mile south of Crenshaw in 1836. Alonzo Ferman and John Johnson later bought the sawmill, and the site became known as Ferman's Mills. The Ferman house and sawmill are featured in this sketch from Caldwell's atlas of Jefferson County in 1878. The sawmill burned in 1905 and was never rebuilt.

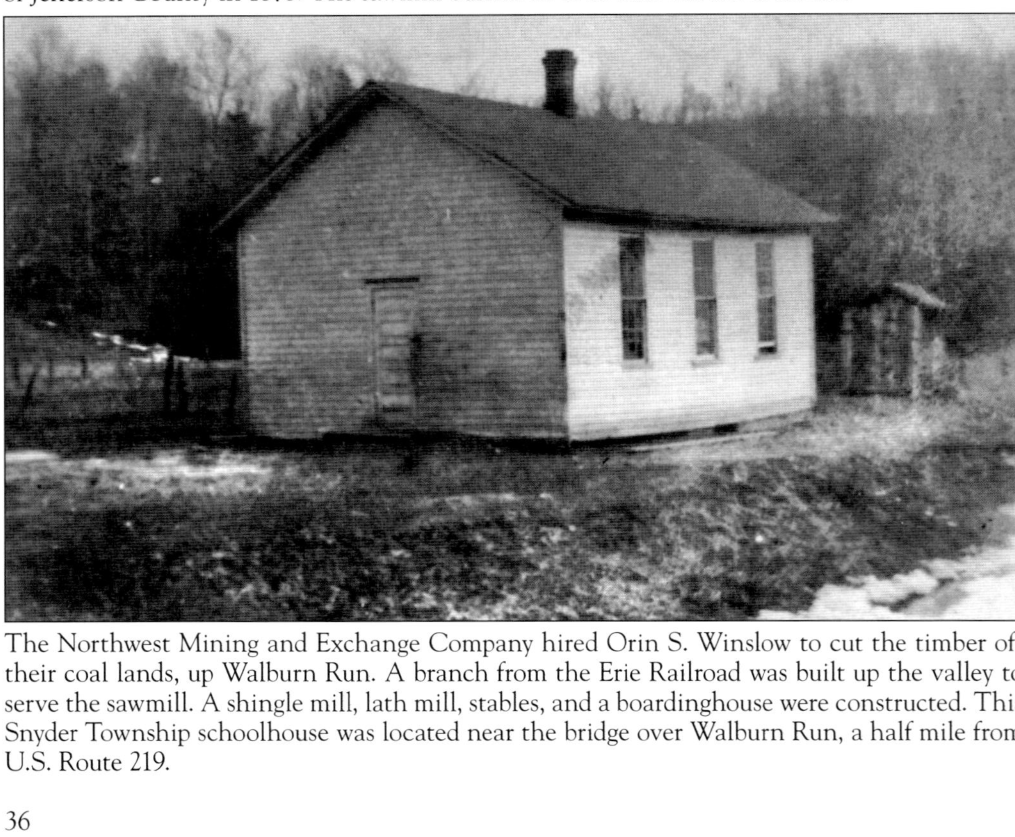

The Northwest Mining and Exchange Company hired Orin S. Winslow to cut the timber off their coal lands, up Walburn Run. A branch from the Erie Railroad was built up the valley to serve the sawmill. A shingle mill, lath mill, stables, and a boardinghouse were constructed. This Snyder Township schoolhouse was located near the bridge over Walburn Run, a half mile from U.S. Route 219.

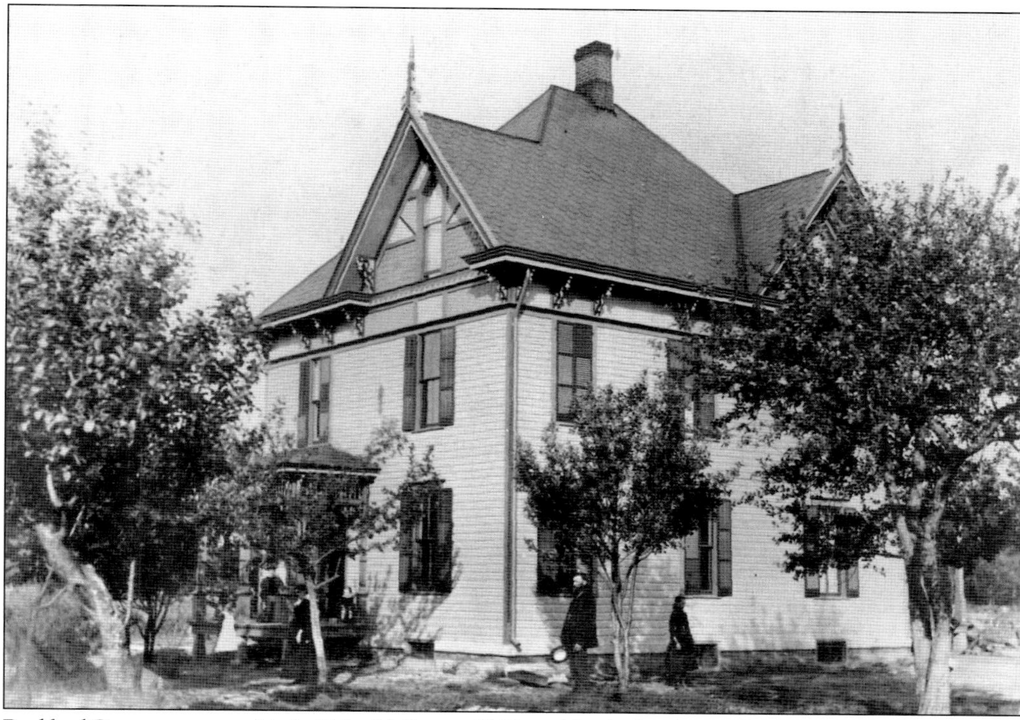

Redford Segers came to Little Toby Valley in 1863 and built this beautiful frame house across from Walburn Run Road and U.S. Route 219. The house has a beautiful black cherry spiral staircase up the three floors and additional woodwork, all handcrafted by Segers himself. He worked at several mills in the area, including the mill at Brockport, and the Buzard and McCain and Carrier sawmills north of Brockwayville.

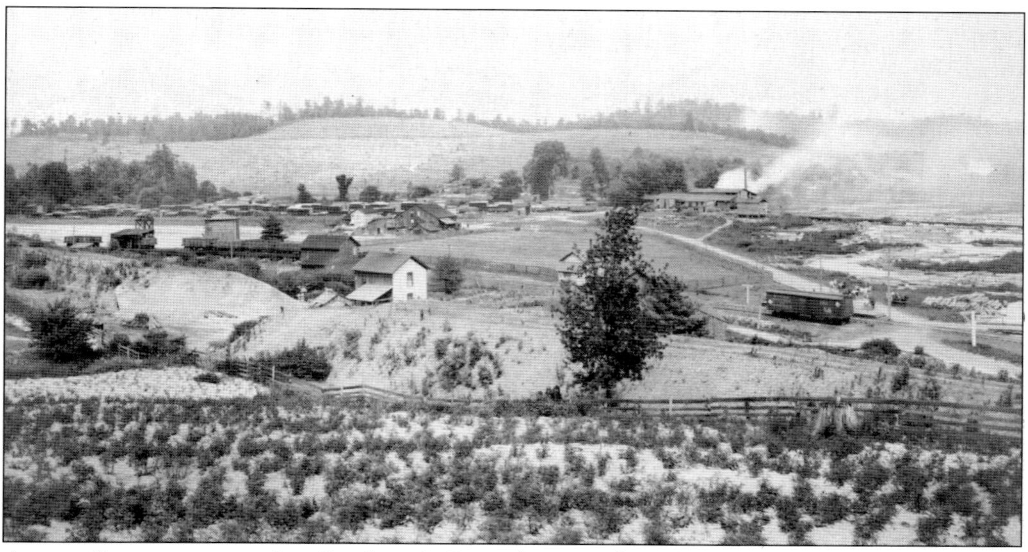

A sawmill was constructed on Rattlesnake Run, about a mile and a half south of Brockwayville, in 1845 by William McCullough. Six years later, Norman B. Lane partnered with Daniel Kingsbury and built a double-steam sawmill at the mouth of Mead Run in Brockport. Lane and partners purchased the McCullough mill and moved to Brockwayville. The village that sprang up around the mill complex became known as Lanes Mills.

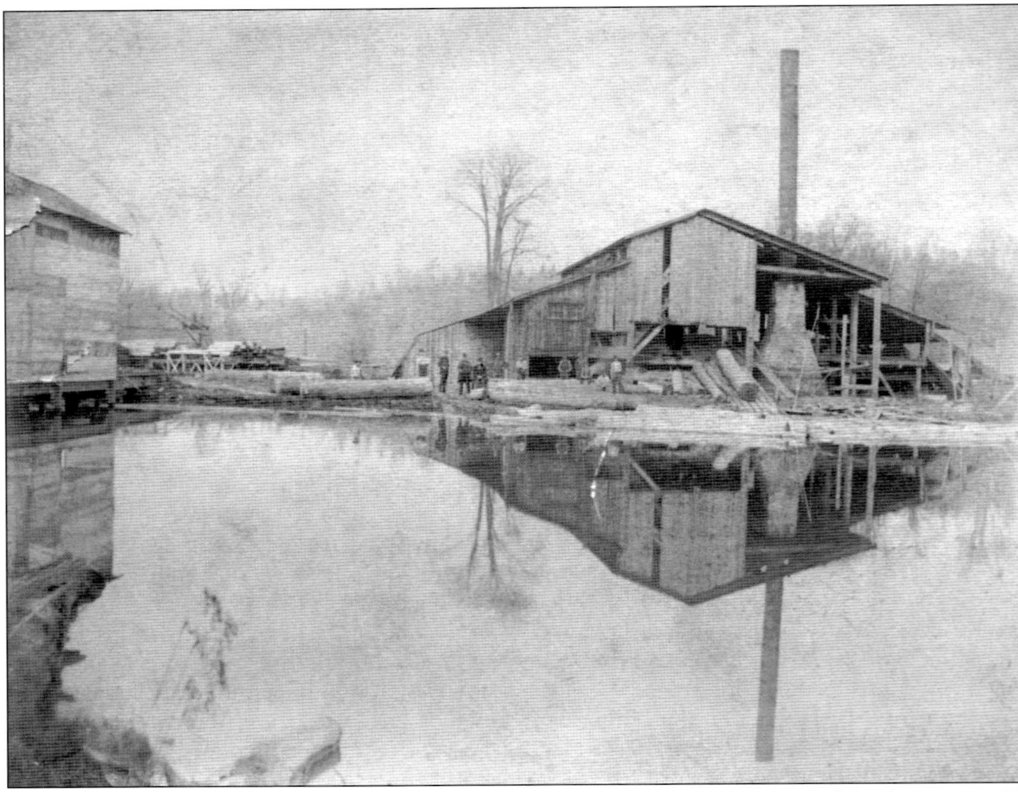

Lane and partners extensively upgraded the mill, and it was considered one of the best sawmills between Buffalo and Pittsburgh. Lane's partners sold their shares to Robert Humphreys in 1866, and the firm became known as Lane and Humphreys. To help increase the productivity of his employees, Lane and Nick Brockway had a law passed that forbade the sale of liquor in Snyder Township.

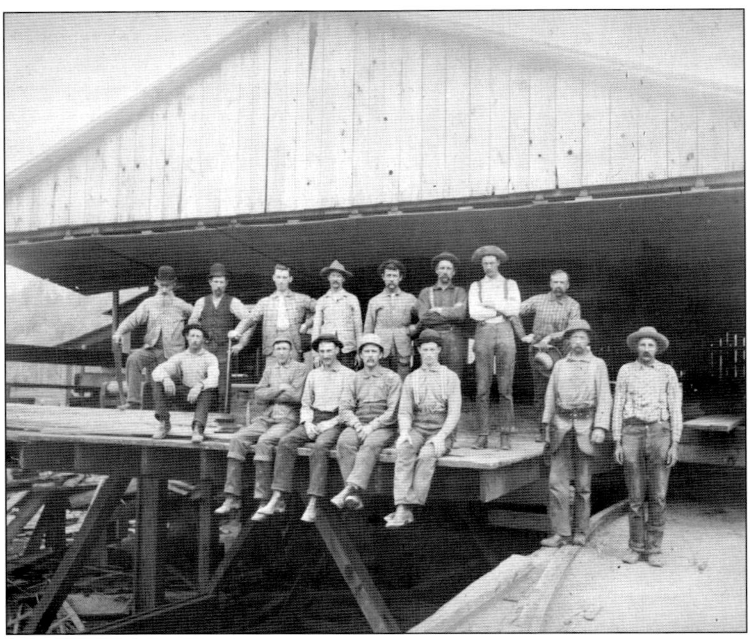

Norman Lane sure knew how to pick a spot for an industry. The Buffalo, Rochester, and Pittsburgh, and Ridgway and Clearfield Railroads were built through his mill site in the early 1880s. In order to get his lumber to market before the railroads, he rafted it down Little Toby Creek, the Clarion River, the Allegheny River to Pittsburgh, and even down the Ohio River to points along the Mississippi.

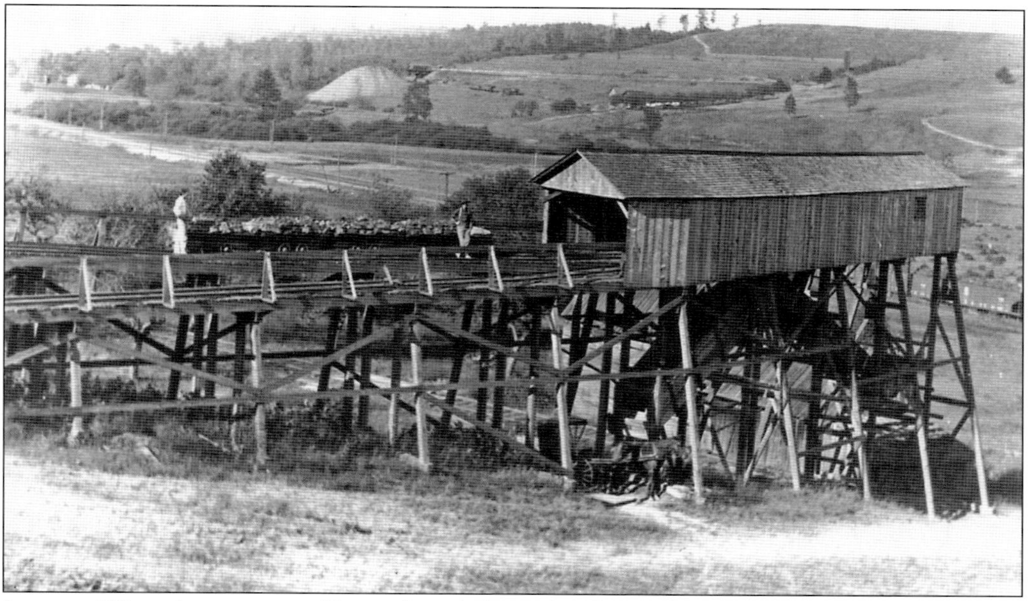

Lane and Humphreys eventually purchased the coal rights under the hills surrounding the mill. After the timber was cut and Lane and Humphreys dissolved in 1897, Norman Lane and son Fred went into the coal mining business. This gravity-operated tipple was on the hill to the north and east of the sawmill and shipped its product out on the Ridgway and Clearfield Railroad.

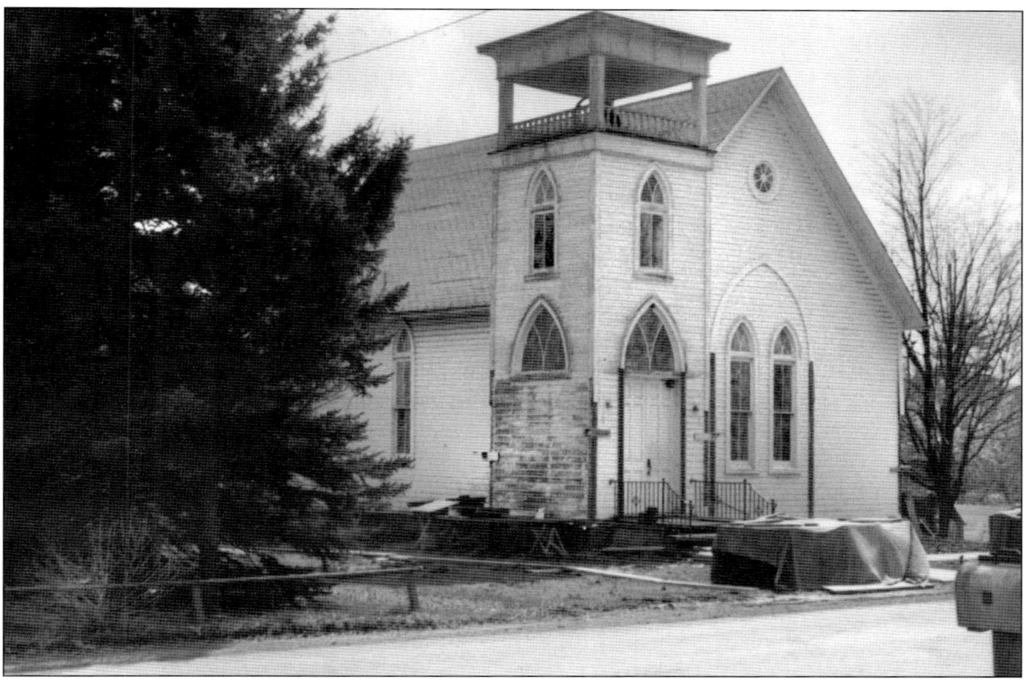

The Lanes Mills United Methodist Church was built in 1894 by Lane and Humphreys who furnished materials and land, which was east of the sawmill next to the schoolhouse. A social hall was built next to the church but was torn down for a parking lot in the 1940s. The church was encased in brick, and an educational wing and parsonage were added in the 1960s and 1970s.

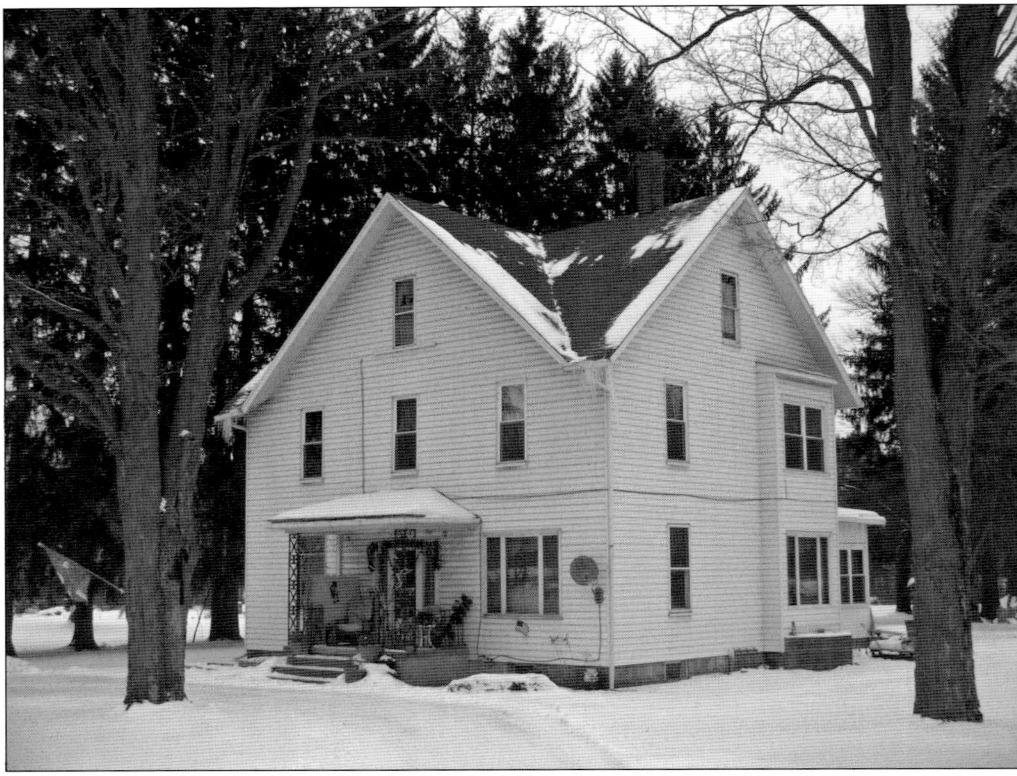

Robert Humphrey, partner to Norman Lane for 33 years in the lumber firm Lane and Humphrey, built this frame house on the corner of Rattlesnake Road and U.S. Route 219 in 1899. Norman Lane passed away in 1907 and Robert Humphrey in 1913. The house has recently experienced several owners using it as a beautiful bed and breakfast.

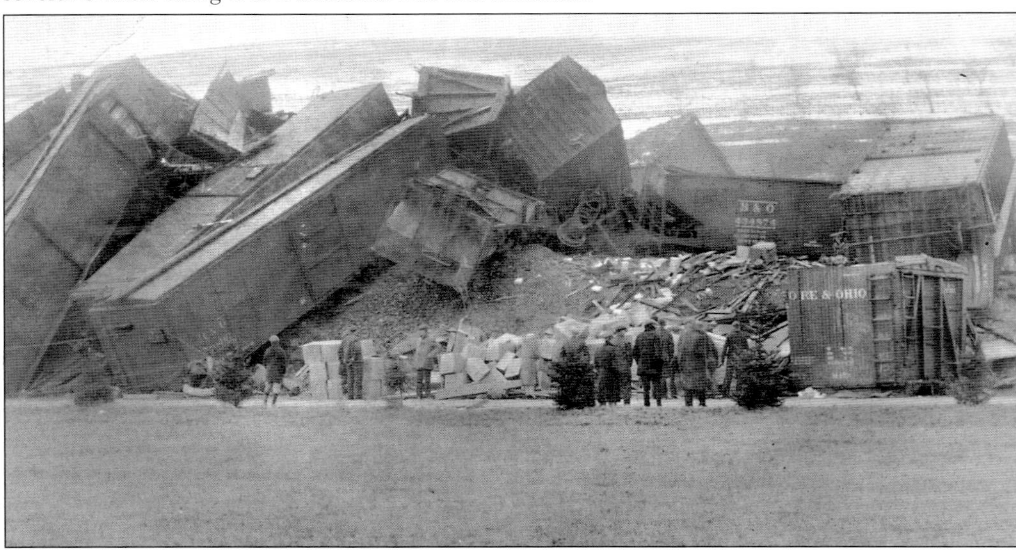

The Baltimore and Ohio Railroad bought the Buffalo, Rochester, and Pittsburgh Railway in 1930, and B&O lettering would be seen on cars through Brockway for several more decades. The railroads in Brockway had some vicious wrecks, as seen in this 1933 wreck near Lanes Mills that demolished 32 cars.

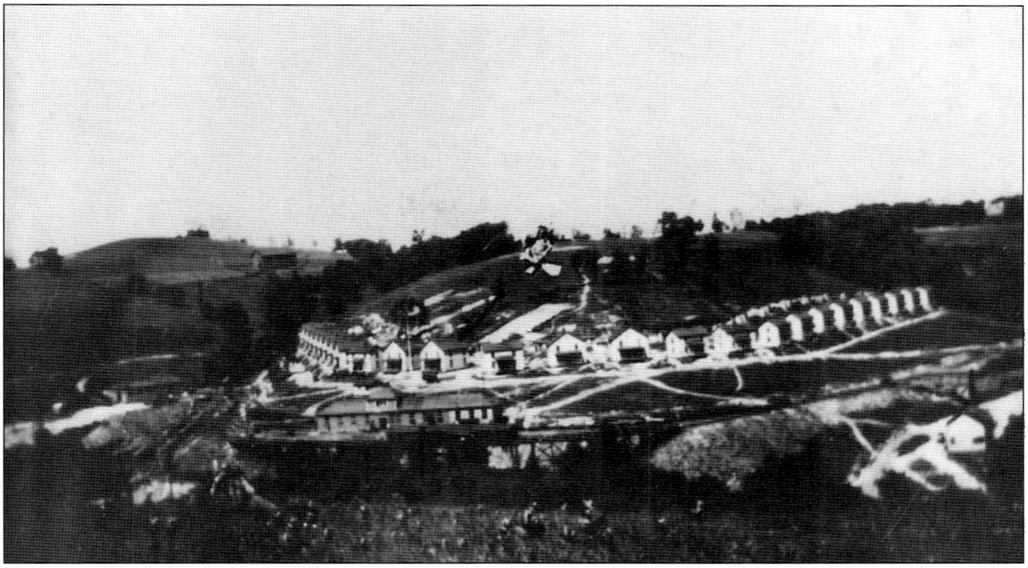

The Granville colliery of the Northwest Mining and Exchange Company opened in 1917 about a mile and a half south of Brockwayville. A three-track spur was constructed up the valley to the mines from the Buffalo, Rochester, and Pittsburgh Railway. The plant was estimated to be able to load 2,000 tons of coal a day and employ 200 miners. A flag-raising ceremony occurred on October 27, 1917.

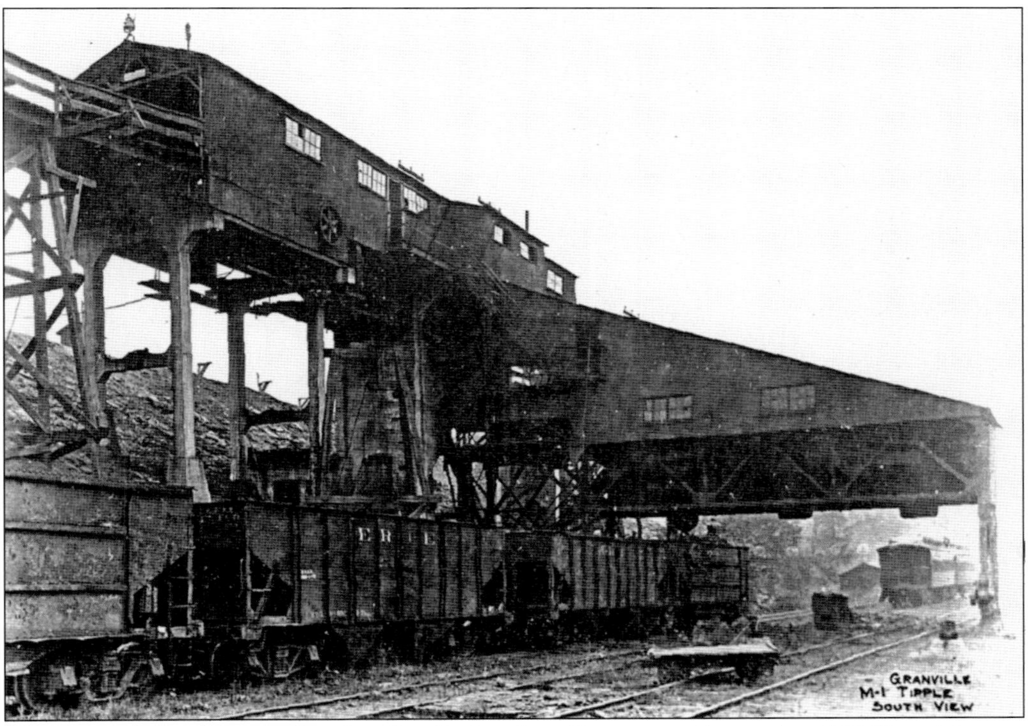

The Granville tipple started loading Erie Railroad coal hoppers in September 1917. Electricity was supplied from the huge power plant at Helens Mills, up on the upper end of Little Toby Valley. The premium-quality coal seam to be mined was at least 4 feet thick, and the technologies employed at the time earned it the reputation of the most modern coal mine in Pennsylvania's northwest.

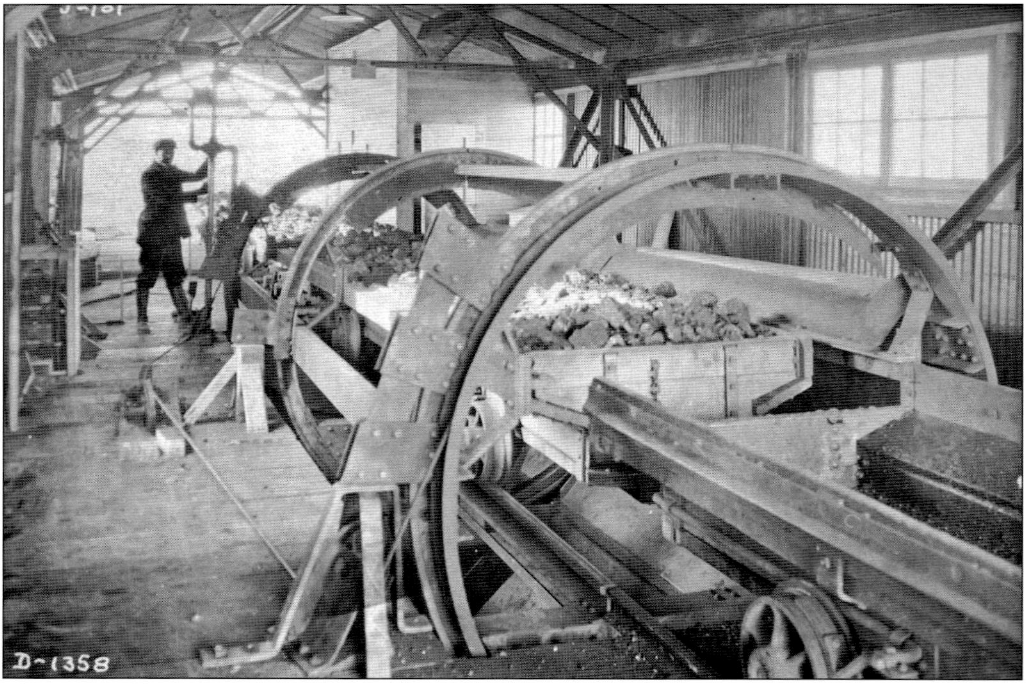

The Granville tipple was constructed of concrete and metal. The coal unloader in the tipple was automatic and, with swivel couplers and a system of cables and pulleys, allowed two cars of coal to be unloaded at the same time. It was steam-driven, using a reversible steam valve that was manually operated. The mine spoils were hauled by cable car to a giant slate dump south of the tipple.

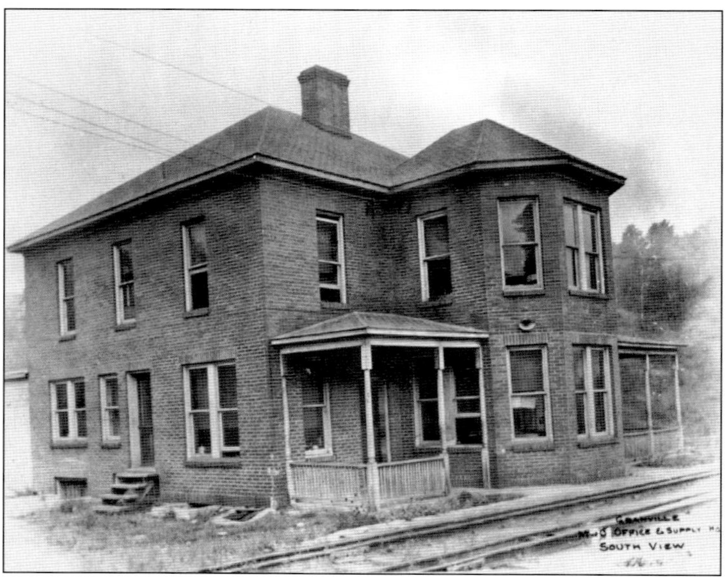

The Northwest Mining and Exchange Company office building at Granville also housed supplies and acted as the scale house. It was located northeast of the tipple along the set of three tracks that served the operation. A passenger train with heated coaches would bring the miners to and from their homes in Brockwayville. The mine expected to run for 25 years but was actually exhausted in about a decade.

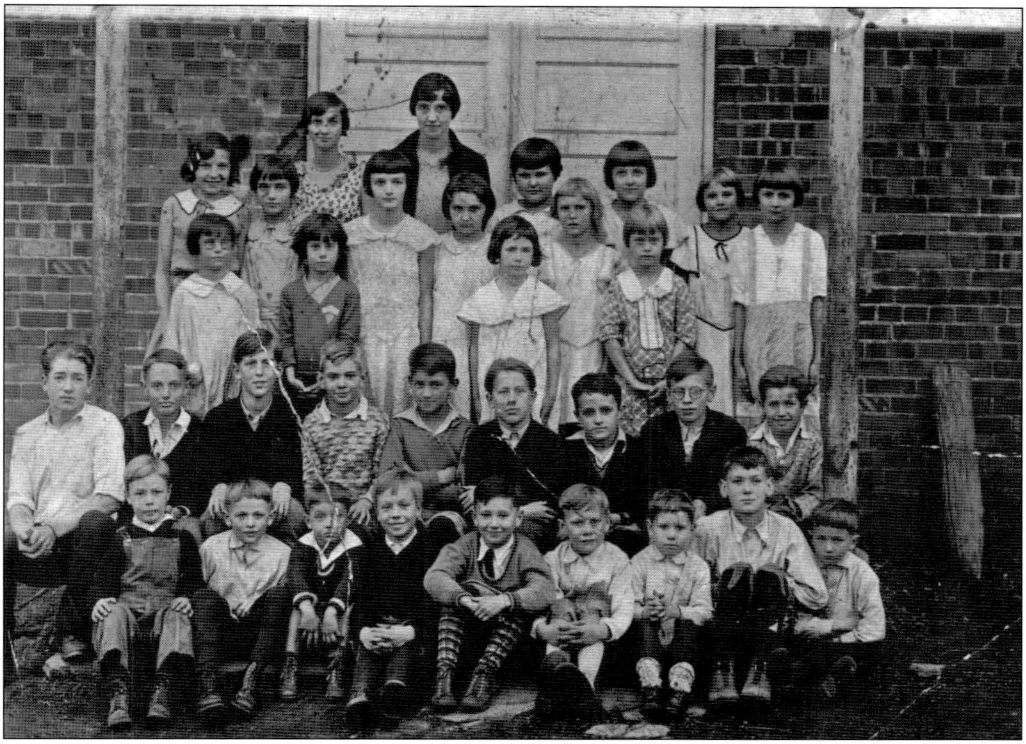

A brick schoolhouse was constructed at Granville to educate the youth of the miners in the village and surrounding area. This photograph was taken during the 1929–1930 school year, a few years after the mine had closed. It was also the year the stock market crashed, sending the country into the Great Depression. One could not tell this by the expressions on the faces of the front row.

A steam crane lifts a girder during construction of the Dellwood Viaduct, or "Lanes Viaduct," just south of the Brockway Machine Bottle Company's original glass plant. The viaduct is considered the southern terminus of the Pittsburg, Shawmut, and Northern Railroad and the northern terminus of the Pittsburgh and Shawmut Railroad, the latter being the moneymaker, after the two split from the same company in 1916.

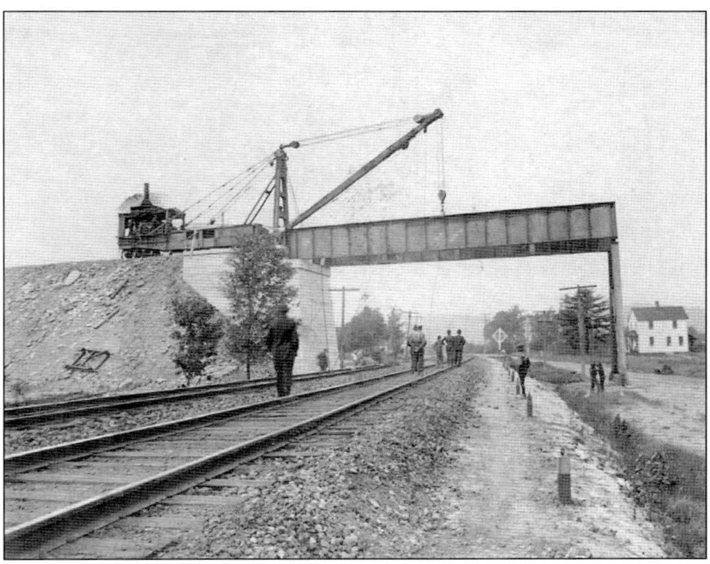

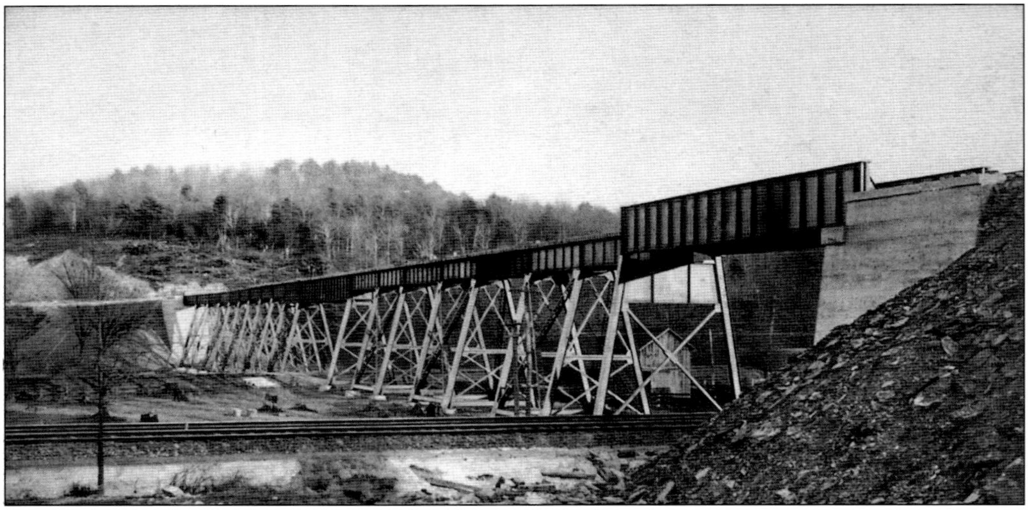

The Pittsburg, Shawmut, and Northern Railroad viaduct at Dellwood stands completed in 1907. The bridge spans the Buffalo, Rochester, and Pittsburgh Railway in the foreground, Rattlesnake Run just before it flows into Little Toby Creek, the Ridgway and Clearfield Railroad, and a spur from the R&C to the Brock Mines. The Buffalo and Pittsburgh Railroad still uses the viaduct to get cars to the glass plant in Crenshaw.

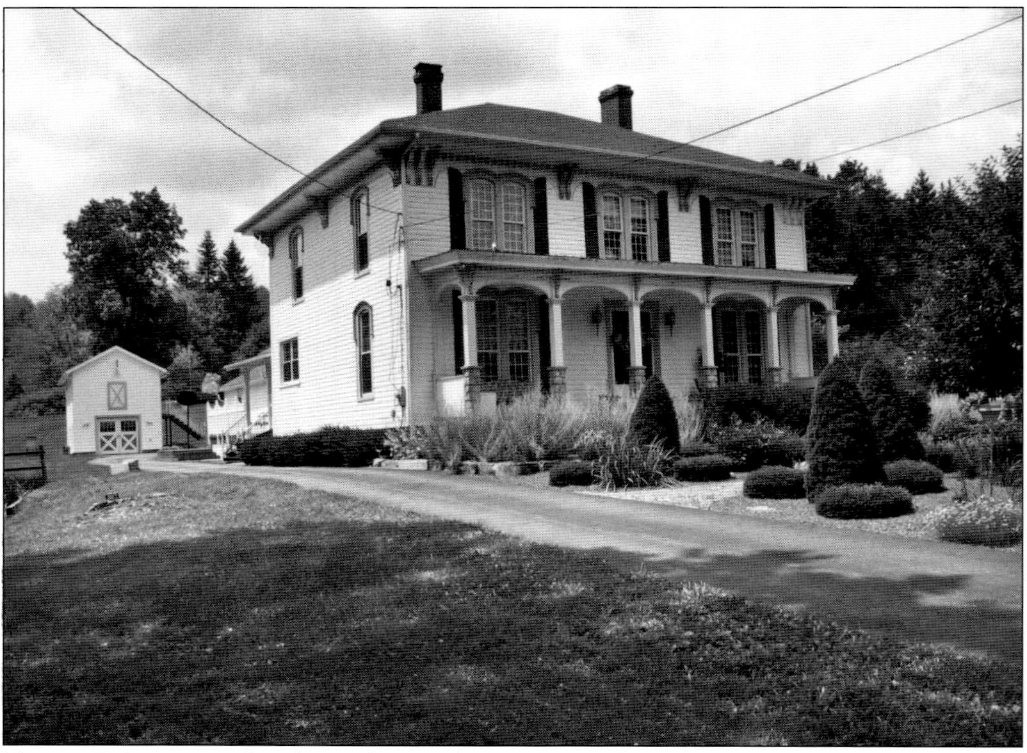

Norman B. Lane moved to the southern end of Brockwayville and built his beautiful home in 1857. The home passed through family and eventually to his granddaughter Naomi Lane Eisenman, who donated an incredible number of artifacts to the Taylor Memorial Museum. Several tenants occupied the apartment in the house throughout the years, including Irvin Keith and family, while he established his metal fabrication business in the Grande Opera House.

Two

Middle Toby Valley and Brockway

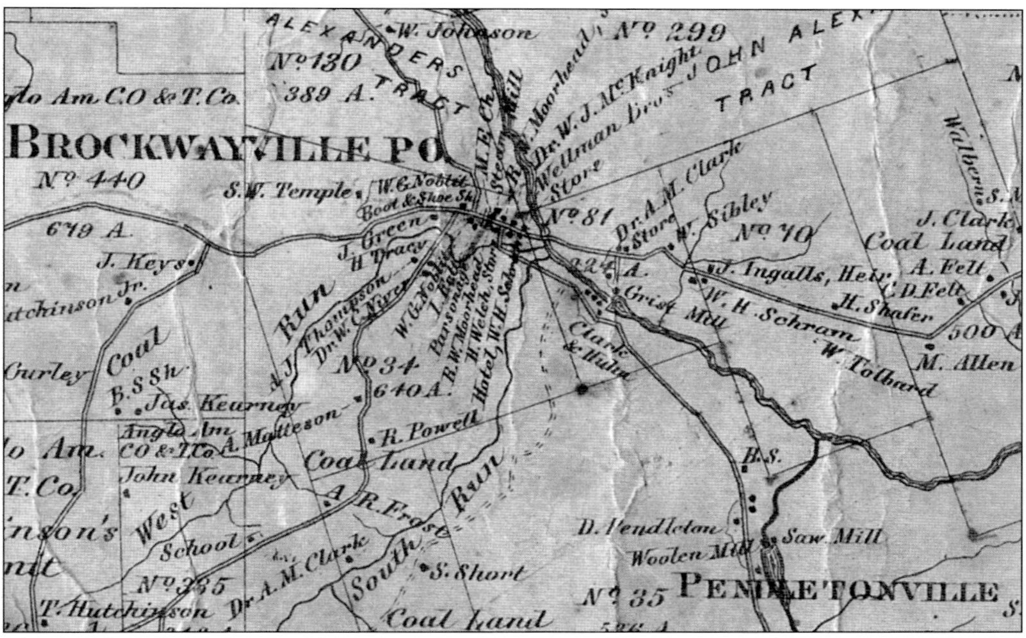

The Middle Toby Valley–Brockway region focuses primarily on the borough of Brockway. The map shown above was cropped from A. Pomeroy's 1866 map of Jefferson County, showing Brockwayville within the current borough lines. Much of Brockwayville at the time was west of Little Toby Creek, but the industrial revolution would cause eastward expansion of the town.

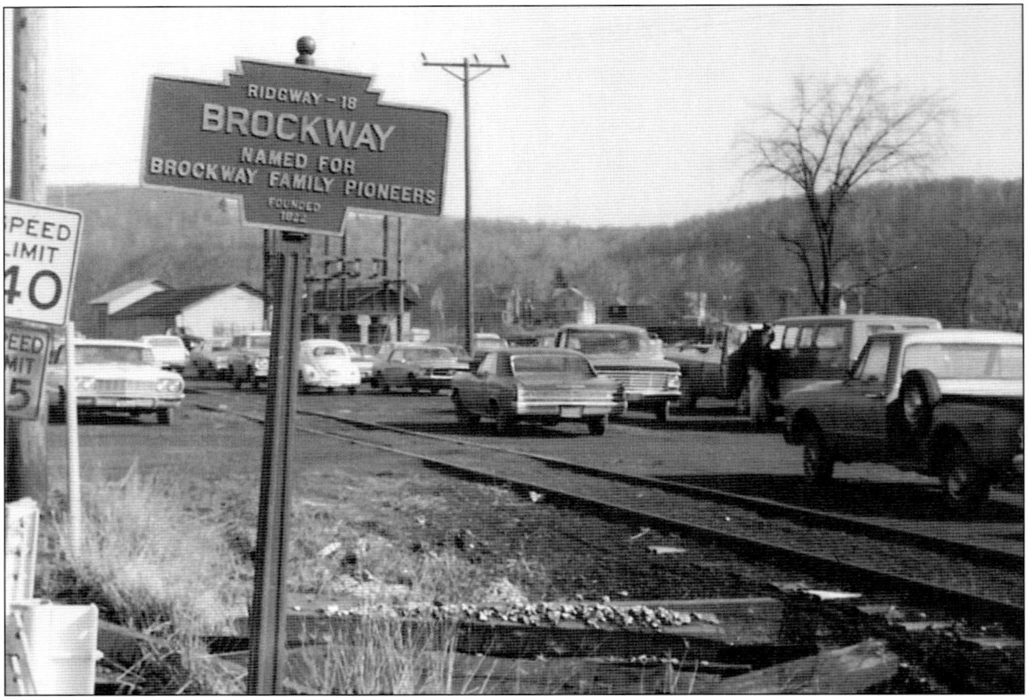

This Brockway signpost stood between U.S. Route 219 and the Ridgway and Clearfield Railroad, just east of the original Brockway Glass Company plant on the southern end of Brockway. The employee parking lot sits to the right, and Little Toby Creek meanders through the woods behind the parking lot toward the business end of Brockway.

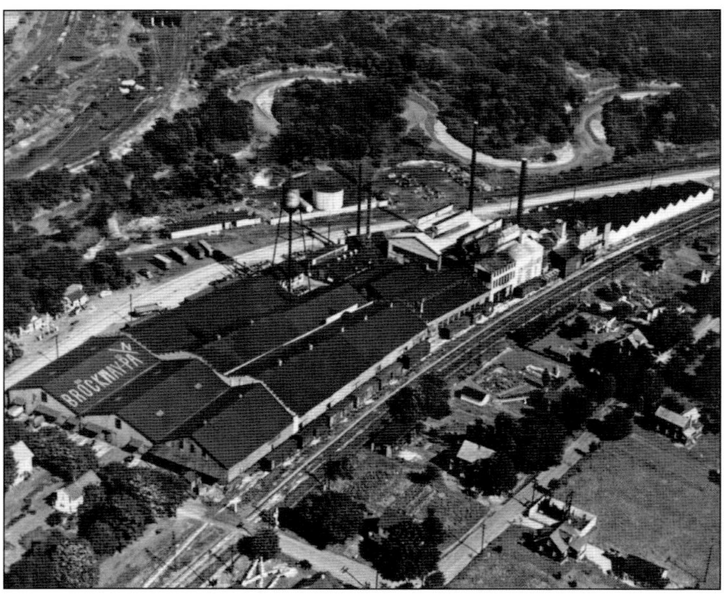

The Brockway Glass Company started as the Brockwayville Glass Company in 1897. The plant was closed due to poor equipment, but was purchased, run, and sold again several more times over the next 10 years. H. B. McCullough purchased the factory, and 12 glassworkers from Olean, New York, invested $34,000 to get the plant up and running again. The organization was named the Brockway Machine Bottle Company.

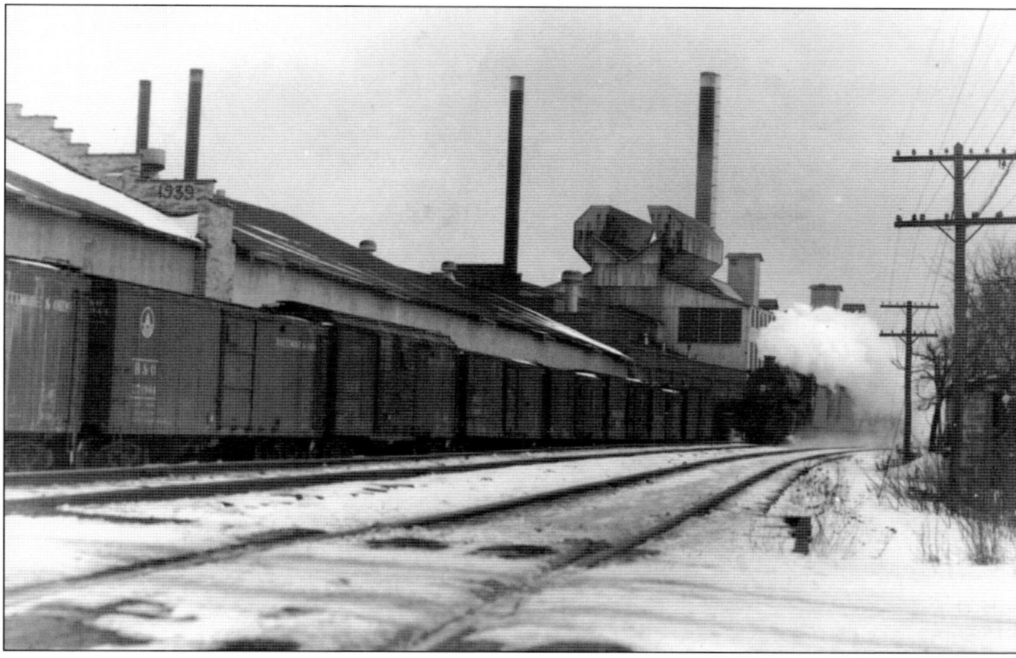

The upgraded Brockway Machine Bottle Company plant made its first bottle on October 17, 1907. This tiny company became the second-largest glass container manufacturer in the world by the 1980s. It employed over 12,500 men, had annual sales of close to $1 billion, and had 600 shareholders holding almost five million shares of Brockway stock, which paid dividends for over 50 years.

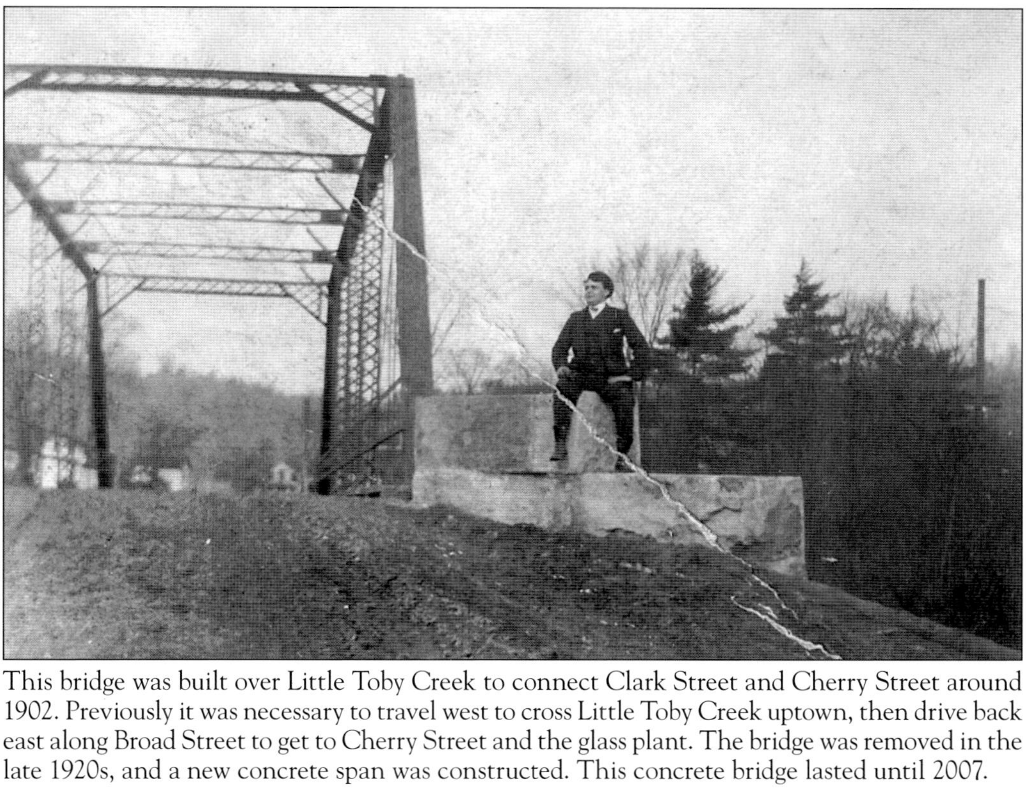

This bridge was built over Little Toby Creek to connect Clark Street and Cherry Street around 1902. Previously it was necessary to travel west to cross Little Toby Creek uptown, then drive back east along Broad Street to get to Cherry Street and the glass plant. The bridge was removed in the late 1920s, and a new concrete span was constructed. This concrete bridge lasted until 2007.

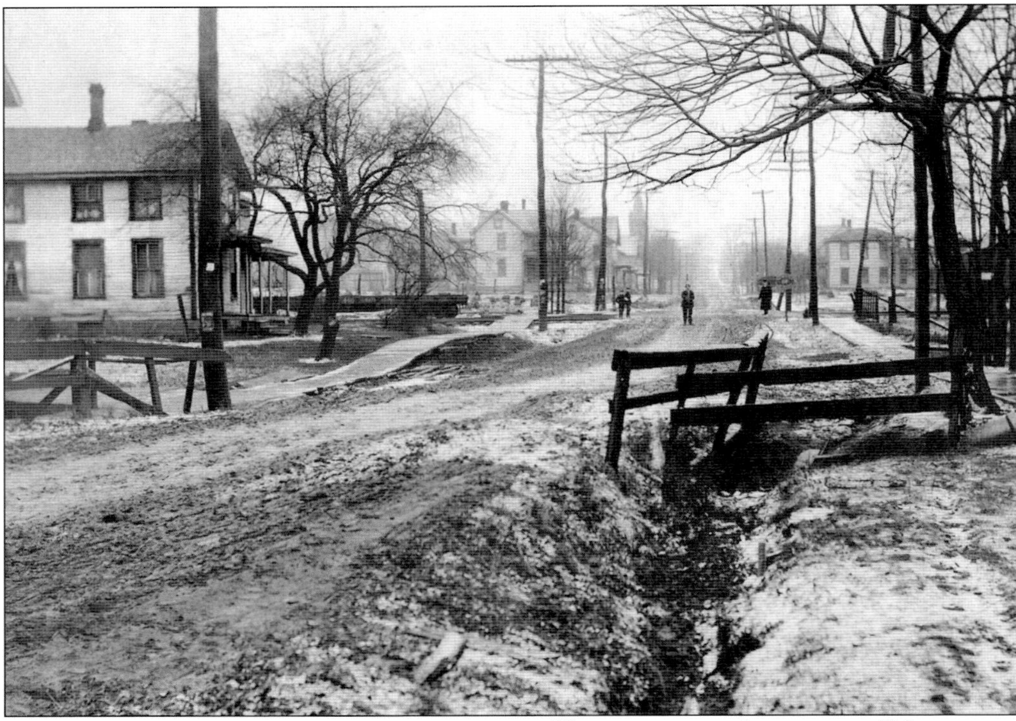

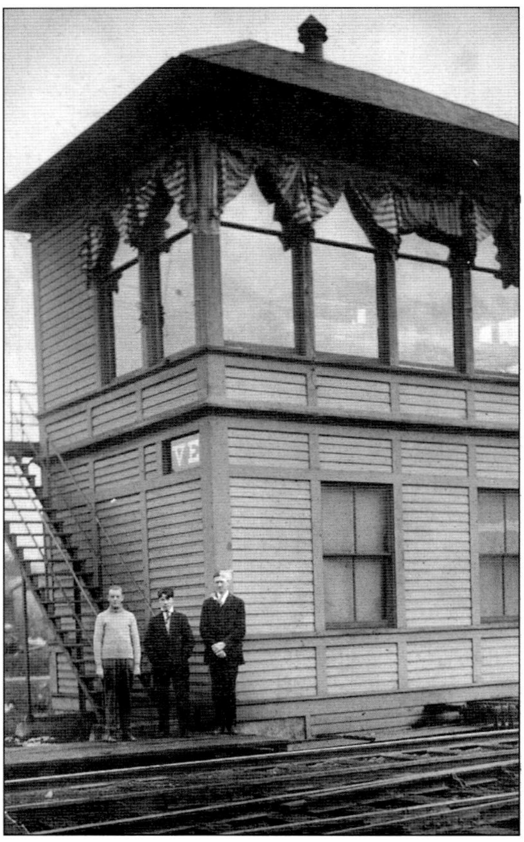

This street scene faces east up "Mount Vista," a hill that U.S. Route 219 now climbs on its way out of Brockway towards Ridgway. The railroad crossing is the Ridgway and Clearfield Railroad, built in 1884 as a connection between the low grade of the Allegheny Valley branch of the Pennsylvania Railroad at Falls Creek and the Pennsylvania-owned Philadelphia and Erie Railroad in Ridgway.

The VE Tower of the Ridgway and Clearfield Railroad sat at the east corner of Clark and Main Streets. It was the railroad's dispatch center and was removed in the late 1920s. The parking lot of the Sheetz store occupies the site in 2010, but the old iron plate girder bridge that carried the R&C across Little Toby Creek still sits to the south behind Sheetz.

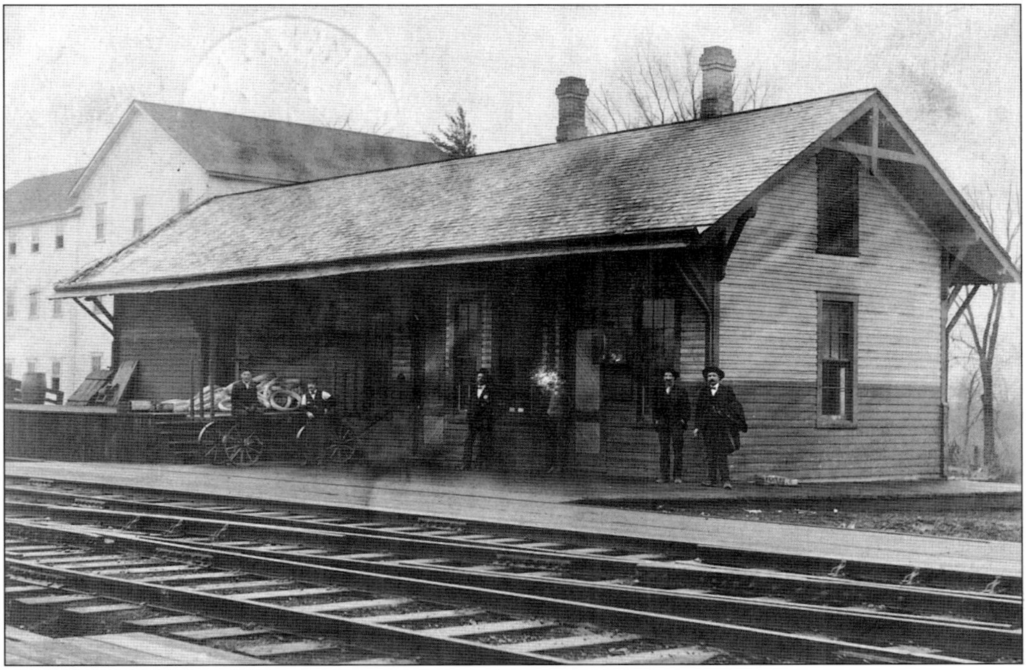

The Ridgway and Clearfield Railroad depot was built on the east end of Brockwayville beside the old Kirkpatrick Hotel, standing behind the depot. The R&C was Brockwayville's connection to the famous Pennsylvania Railroad, with connections to other Pennsylvania lines in Falls Creek and Ridgway. The R&C was leased by the Pennsylvania Railroad, but was primarily a coal-hauling line for the Erie Railroad's Northwest Mining and Exchange Company.

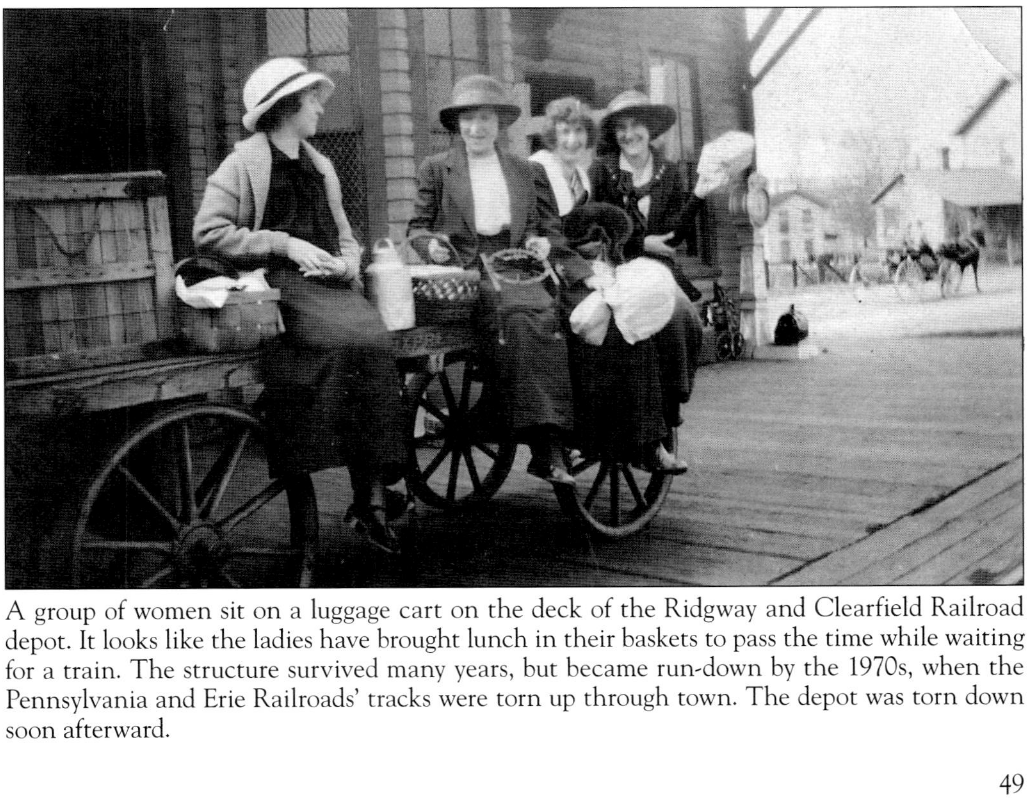

A group of women sit on a luggage cart on the deck of the Ridgway and Clearfield Railroad depot. It looks like the ladies have brought lunch in their baskets to pass the time while waiting for a train. The structure survived many years, but became run-down by the 1970s, when the Pennsylvania and Erie Railroads' tracks were torn up through town. The depot was torn down soon afterward.

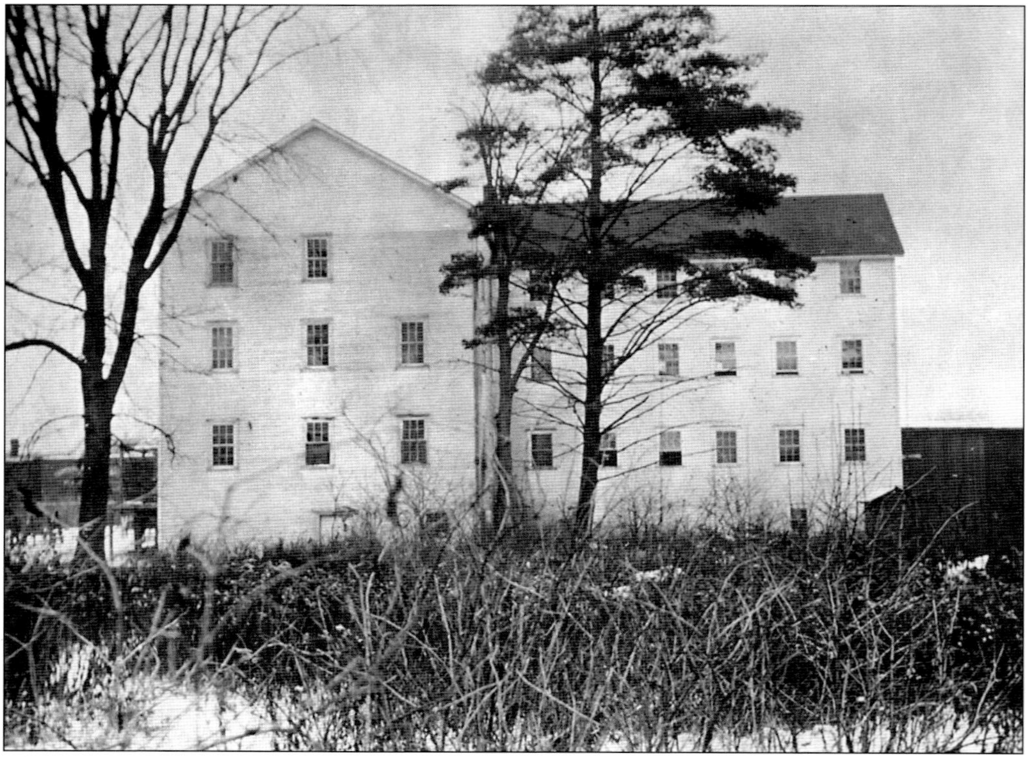

The Kirkpatrick Hotel was built before 1904 and was used to possibly house the railroad workers on the east side of town. It was also used by the Eureka Milling Company, owned and operated by Charles McCauley and Arthur McKay. It was sold to the Brockway Macaroni and Supply Company in 1904, which used it for several years until it burned in 1908.

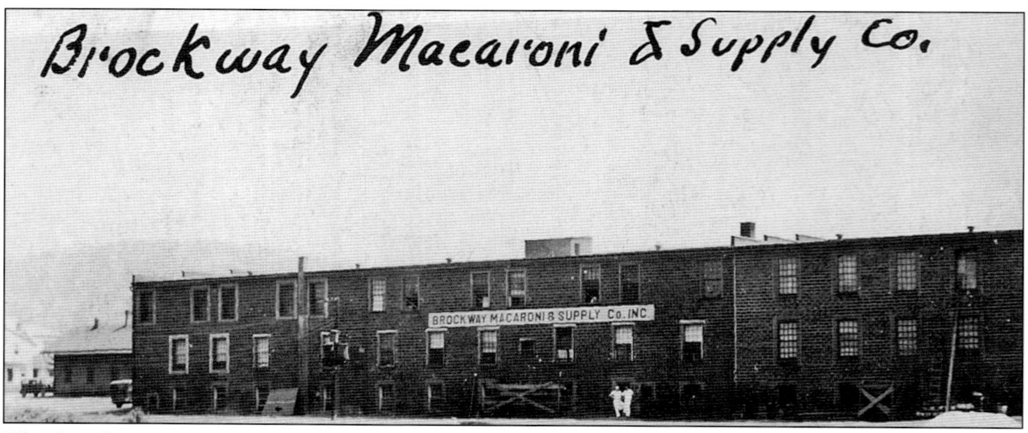

The Brockway Macaroni and Supply Company built a large brick factory to replace the one lost in the 1908 fire. This photograph of the plant was taken in 1936. The company owned another plant in Reynoldsville, so when the Brockway factory burned in a spectacular fire on January 12–13, 1942, it was not rebuilt.

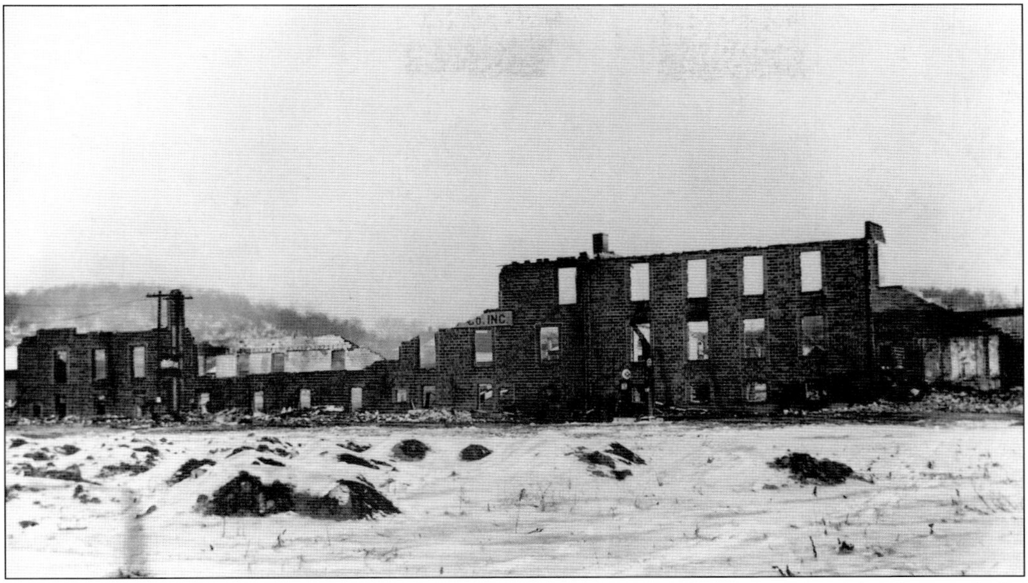

Two hours of effort by firefighters were not enough to save the structure. The focus of the firefighting shifted to saving the Ridgway and Clearfield Railroad depot nearby. The fire was expensive, costing the company $200,000. Rumor was that Italian supporters of Mussolini and the Axis burned the factory in protest of the war.

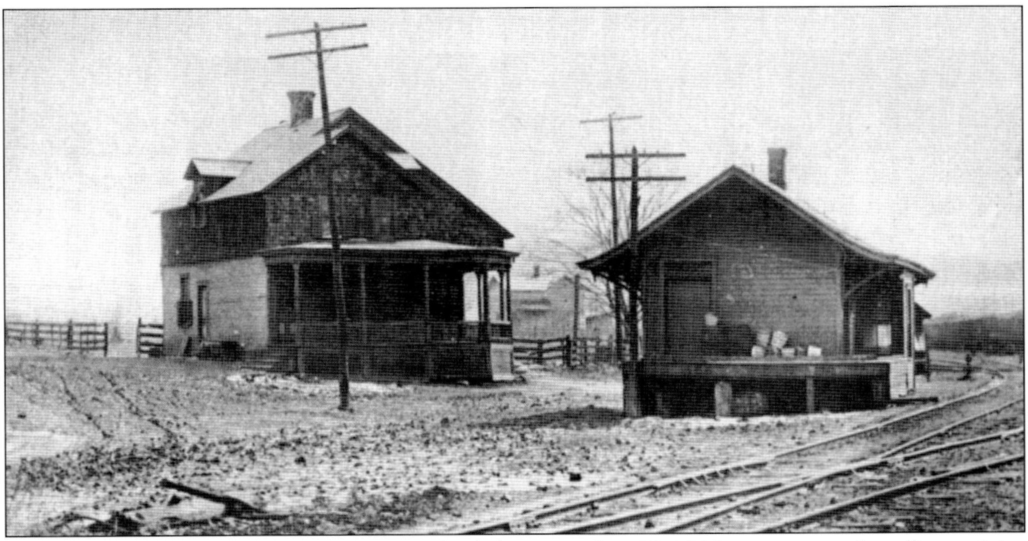

The Erie Railroad built the structure on the left in October 20, 1893, to serve as the offices of the Erie's Bradford division. It was later used as the offices of the Northwest Mining and Exchange Company. It was also used by the Pittsburg, Shawmut, and Northern Railroad as a passenger depot. The building on the left beside the tracks was the Erie Railroad depot.

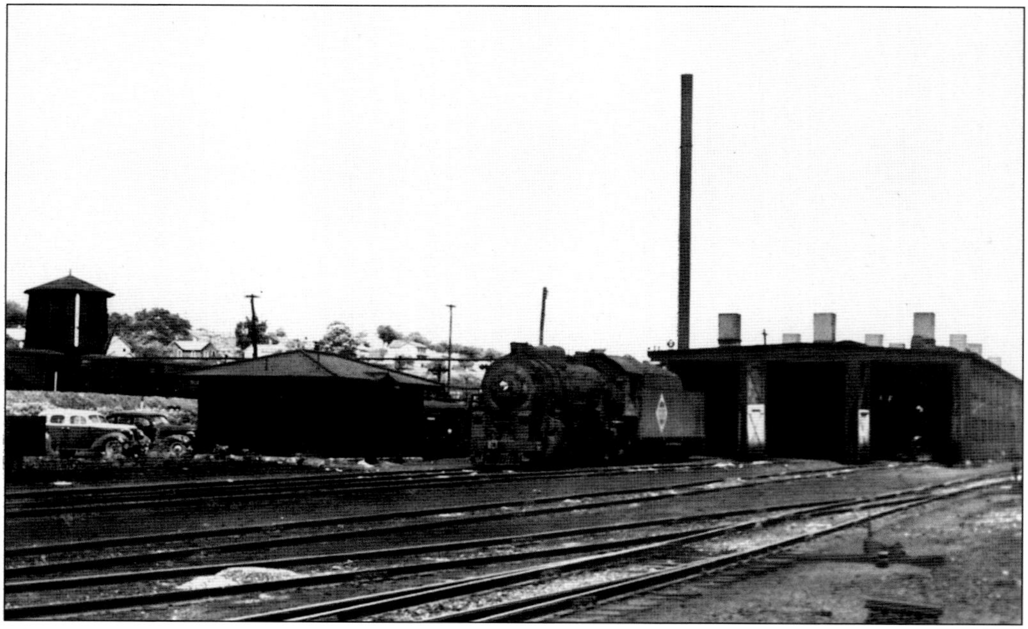

The east end of town held small yards for the Erie Railroad and the Pittsburg, Shawmut, and Northern Railroad. The engine house shown above belonged to the Erie Railroad, while the Shawmut yard was to the northeast. An Erie Railroad workhorse "Mikado" class locomotive waits for its orders at the engine house in the 1950s, at a time when steam locomotives were being replaced by diesels.

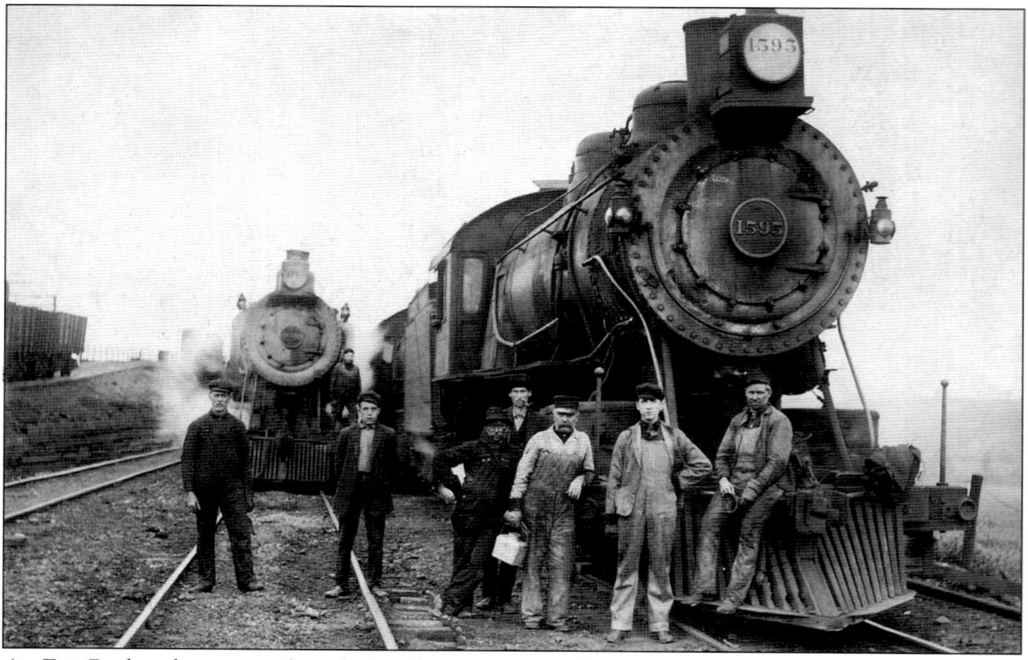

An Erie Railroad crew stands with their locomotives at the yards, which included the engine house, coaling facilities (shown here on the left), a water tank, oil house, scale house, sand house, washroom, ash pit, truck storage, repair shops, and a wye used to turn the locomotives around. There were also multiple storage tracks for the freight cars, which included a large fleet of coal hoppers.

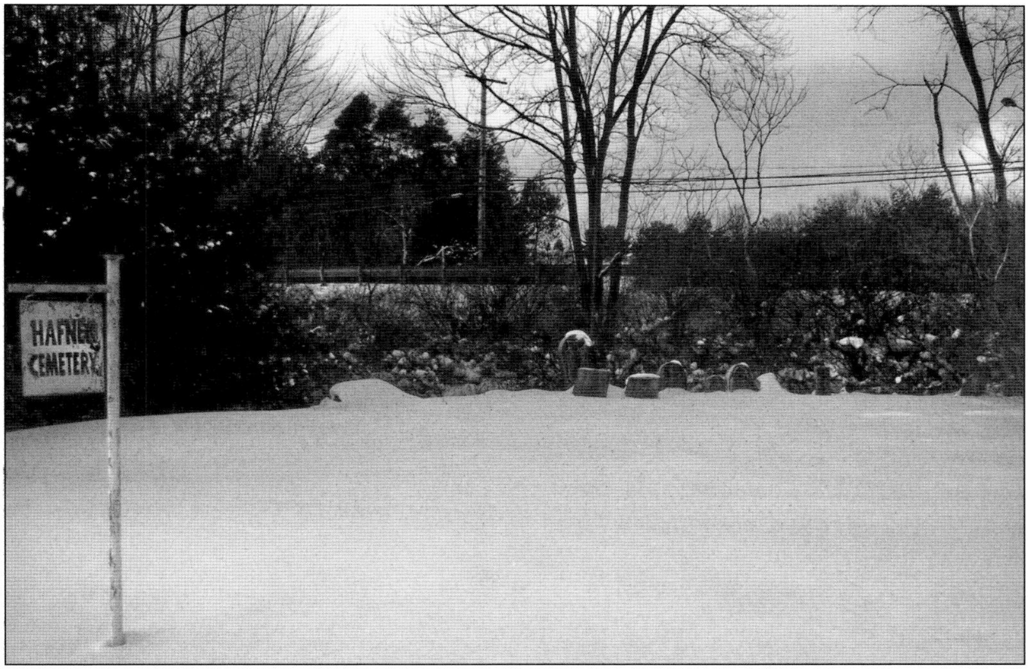

The Hafner Cemetery at the eastern end of Bond Street contains markers from the mid-1800s, including that of Revolutionary War veteran Joel Clark Sr., who died in 1844. The plot also includes the Henry Shaffer family, son of Jacob Shaffer who settled on Bond Street in 1823. In 1842, Henry Shaffer married Pheobe Pendleton, daughter of James Pendleton who owned a sawmill, gristmill, and a carding mill along Rattlesnake Run.

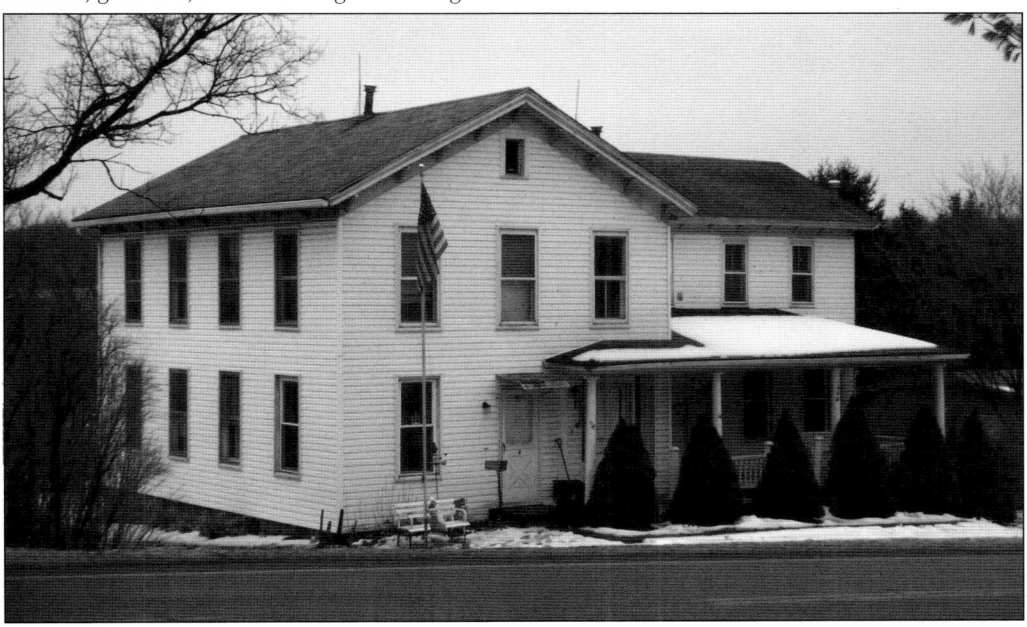

The cornices on this house near the hilltop on the east end of Brockwayville indicate that the house was probably built in the mid- to late 1800s. The John Wrey Smith family owned farmland that surrounded the northeast end of Brockwayville, and this was most likely their farmhouse. They were neighbors of the Shaffer family who lived below them on Bond Street.

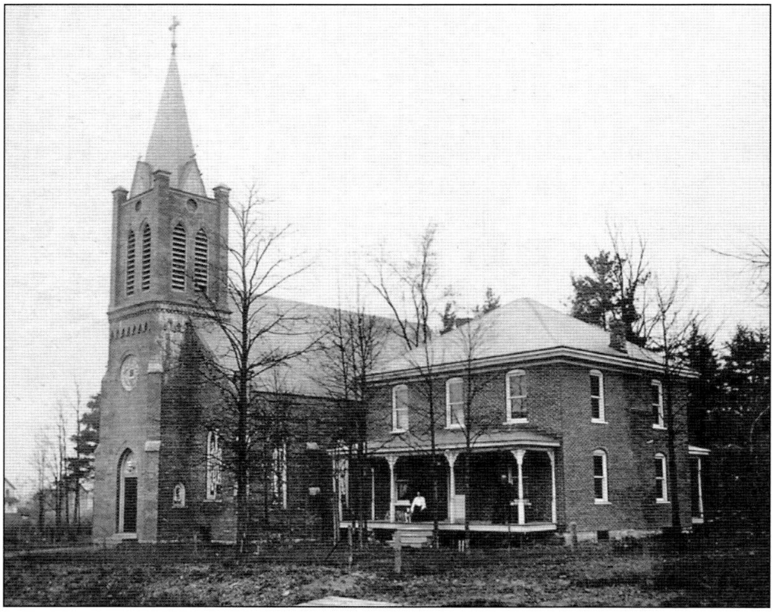

The original St. Tobias Roman Catholic Church, named for Rev. Tobias Mullen, was completed in August 1899 under the motivation of Fr. Bernard Lynch and his congregation. The congregation grew to a size that required six masses each Sunday, so the old church was razed in 1965 to make way for the new one to be built a few hundred yards behind it.

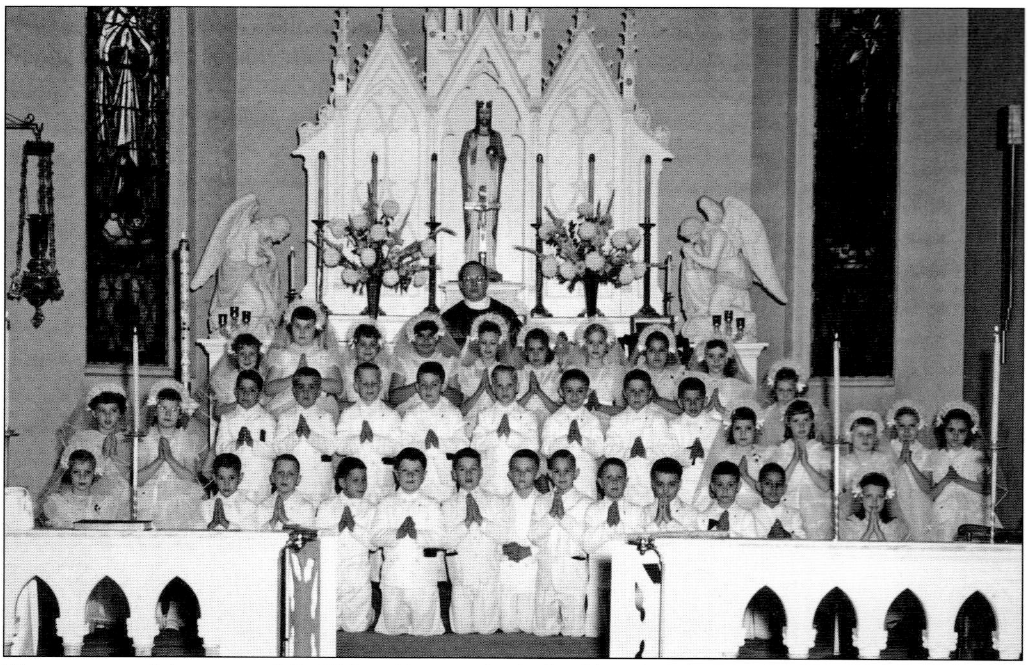

The interior of the original St. Tobias Roman Catholic Church is featured in this photograph. The photograph was taken in the 1950s or 1960s, and proof of the size of the congregation exists with the number of children. The dedication of the new St. Tobias Roman Catholic Church occurred on October 27, 1968, and Bishop Whealon was present to consecrate the main altar.

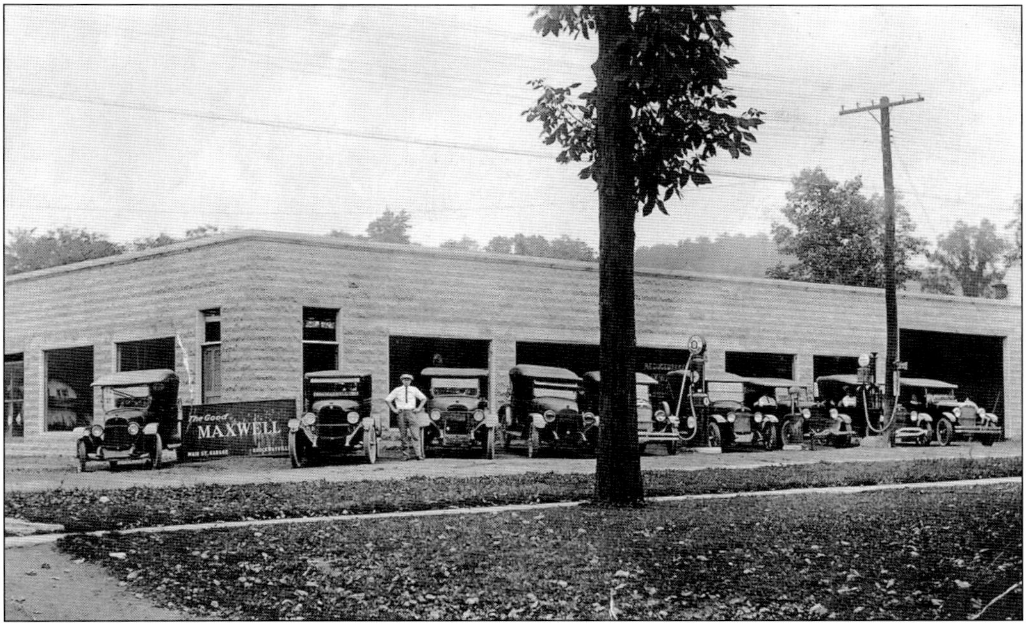

W. Axel Johnson was the proprietor of the Maxwell garage to the immediate west of the Catholic church. The rear of the garage was the site where Wendell August started his first wrought iron forge in 1924. Wendell August was a coal operator and a businessman, and he hired blacksmiths Otto Pisoni and Natale Rossi to create forged and hand-beaten works of art that earned national acclaim.

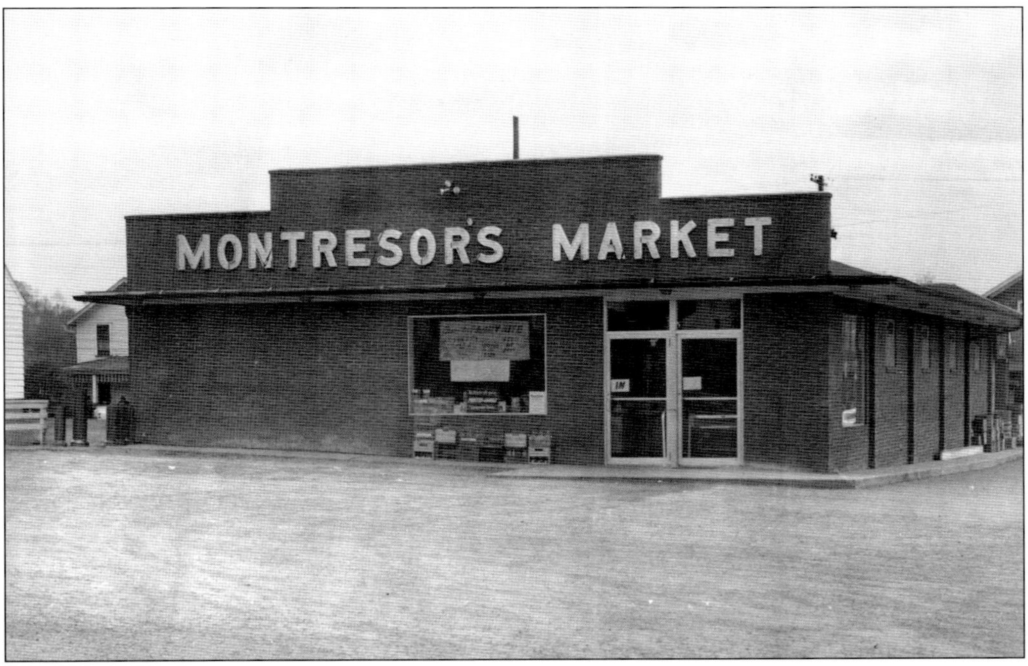

The east end of town had a few grocery stores back in the day, including Montresor's Market shown in this photograph. Coder's Print Shop now occupies the building. Martino's grocery store was nearby on Main Street, which eventually moved west into town, when land became available after the flood control was installed in the late 1950s.

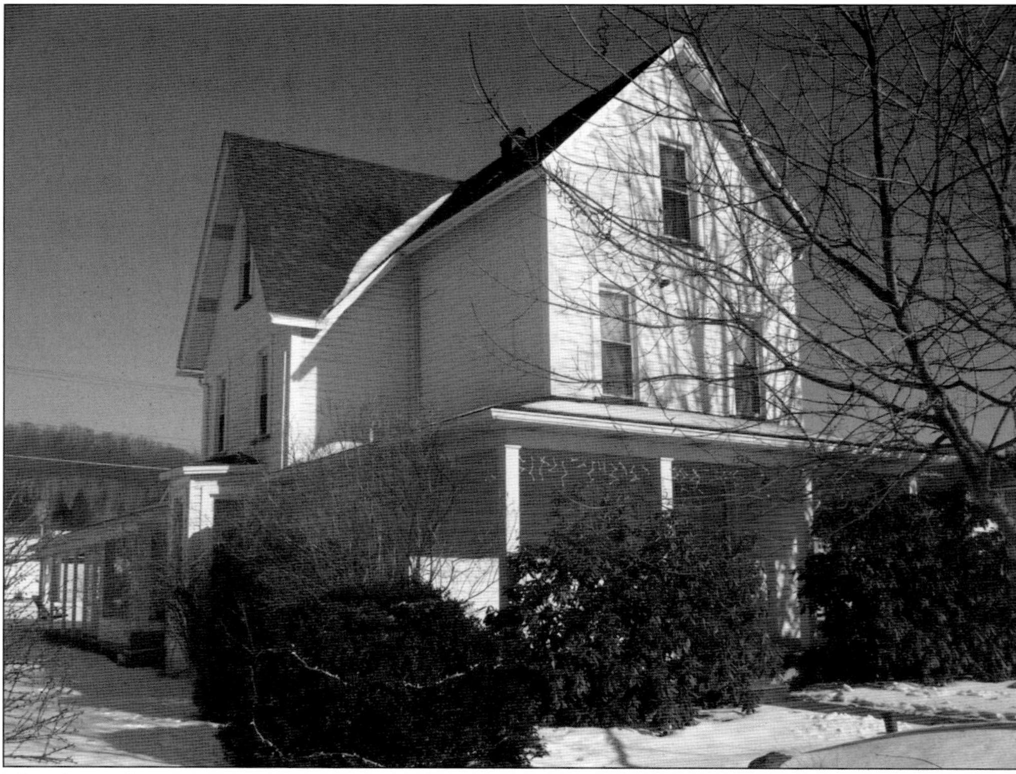

This large house sits on Main Street between Buzard and McCain Streets, a block west of the Johnson garage. A number of old, large homes line Main Street on the east end, and tracing their histories became difficult without spending a lot of time at the Jefferson County Courthouse in Brookville. Most of the homes along Main Street are well kept, adding to the pride of the community.

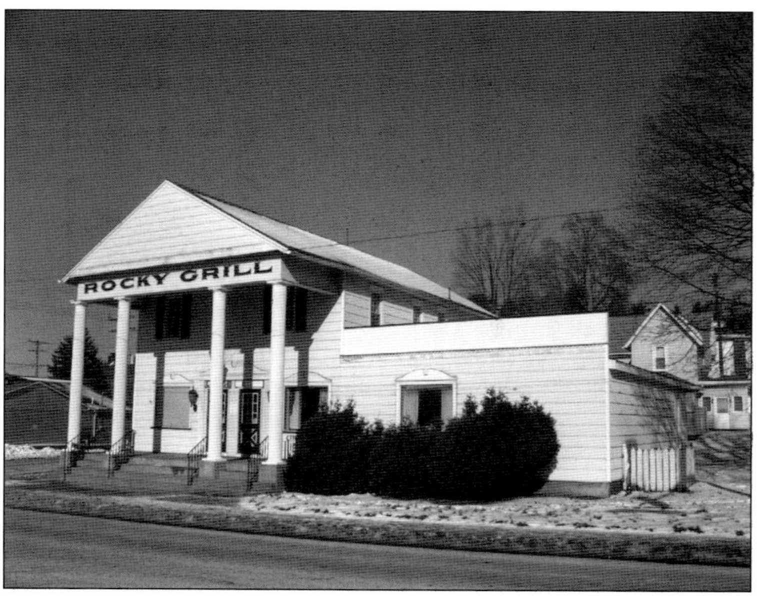

Alonzo Brockway's cabin of 1822 was most likely near the current location of the Rocky Grill. The building was at one time Monaco's Grocery Store, but Joe Scarnati purchased it in 1933 and converted it into a bar and restaurant. A large mural that hung on the wall in the restaurant reminded Joe of the Rocky Mountains, so he named the restaurant the Rocky Grill.

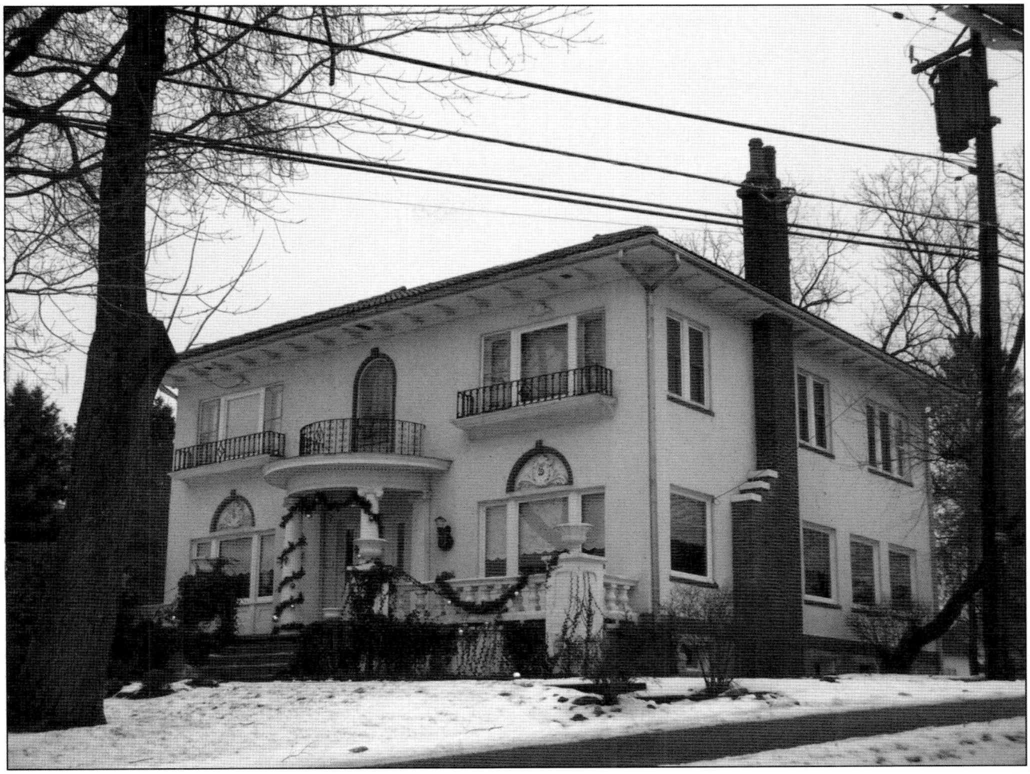

This beautiful house sits at the top of a sweeping lawn on the east side of Evergreen Street, which was once called Railroad Street. The house was built by John O. Nava, who ran a machine shop north along Evergreen Street and was employed by the Brockway Glass Company for many years. The house was purchased by Joe Scarnati, owner of the Rocky Grill discussed earlier.

The Brockway Light, Heat, and Power Company plant opened in 1921 on the corner of Evergreen and James Streets. The electric generation station cost between $80,000 and $100,000 and used engines manufactured in Ridgway to electrify the town of Brockwayville for the first time. The Pennsylvania Electric Company ("Penelec") of Johnstown took over the plant in 1958, and it was eventually torn down.

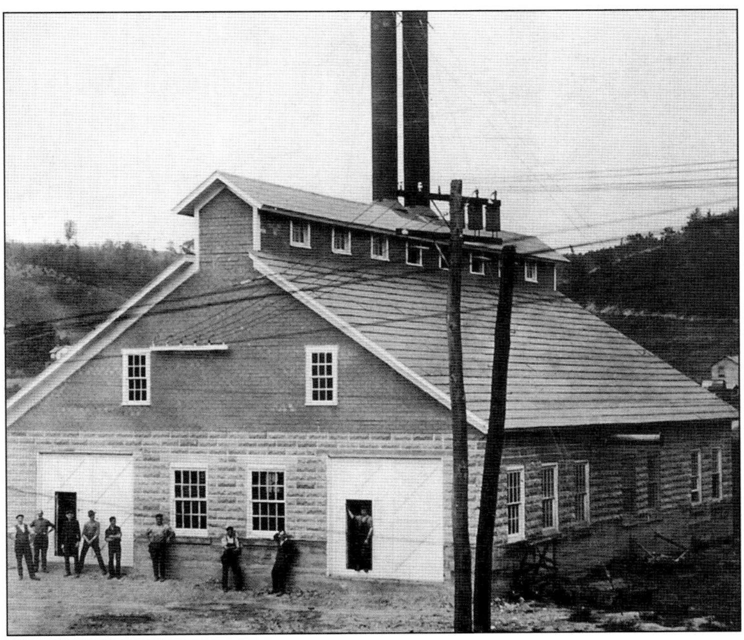

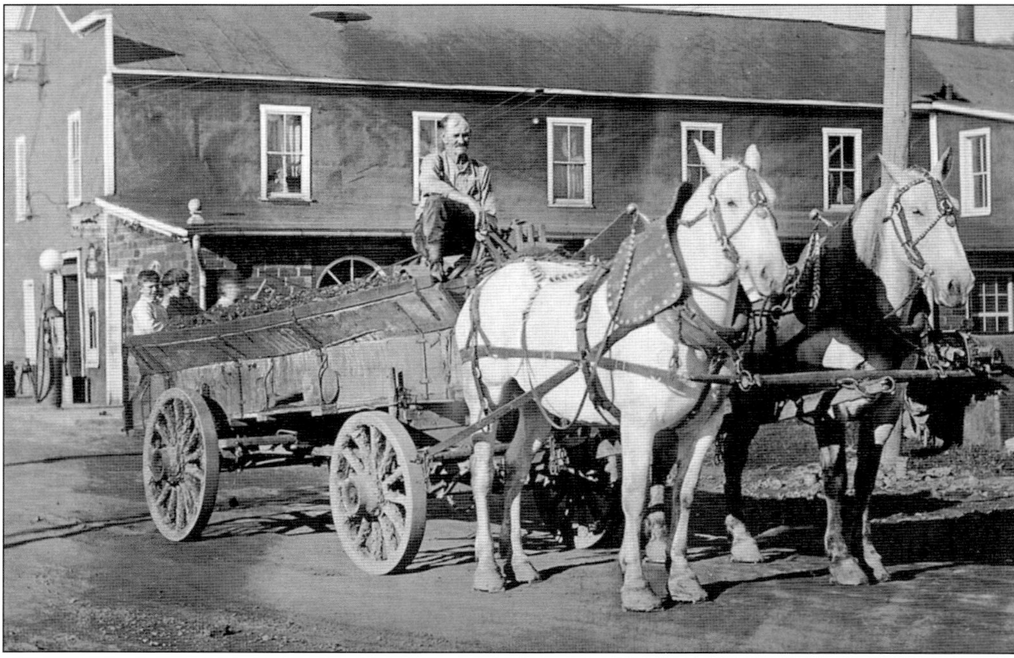

Elmer Allen hauled coal from local mines in his wagon to feed the boilers of the Brockway Light, Heat, and Power Company on Evergreen Street. Behind Allen is the John O. Nava Machine Shop, in which they conducted general machine work and manufactured the Brockway Battery, the first "non-buckle plated battery in the industry," according to Lew Reddinger.

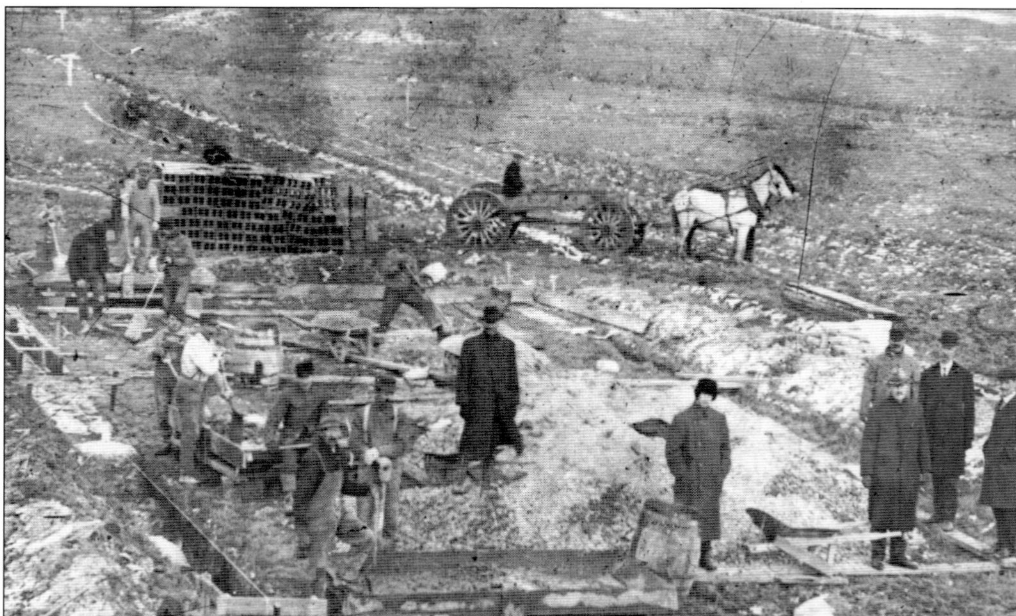

This building would house the Universal Electric Motor business, which ended up being one of the biggest scams in the industry. The building was occupied by the Babcock and Bethune Shock Absorber Company between 1913 and 1916 and by an ice cream plant until it burned in 1921. Wendell August built a new forge on the site in 1926, after his first forge in the Johnson garage burned down.

R. F. Davis built a restaurant and lodging house in 1900 at the current intersection of Routes 219 and 28 to feed the railroaders of the Erie and Pennsylvania Railroad yards. The little restaurant went through some exterior additions and several name changes, including the Broadway Inn and Calhoun's Saloon. It is still operating under the name of Birdie's.

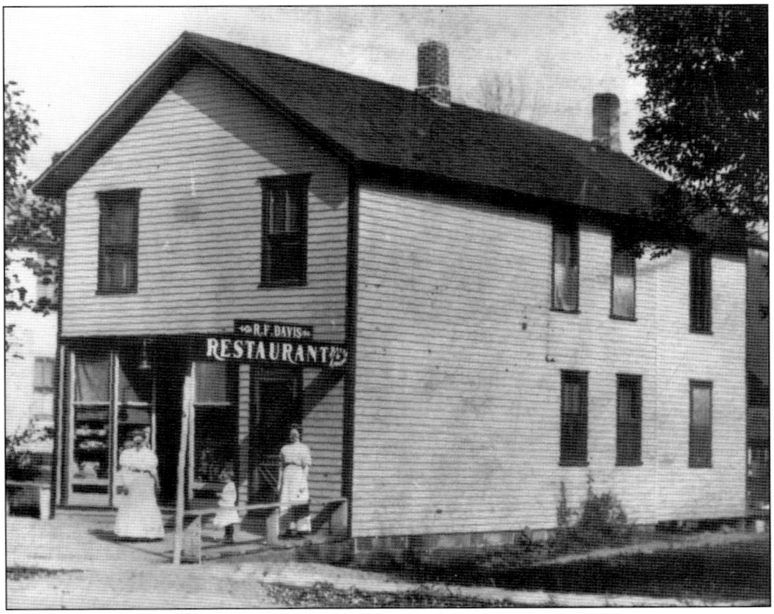

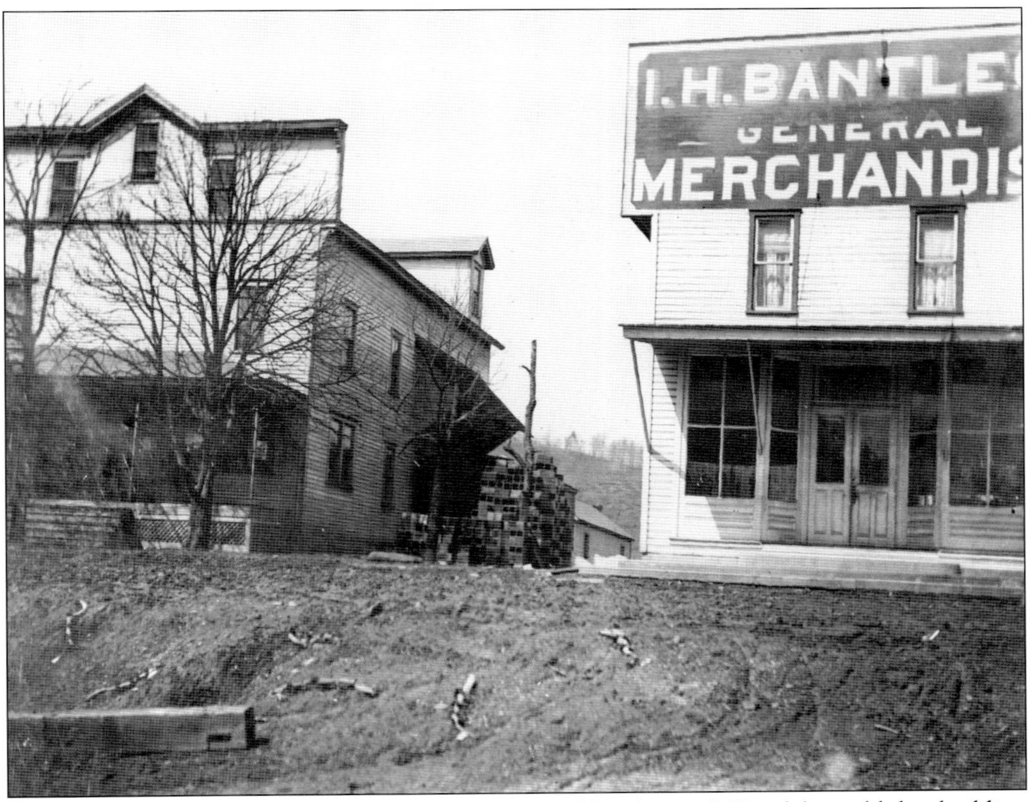

McCauley and McKay started the Eureka Mill in the old Kirkpatrick Hotel, but sold that building to the Brockway Macaroni and Supply Company in 1904. They proceeded to build a new three-story grist mill on the north side of Main Street. It once housed Cramer Lumber, but was torn down for the Dollar General store. The I. H. Bantleon general store was Agway and is now Napa Auto Parts.

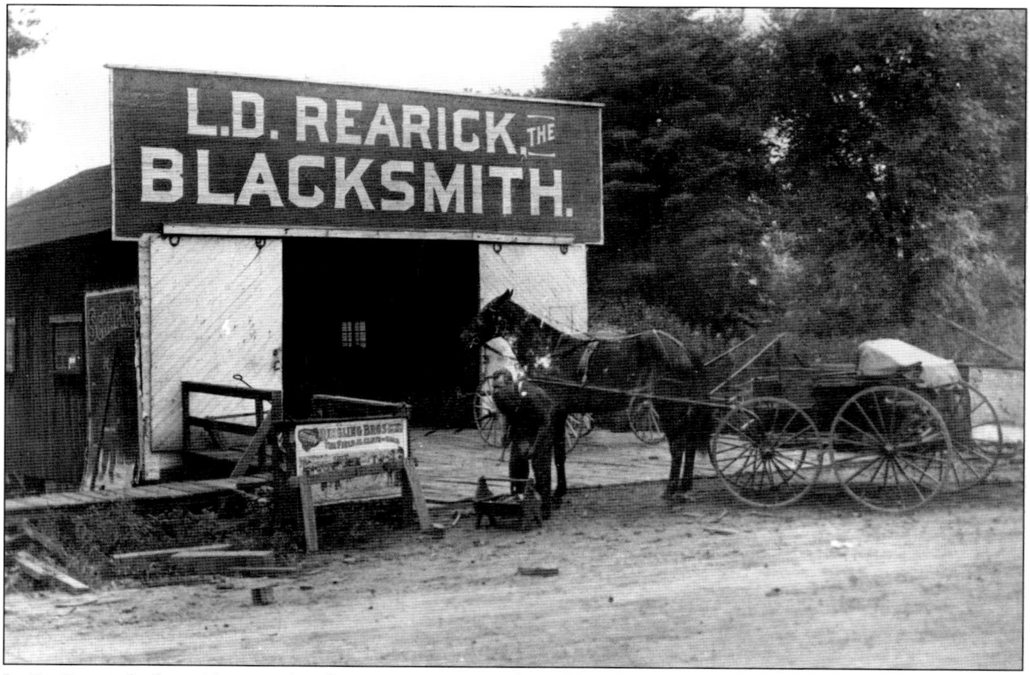

L. D. Rearick shoed horses for the community at his old-time blacksmith shop, across Main Street from the I. H. Bantleon general store. The sign on the left is advertising the Ringling Brothers' spectacle, "The Field of the Cloth of Gold." The site is now occupied by the Gulf Station and automobile repair center.

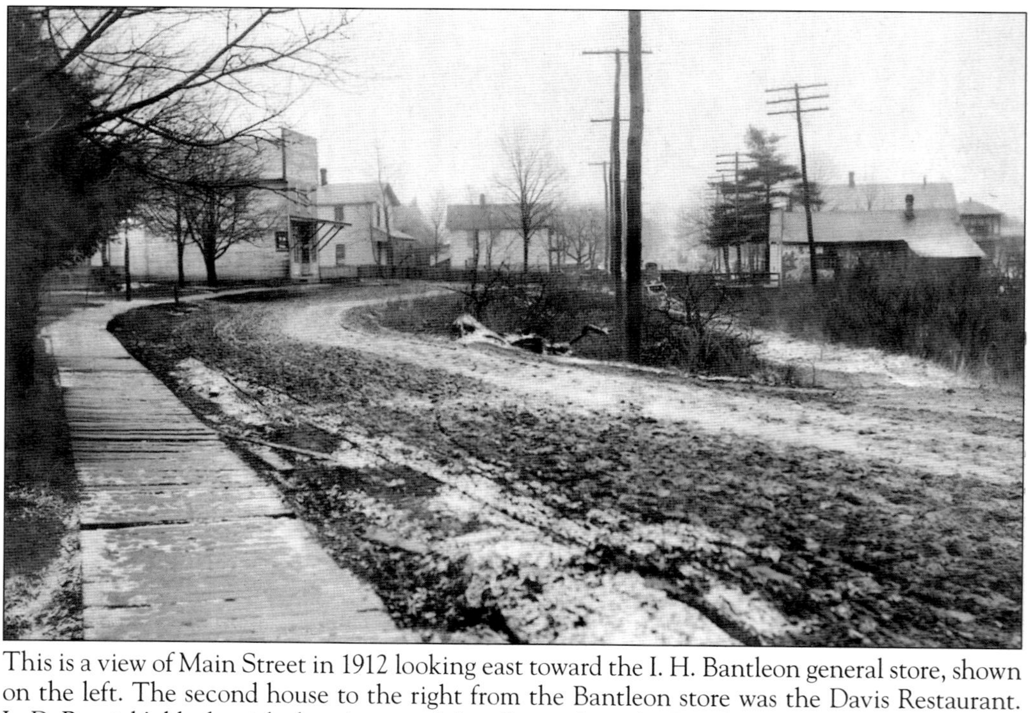

This is a view of Main Street in 1912 looking east toward the I. H. Bantleon general store, shown on the left. The second house to the right from the Bantleon store was the Davis Restaurant. L. D. Rearick's blacksmith shop is across Main Street from the Bantleon store. The curve in the muddy street was necessary to avoid the old milldam of Alonzo and James Brockway.

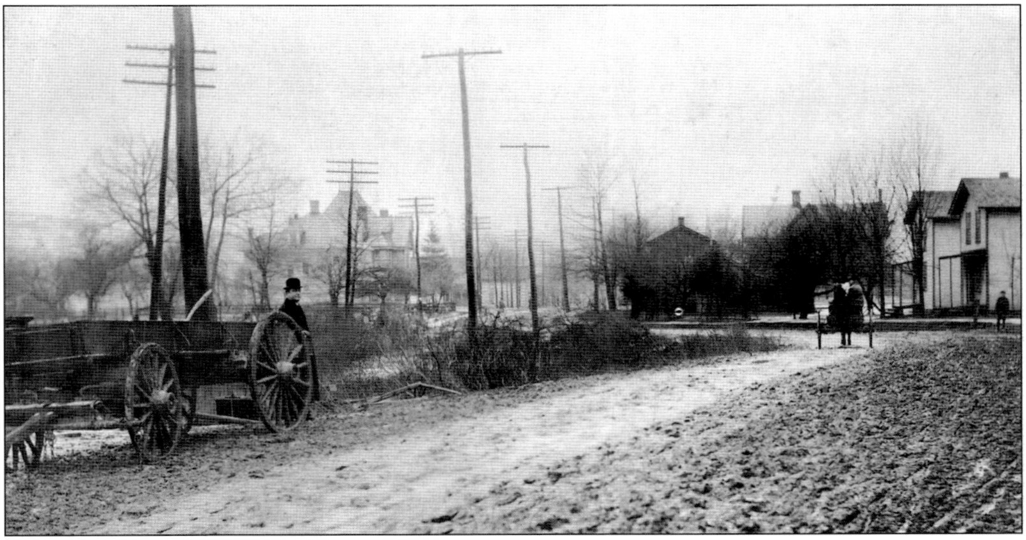

This view is from Main Street in front of the Bantleon store looking east about 1912. Driving Main Street today is a pleasant experience, but the look on the face of the gentlemen on the left says otherwise. His wagon's wheels are caked with mud, and the ruts along the street indicate a rather uncomfortable ride. Main Street would be straightened and paved with Shawmut bricks next year.

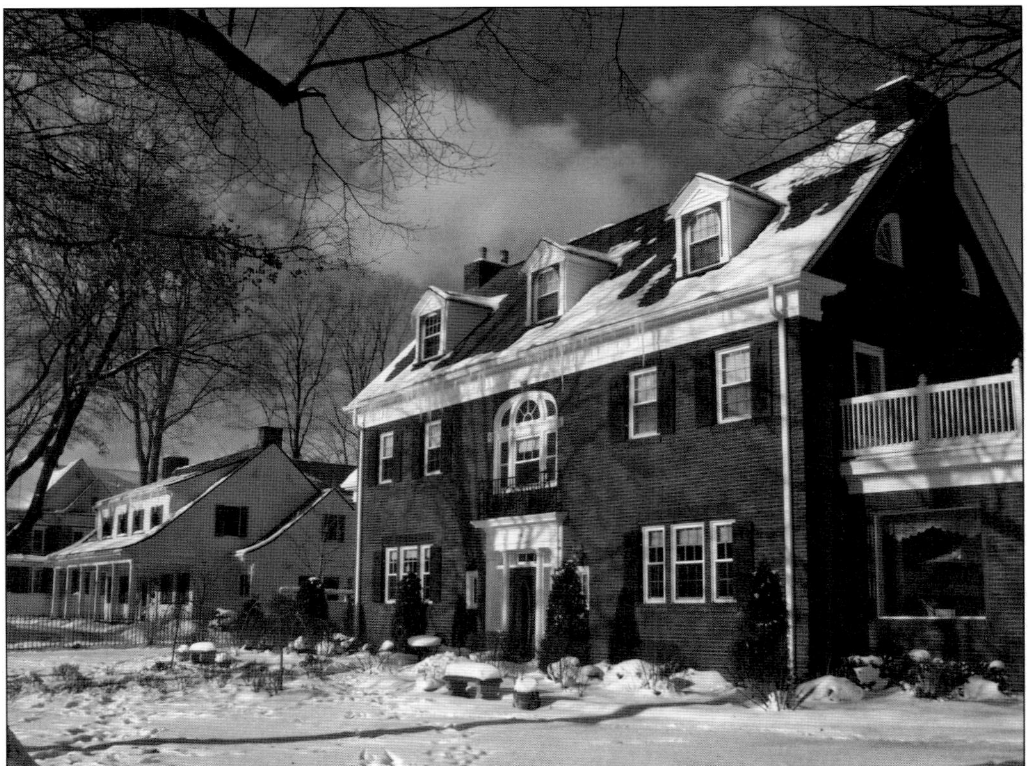

These two houses were built by Wendell August in the 1920s. Wendell August grew up in Brockwayville and lived in the house on the right for a few years. Unfortunately the tragic death of a son in a plane crash and an unpleasant family situation forced him to move his forge to Grove City, where it remains today as a highly successful artistic metalworking establishment.

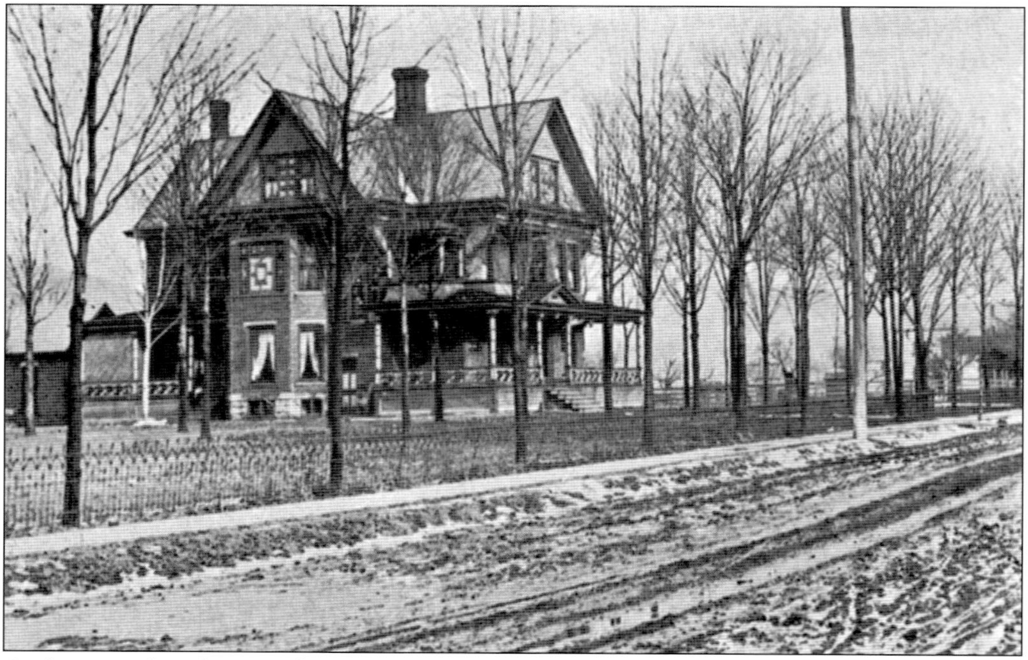

At the time this photograph was taken in 1910, H. B. McCullough occupied this house at the corner of Tenth Avenue and Main Street. It was built by Reynolds L. Buzard in 1886, while he was establishing a lumbering operation at the mouth of Baghdad Run with William G. McCain. Reynolds L. Buzard died in 1902 from complications caused by bronchitis.

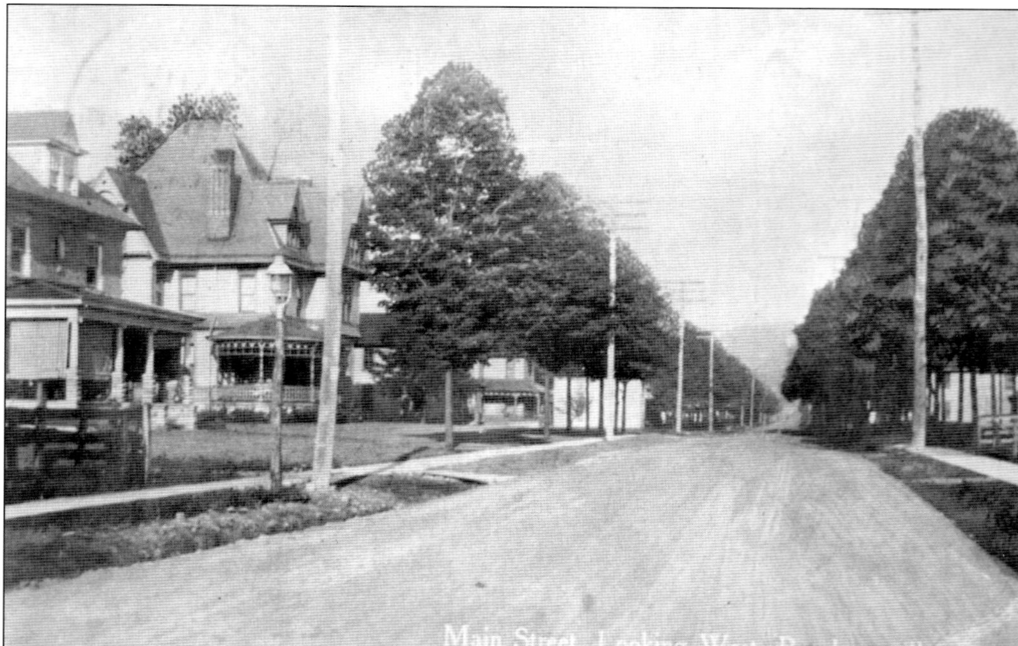

The house on the left was occupied by Charles R. McCauley of the Eureka Milling Company. The huge house beside it was occupied by A. R. Chapin, cashier of the First National Bank. It was built by William G. McCain, who owned the W. G. McCain and Sons general store in the old Excelsior building on west Main Street. He sold the business to Beadle and Company in 1898.

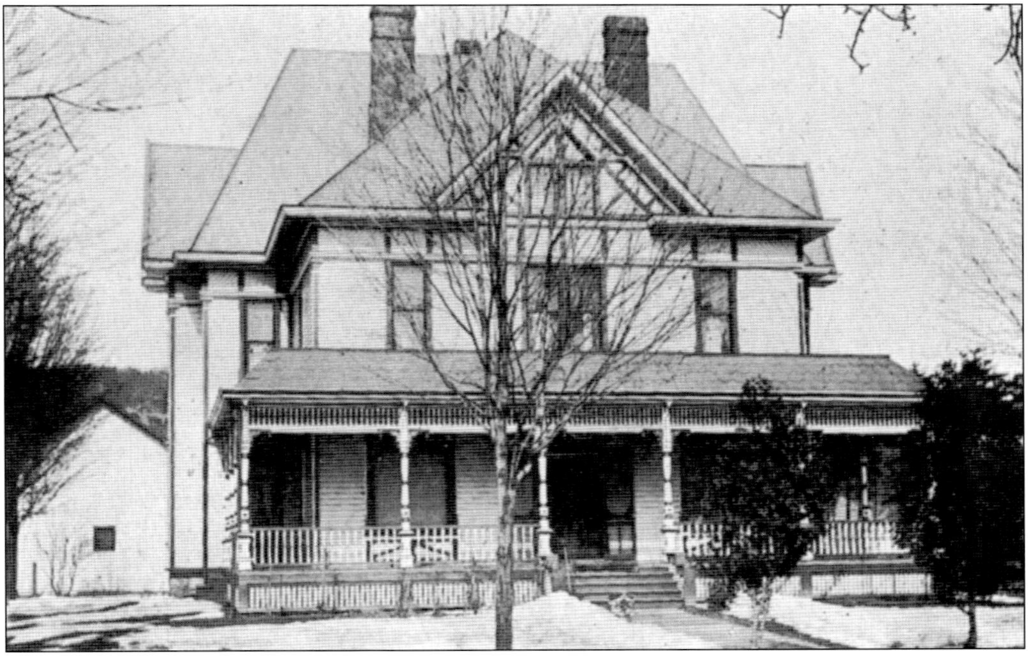

H. B. Cooper lived in this large home, which stood immediately to the east of the Presbyterian church. Cooper was a partner in the Bond and Cooper general store on the west end of town. It is uncertain whether Cooper built the house, but the house met an unfortunate but necessary demise, when it was destroyed to erect a parking lot for the new Presbyterian church in the 1960s.

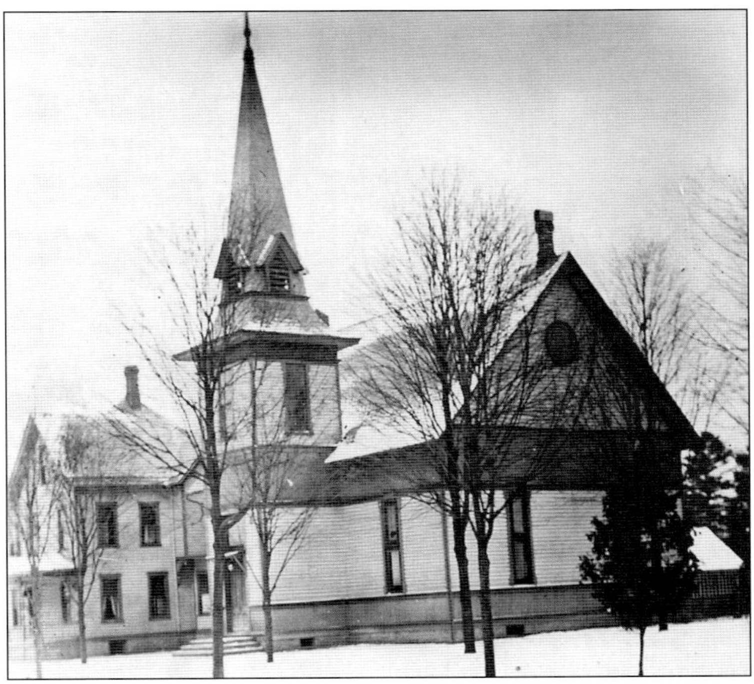

The original Presbyterian church was built in 1888, after services were held in the Methodist church. The final worship service in the old building was conducted on August 12, 1962. The church and manse were razed to begin construction of a brick church with a white aluminum spire and a complete educational wing. After again temporarily using the Methodist church, the structure was completed on July 19, 1964.

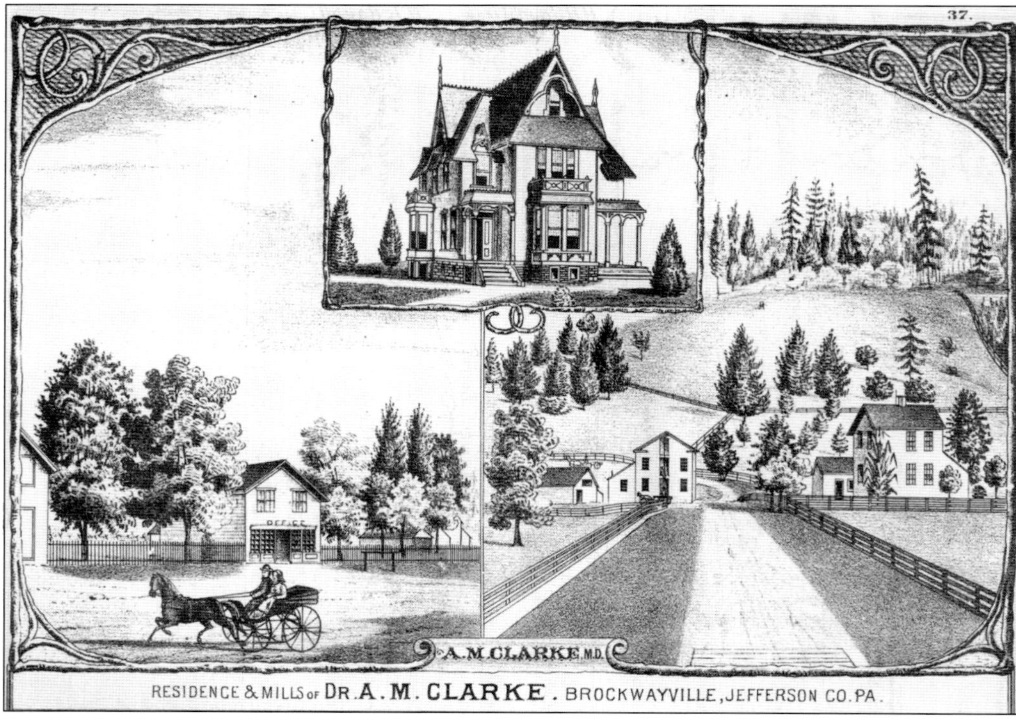

Dr. Asaph Milton Clarke's beautiful home and gristmill at the end of Ninth Avenue is featured in this sketch from Caldwell's 1878 atlas of Jefferson County. Dr. Clarke purchased the sawmill of Alonzo and James Brockway in 1848, and added a gristmill. The "Father of Brockway" passed away on May 22, 1884, and his mill burned down on June 25, 1887.

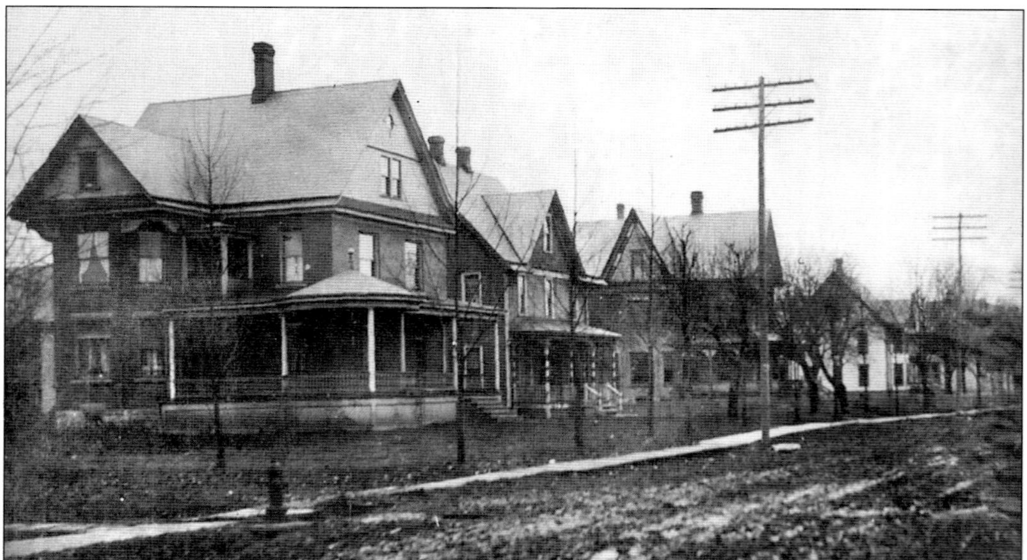

These houses along the south side of Main Street include the homes of Benson Taylor, Sidney Almay, William Bond, and James Bond. Taylor Memorial Park was named for Benson Taylor's son Vernon. Descendants of the Almay family still occup their house. William Bond first settled in Sugar Hill, a settlement 4 miles west of Brockwayville, and his original house still stands on James Bond Road.

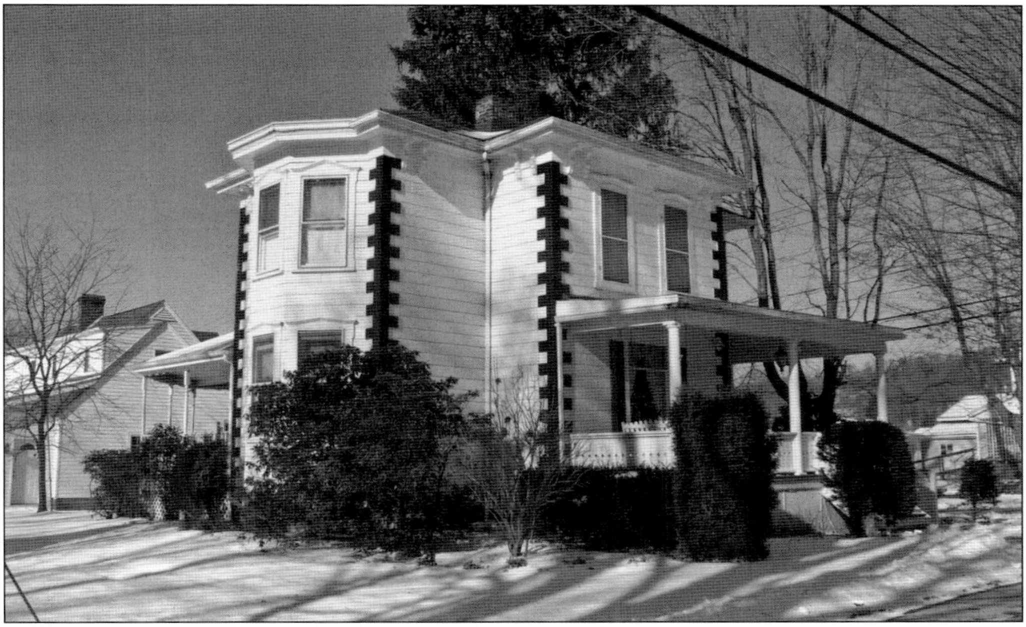

This house sits at the southwest corner of Eighth Avenue and Alexander Street. It does not appear on the A. Pomeroy map of Jefferson County in 1866 but shows up in the Caldwell atlas of Jefferson County in 1878. The name associated with the house is Capt. A. H. Tracy, whose name appears on the 1866 Pomeroy map as a cabinet maker on the west side of town.

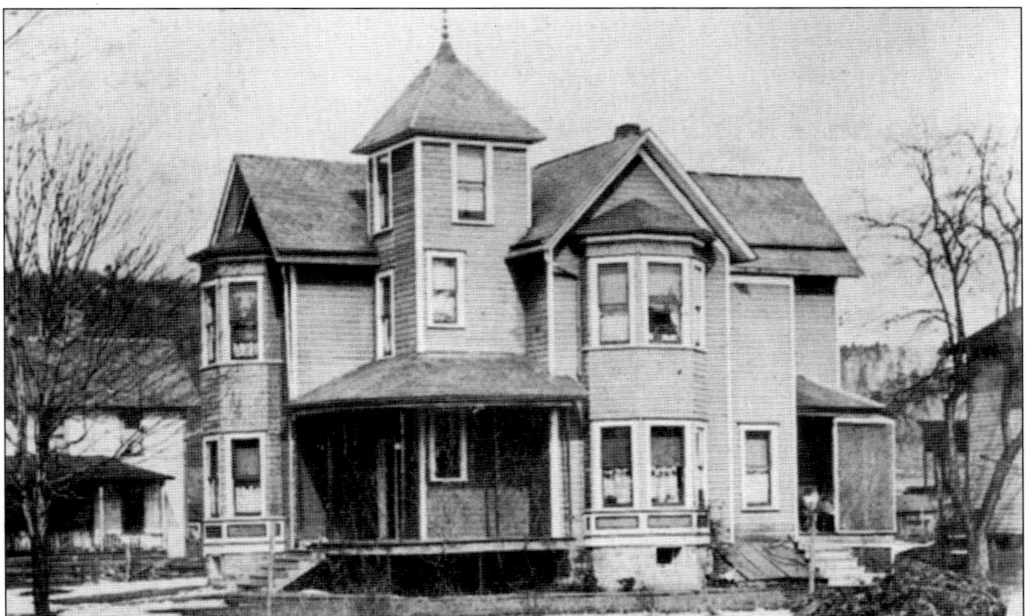

Harry Zell lived on the southeast corner of Eighth Avenue and Alexander Street and was an agent for the Pennsylvania Railroad. In 1902, he was elected president of an organization formed to construct a cultural center that would allow concerts, lectures, traveling theatrical performances, and the display of local talent to take stage. The organization constructed the Grande Opera House on the northwest corner of Seventh Avenue and Main Street in 1903.

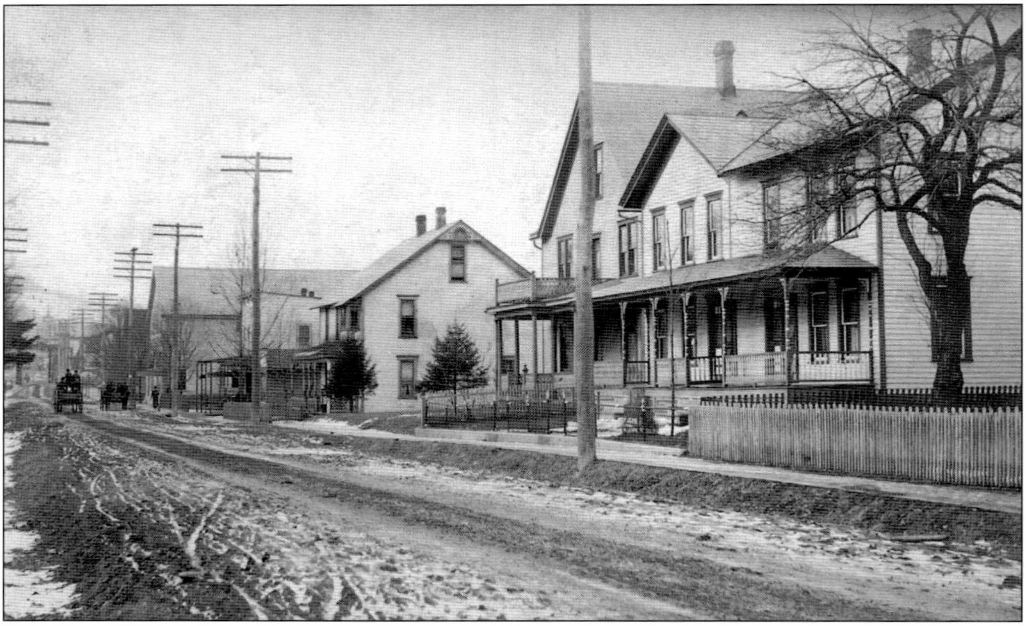

Another view of Main Street looking west from Eighth Avenue features the left center house of James E. Kester, the gentleman responsible for snapping over half of the photographs in this book. His studio was on the second floor, with ample natural lighting from windows and skylights. The house to the right of Kester's was the residence of Dr. George Humphreys who located in Brockwayville in 1896.

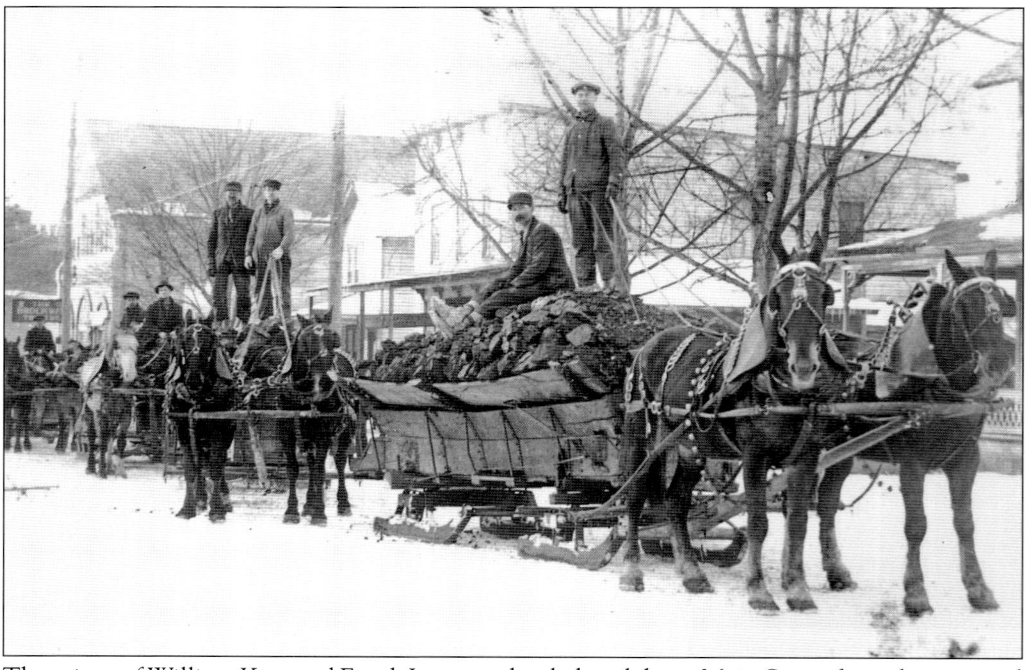

The mines of William Keys and Frank Lemmon hauled coal down Main Street from the west end during World War I in competition to see who could haul the biggest load. They were hauling the coal to the Ridgway and Clearfield branch of the Pennsylvania Railroad near the McCauley and McKay gristmill for shipment out of town for war purposes.

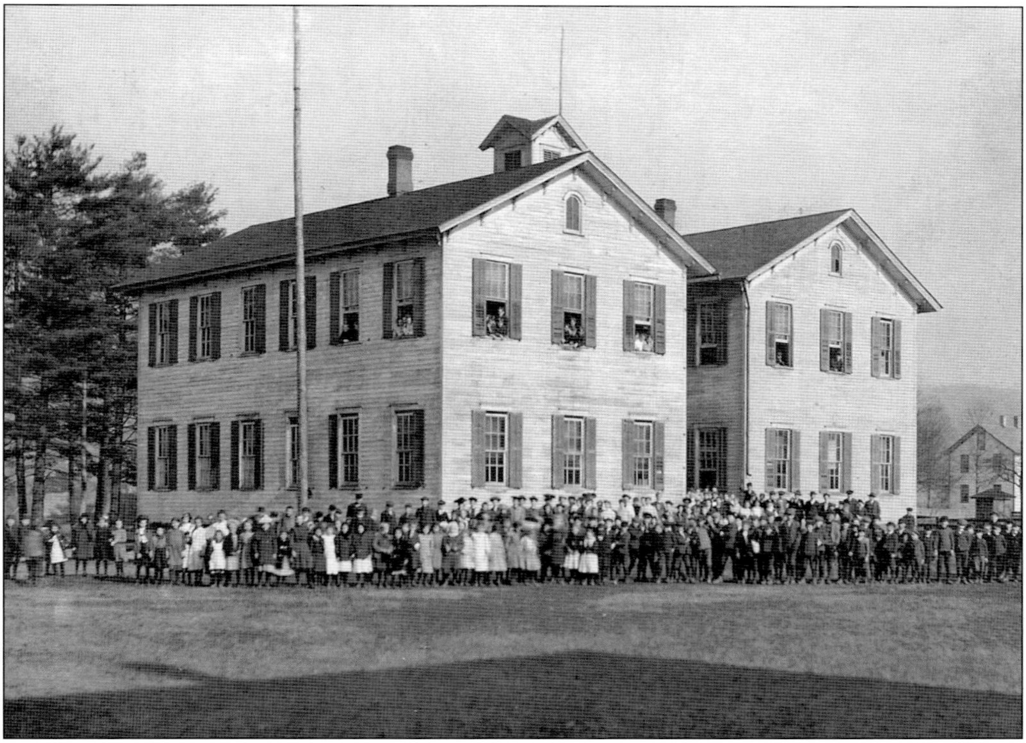

The original Seventh Avenue school shown here was constructed around 1880. The entire structure was moved off Seventh Avenue for the construction of the new brick Seventh Avenue school in 1921. The old buildings were arranged in an "L" shape and converted to apartments. The "Bedner Apartments," as they are now known, are still standing near the senior little league baseball field.

Photographs of the interior of the original schools in Brockway are rare. Most school photographs are of the children and teacher standing outside the school. This 1908 photograph was an exception, featuring the inside of the original Seventh Avenue school's first science laboratory classroom. A laboratory desk sits in the front center of the room, and old glass bottles of chemicals fill the cabinet on the far left.

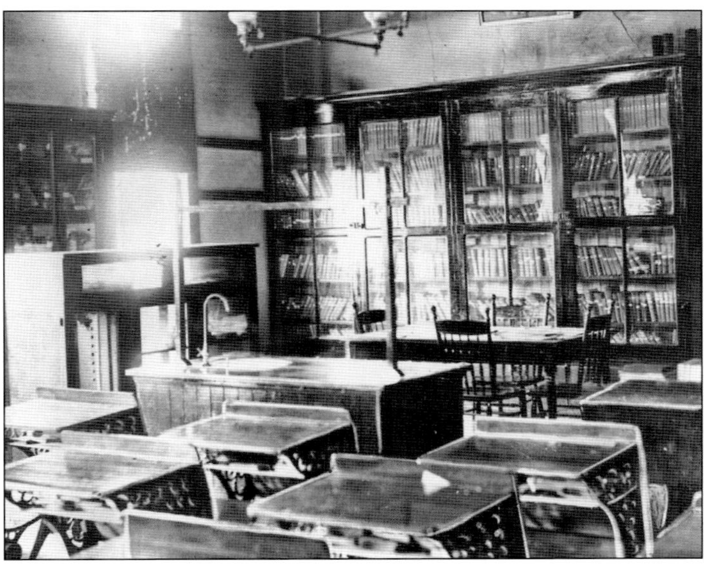

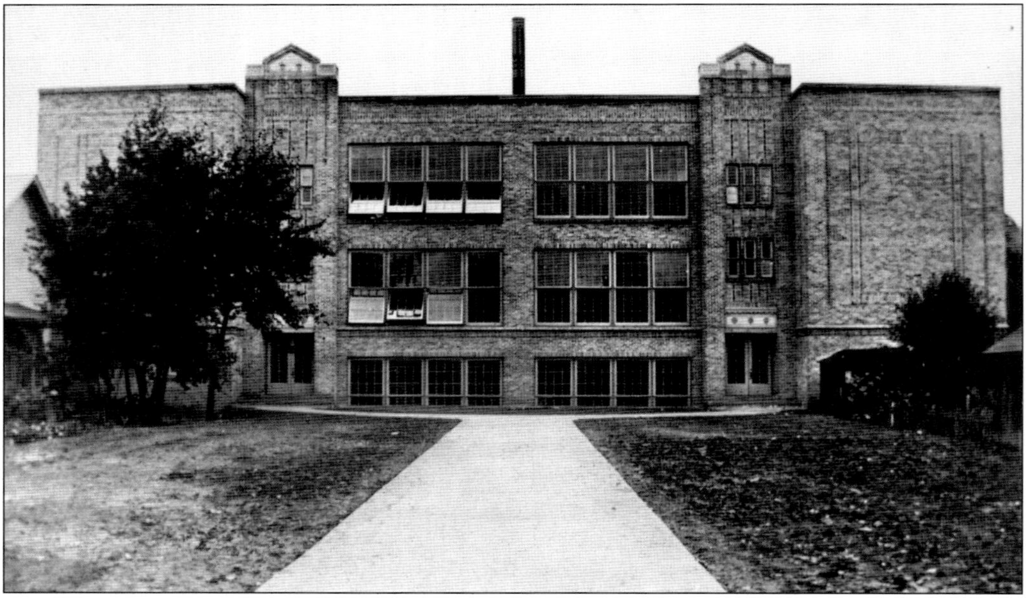

In 1921, the old wooden school was moved off Seventh Avenue to make room for a three-story brick building for grades 1 through 12. The building was completed in 1923 and provided 49 years of educational services to the community. The building was torn down for the construction of a home for the elderly, called the Toby Terrace Apartments.

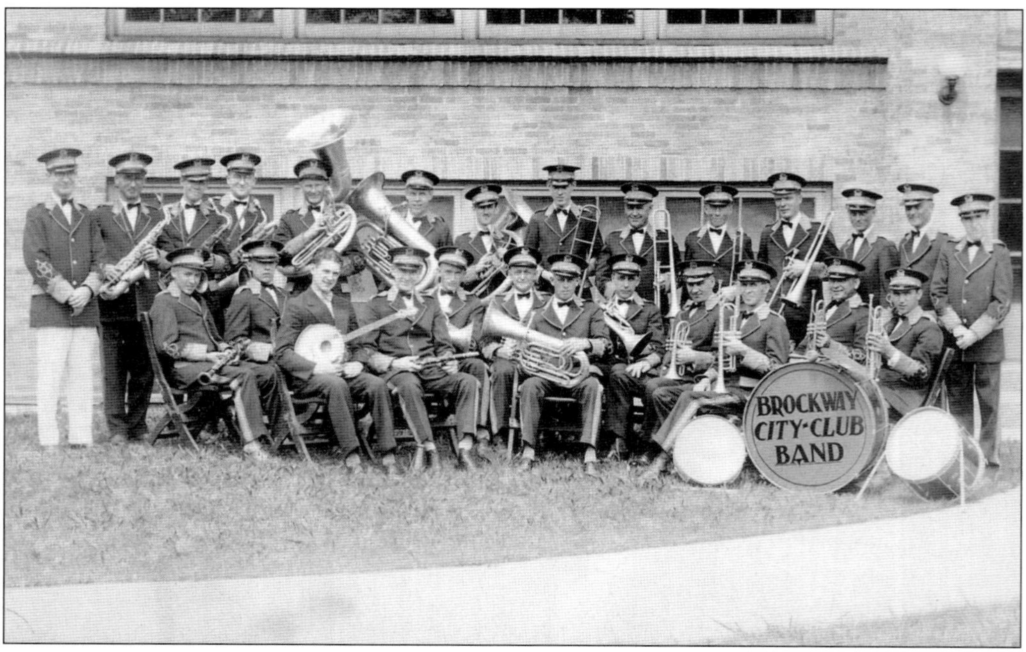

The Brockway City Club Band, under the baton of Don Gillung, played many street concerts throughout the 1920s and 1930s. The Brother Worker's Concert Band, conducted by Joseph Angelo, was another local ensemble that entertained the citizens of Brockway for a number of years. When the Brother Worker's Concert Band disbanded, many of the members joined the Brockway City Club Band.

The horse racing track and grandstand stood where the Kids Kingdom portion of the Taylor Memorial Park now stands. It was not the only racetrack in Brockway; an automobile racetrack once sat on the hill to the north of town near the St. Tobias Catholic Cemetery. The evening sky over Brockway on race nights would be filled with the track lights and the sounds of big engines.

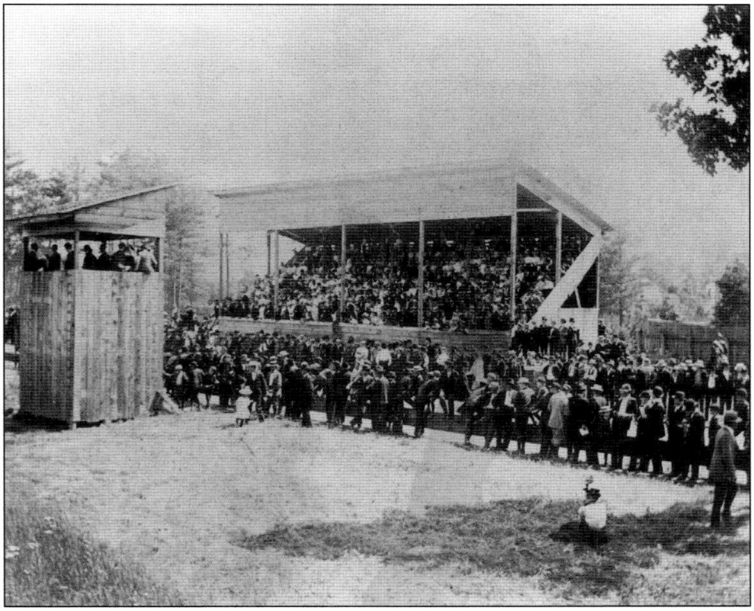

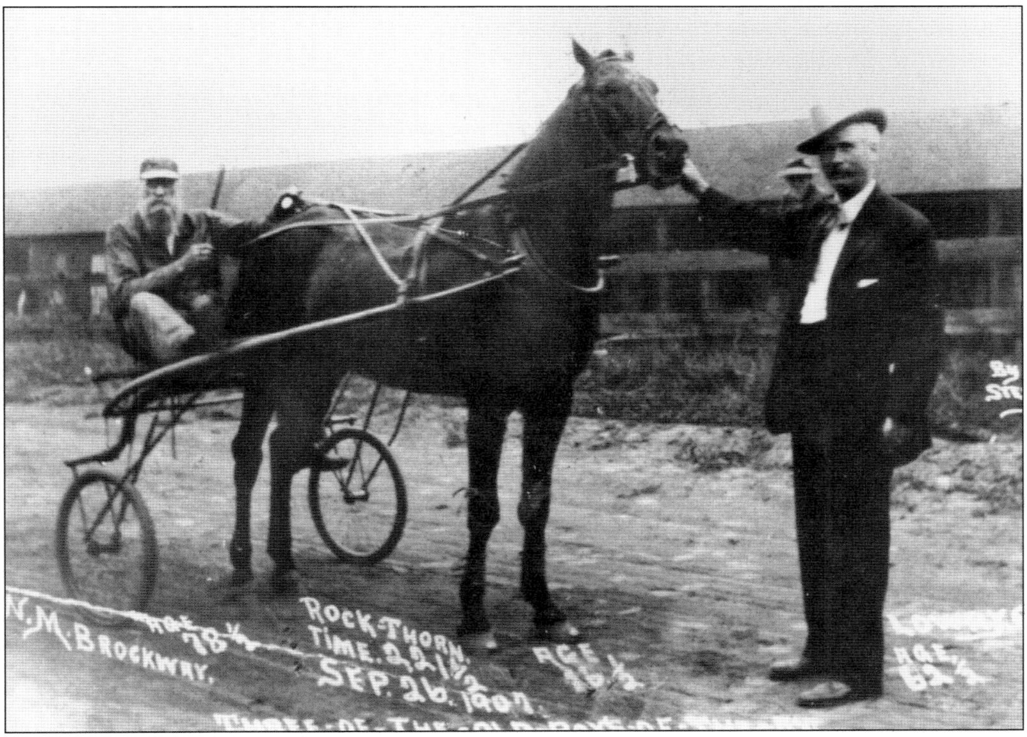

Capt. Nichols Mason Brockway, Civil War veteran of Company G, 57th Regiment, Pennsylvania State Militia, sits behind his horse, named Rock Thorn, on September 26, 1907. As indicated on the photograph, Nick Brockway was 78-and-a-half years old, and his horse 16-and-a-half years old, both considered old-timers. Nick Brockway probably raced Rock Thorn at the Ridgway, Helens Mills, and Brockwayville horse tracks.

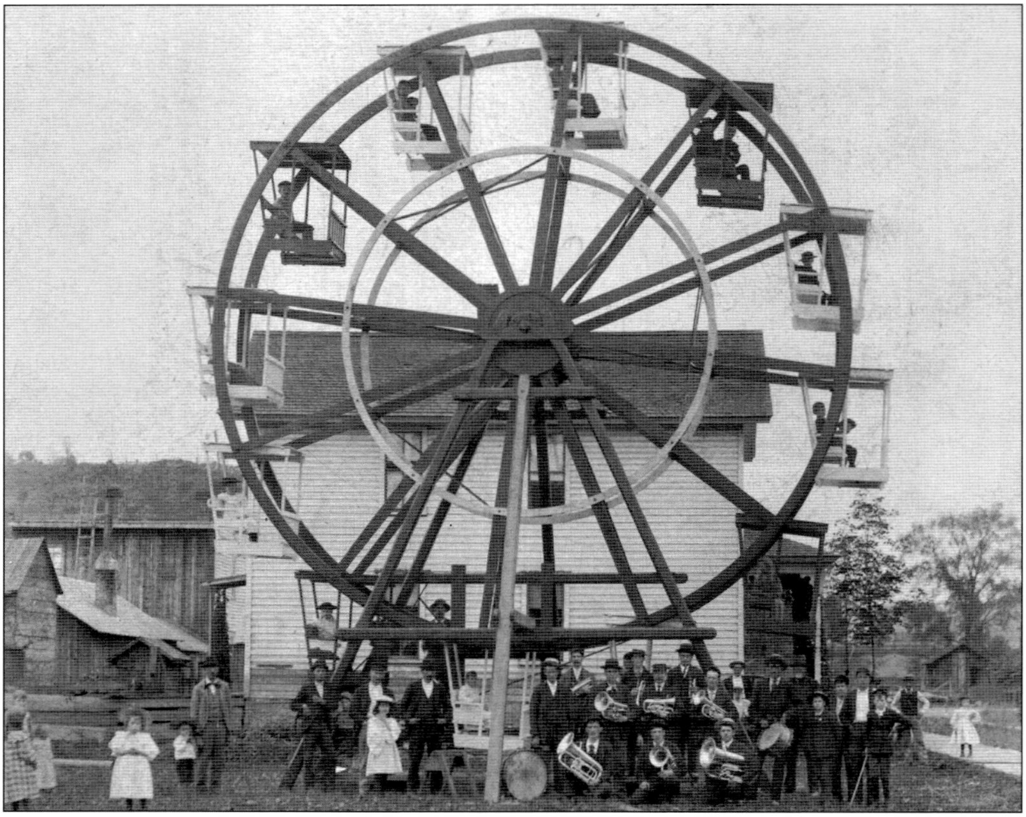

Henry Perry Dull, a local lumberman, used his resources to entertain the folks of Brockwayville with his Ferris wheel in what would become Taylor Memorial Park. He also ran a small carousel near his Ferris wheel, and both would be up and running for the weekends. He also took his small fair on tour, appearing in several communities surrounding Brockwayville.

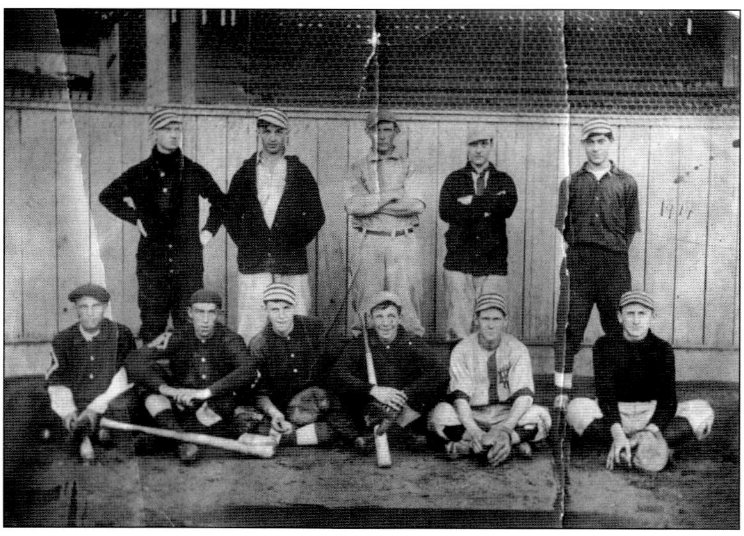

A baseball diamond was a necessity for most of America's towns by the early 20th century. This was Brockwayville's baseball team of 1914. From left to right are (first row) Pete Folvo, Joe Himes, Harry Hooton, Eddy Carlson, Delbert Truesdale, and John Bazzelli; (second row) Russell Young, Bill Briggs, Mose Dull, Irvin McQuone, and Pat Paruso.

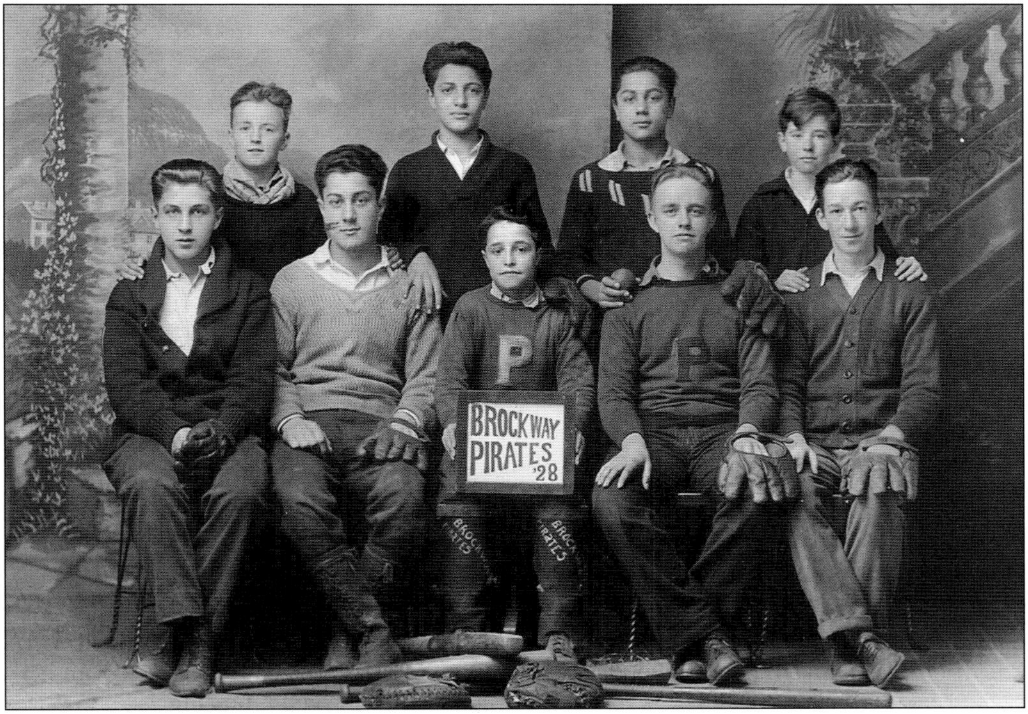

The Brockway Pirates baseball team of 1928 included, from left to right, (first row) I. Chittister, H. Paruso, unidentified, J. Kester, and Joseph P. Sloan; (second row) unidentified, R. Castafero, Pat Paruso, and unidentified. Joe Sloan was the manager of the team, and the Taylor Memorial Museum recently acquired Sloan's manager briefcase and other Brockway Pirates memorabilia.

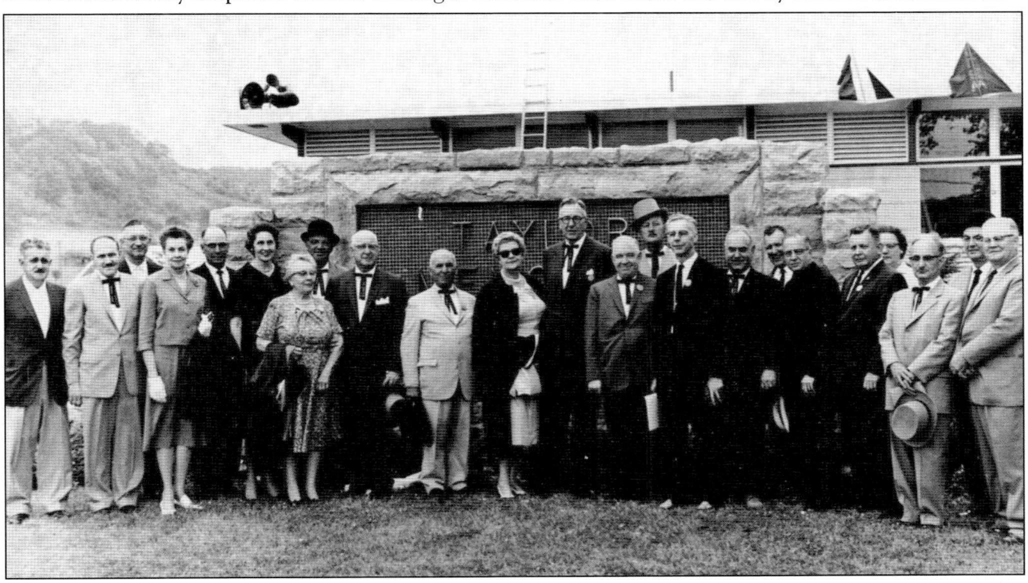

The Taylor Memorial Park was dedicated on July 15, 1961, with members of the Vernon Taylor family present. The park currently includes tennis courts, baseball fields, the Varischetti football field, a skate park, the trailhead of the Clarion–Little Toby Rail Trail, a stage erected by the American Legion, a large swimming pool, a large covered pavilion, the Taylor Memorial Museum, Kids Kingdom playground, basketball courts, and an inline hockey court.

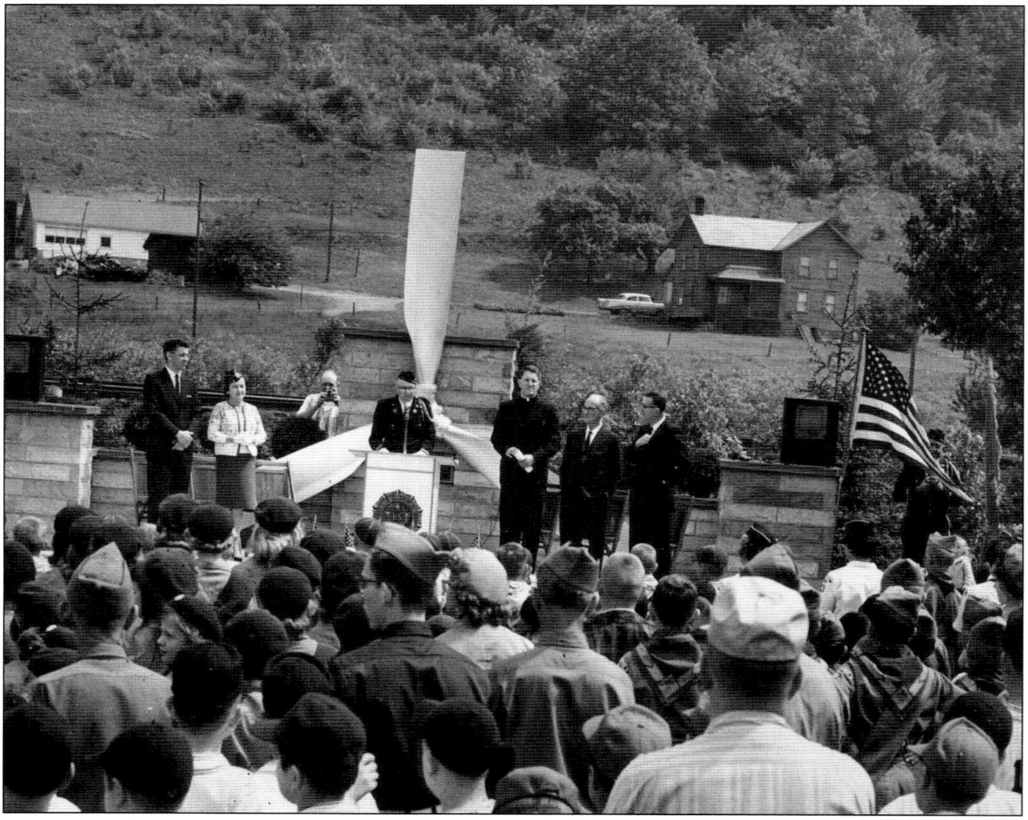

The old American Legion stage was the sight of numerous speeches given by prominent citizens and guest speakers for holidays such as Memorial Day and the Fourth of July. It was built by the Parson-Marnatti Post 95 in 1960. The stage included an antiaircraft gun, an anchor, and a propeller behind the speaker stand, all donated from government agencies.

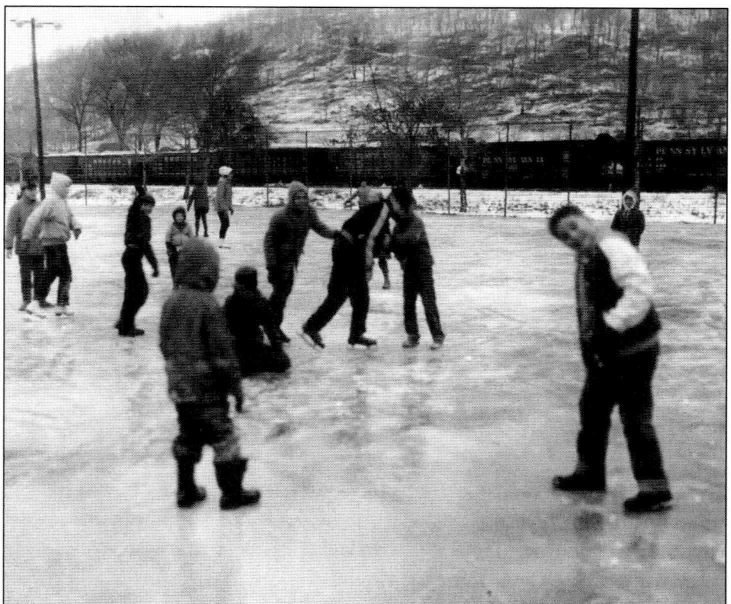

The Ninth Avenue courts originally contained just basketball courts, but in the winter were filled with water and let to freeze for ice-skating. An interesting feature for railroad fans is the line of Pennsylvania Railroad coal hoppers sitting on the Ridgway and Clearfield Railroad beside the park. Today the courts have two basketball courts and an inline hockey court, which are both used extensively during the summer leagues.

The Sons of Italy building was constructed around 1935 on the west side of Seventh Avenue, across from the old brick school. The Brockway Sales Company used the first floor of the building for offices sometime after 1927. The Brockway Sales Company merged with the Brockway Machine Bottle Company to create the Brockway Glass Company, which continued to use the structure until 1954.

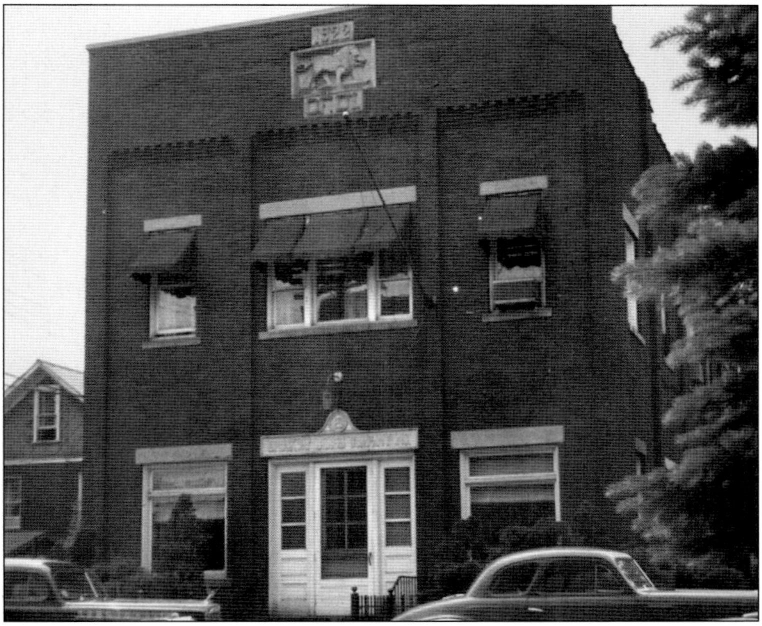

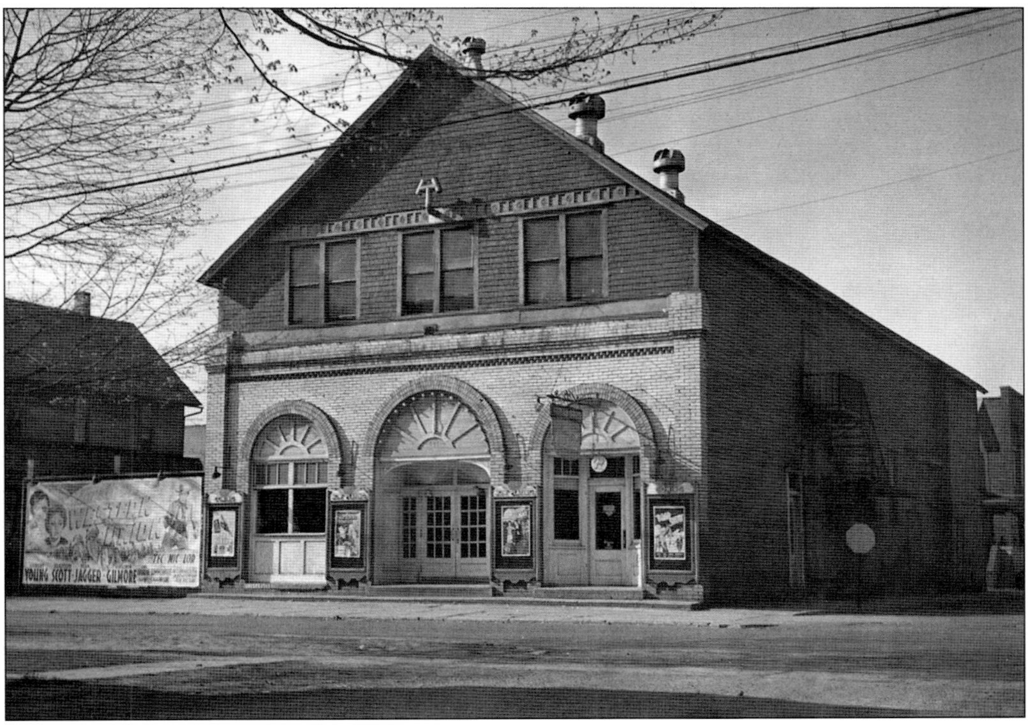

The Grande Opera House was constructed in 1903. It was used for concerts, plays, and graduation ceremonies. Trains brought crowds in from the surrounding areas to experience "big time" performances. The opera house was then changed to a roller skating rink until "motion picture plays" became popular. Electric generators run on gasoline were installed in the building, and the entire interior was renovated.

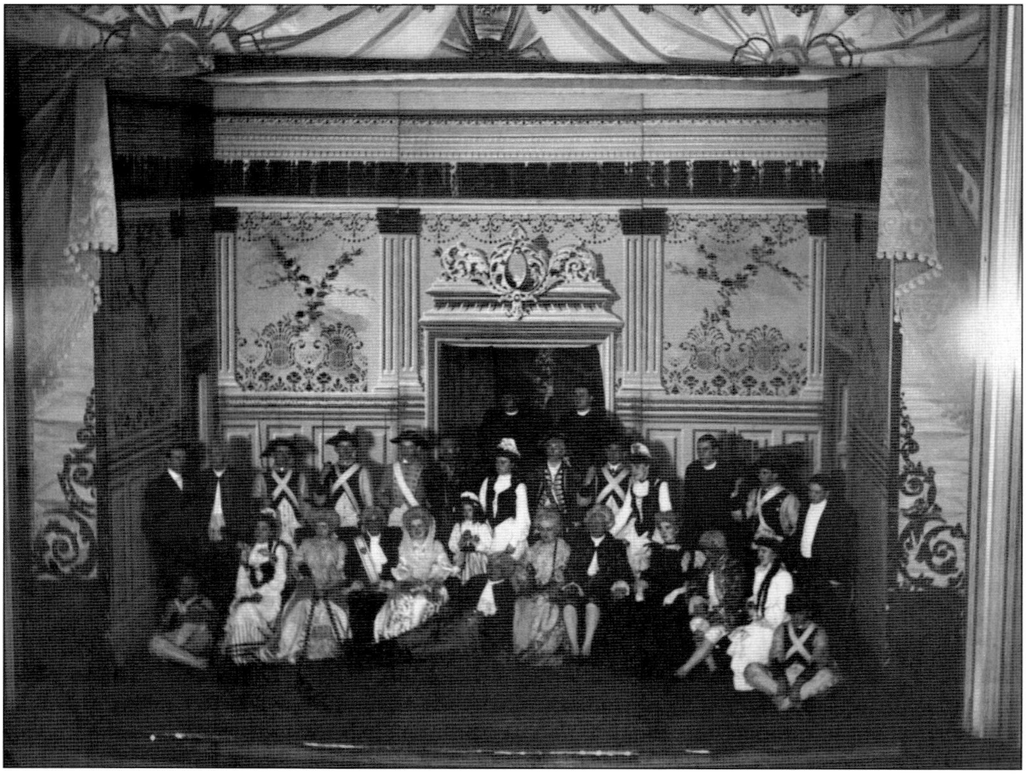

This is the only known photograph of the interior of the Grande Opera House in its heyday. The ticket room, annex, stage, floor, balcony, and paint were all intact for about a century. Keith Brothers found it necessary to remove parts of the stage and add a second floor in the early 2000s, but the company still has some of the original ropes and pulleys from the stage.

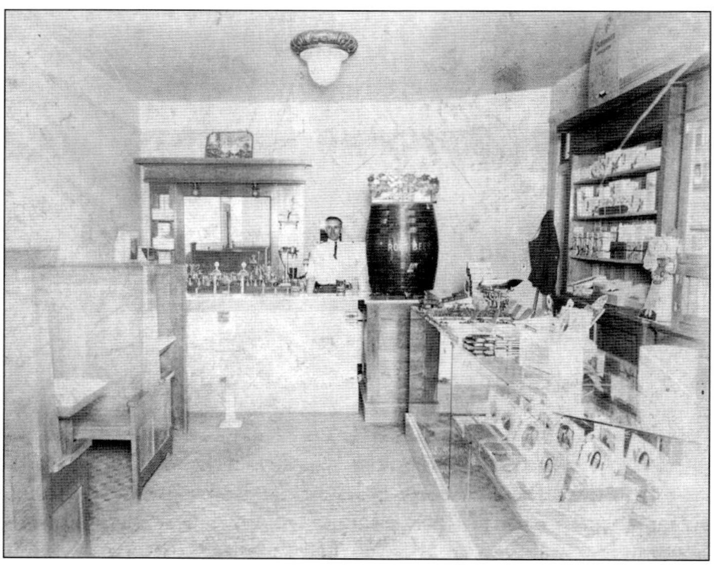

America's favorite thing to do before, during, and after watching a movie is to eat. The Opera House Annex run by George Bedner served sodas, sundaes, and ice cream before and after movies. Joe Kosco sold the building to Irvin and Melvin Keith in 1945, and the Keith brothers began their metal fabrication business. Irvin passed away in 2001 at 92 years, and his son Scott still runs the Keith Brothers business.

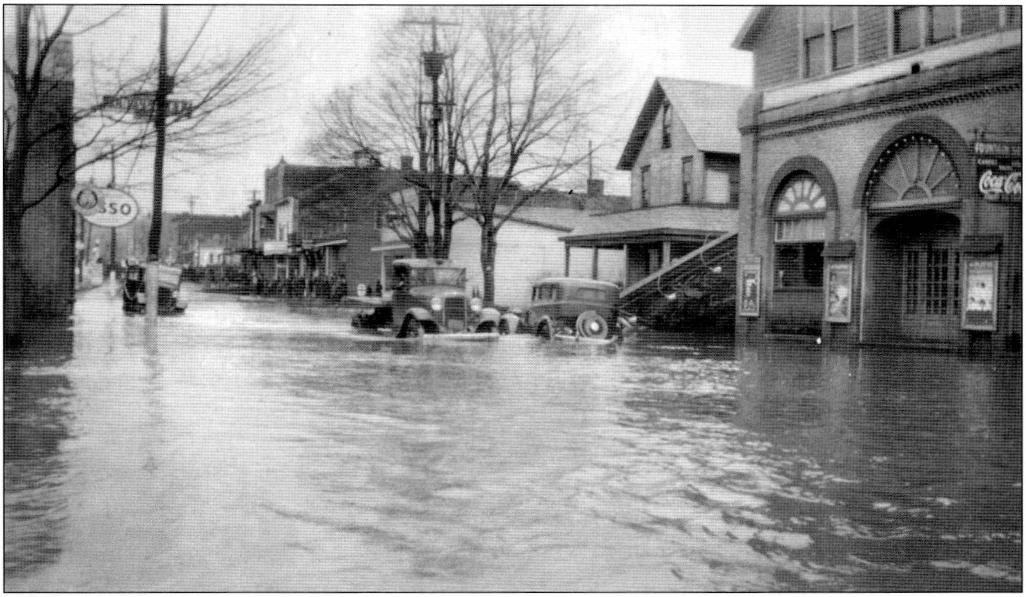

The state of Pennsylvania suffered one of the worst floods in history on March 17, 1936. Named the "Great St. Patrick's Day Flood," water in Pittsburgh reached 11 feet above the sidewalks. Little Toby Creek surged well above its banks, filling the valley between the Baltimore and Ohio tracks on the south and west, to the Pennsylvania tracks on the north and east.

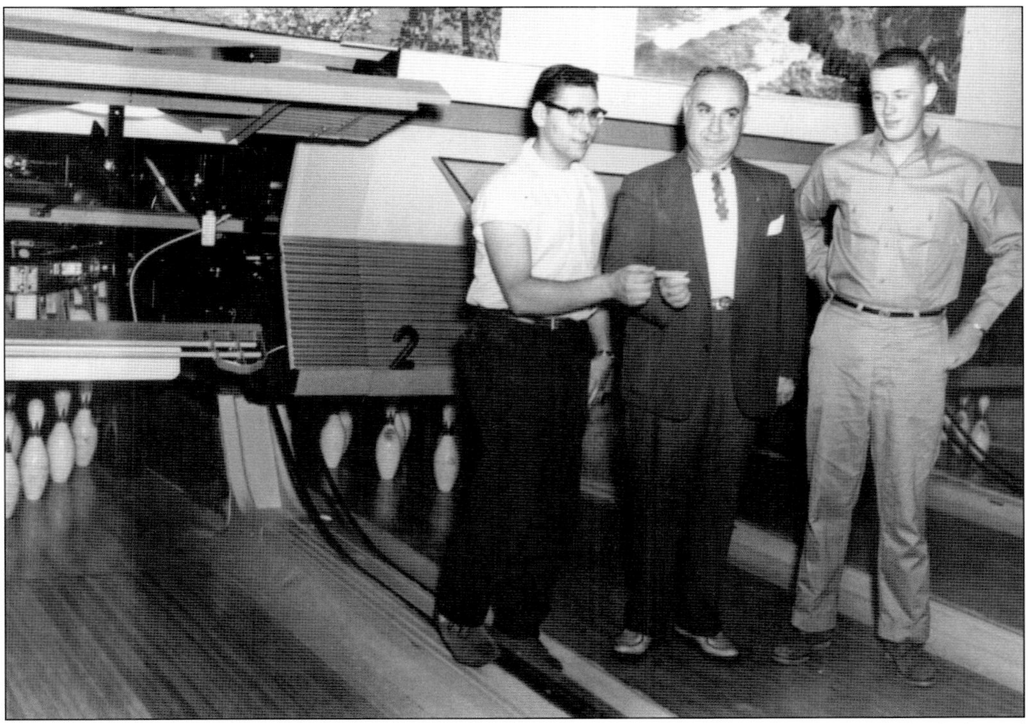

The Hi-Hat bowling lanes sat on the north side of Main Street on the west end of the block shared by the Grande Opera House. Brockway has had several bowling lanes over the years, including the Timber Lanes to the east of Martino's. The Timber Lanes bowling alley was replaced by the offices of Brockway Pressed Metals.

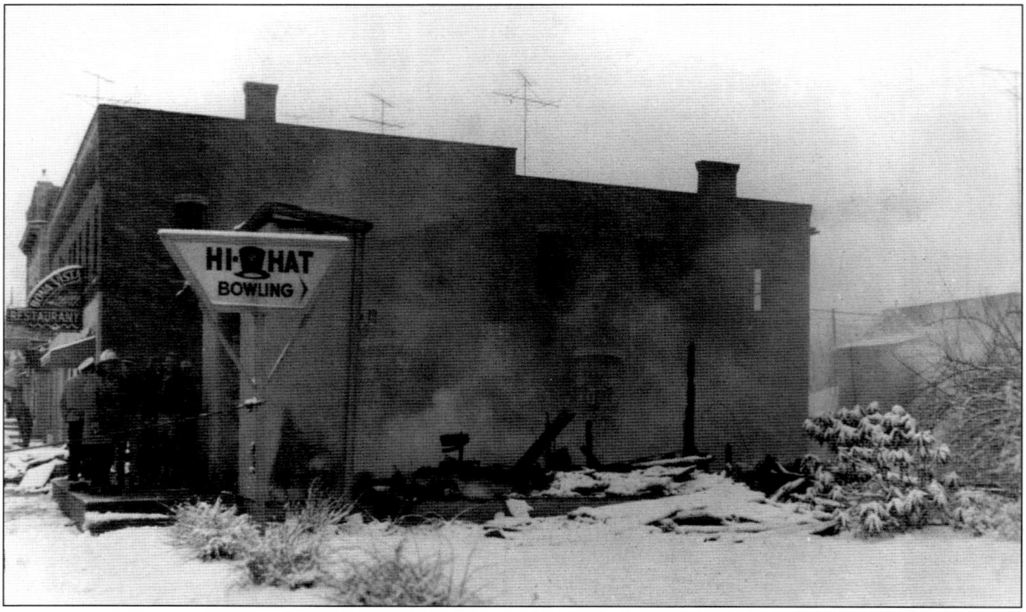

The Hi-Hat bowling lanes and the Fran-Le Shoe store burned to ashes on January 8, 1962. Property damage was estimated at over $150,000, and for the first time in 50 years, the Brockway Volunteer Hose Company had to summon aid from other fire departments. It took Brockway's three pieces of equipment and an additional four pumpers, an aerial ladder, and other emergency equipment to confine the fire.

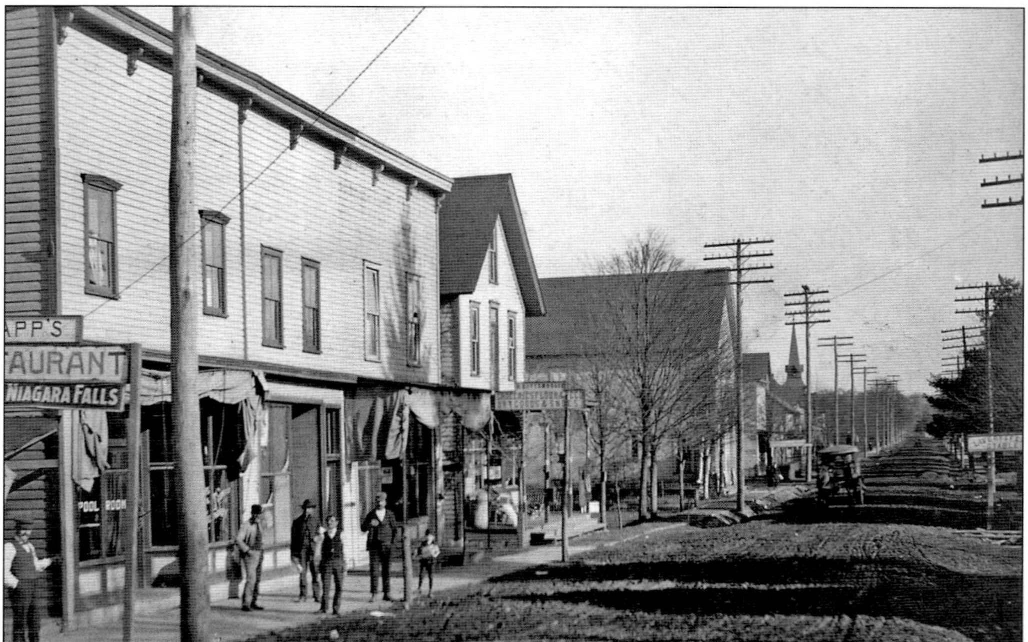

The north side of Main Street, east of the bridge over Little Toby Creek, held Tapp's Restaurant, a poolroom, Smith's Market, and Harvey Rittenhouse's store featuring groceries, flour and feed, dry goods, and shoes. Across Main Street were the John J. Mullany and Sons Livery and Feed Stables. The whole block on the north side was leveled by a fire on September 19, 1909.

Sloan's Restaurant was in the block east of the Main Street Bridge on the north side. Norman P. Sloan was the proprietor, center, with Harry "Shorty" Mathews, to the left, and Hazel Olson and Wray Smith to the right. The boy in the doorway holding the derby is unidentified. The photograph was taken in 1915, after the streets and sidewalks were paved with Shawmut bricks.

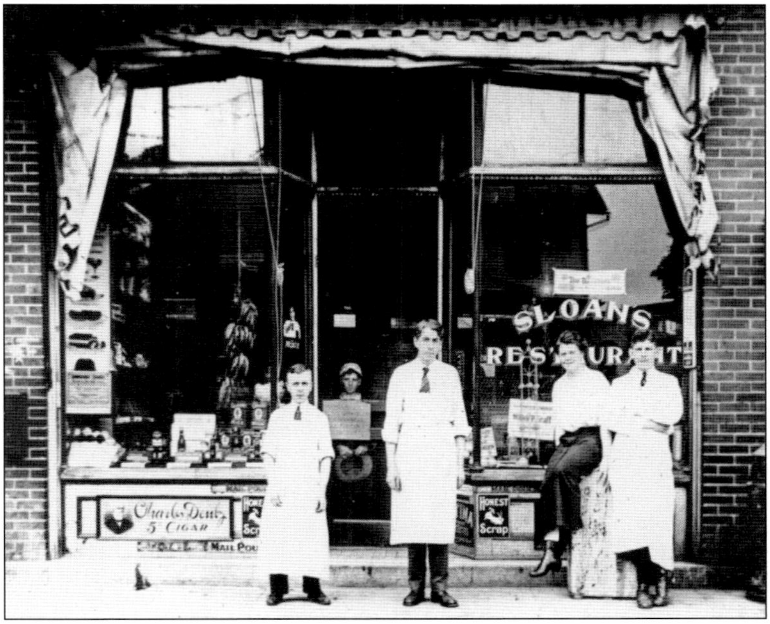

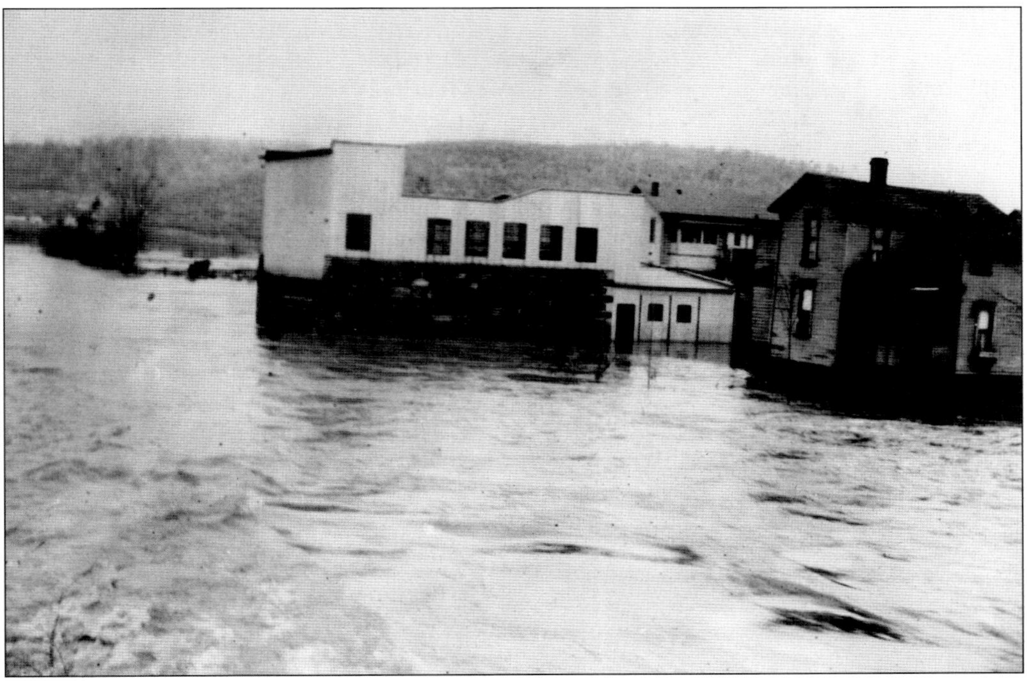

Floodwater photographs have always filled viewers with feelings of intimidation, and this photograph is no exception. It was taken from the Main Street Bridge looking down Little Toby Creek to the north during the St. Patrick's Day flood of 1936. The building in the center is the Paris Cleaners business, and the building to the right is the Angelo house. Behind the buildings are the Bedner Apartments.

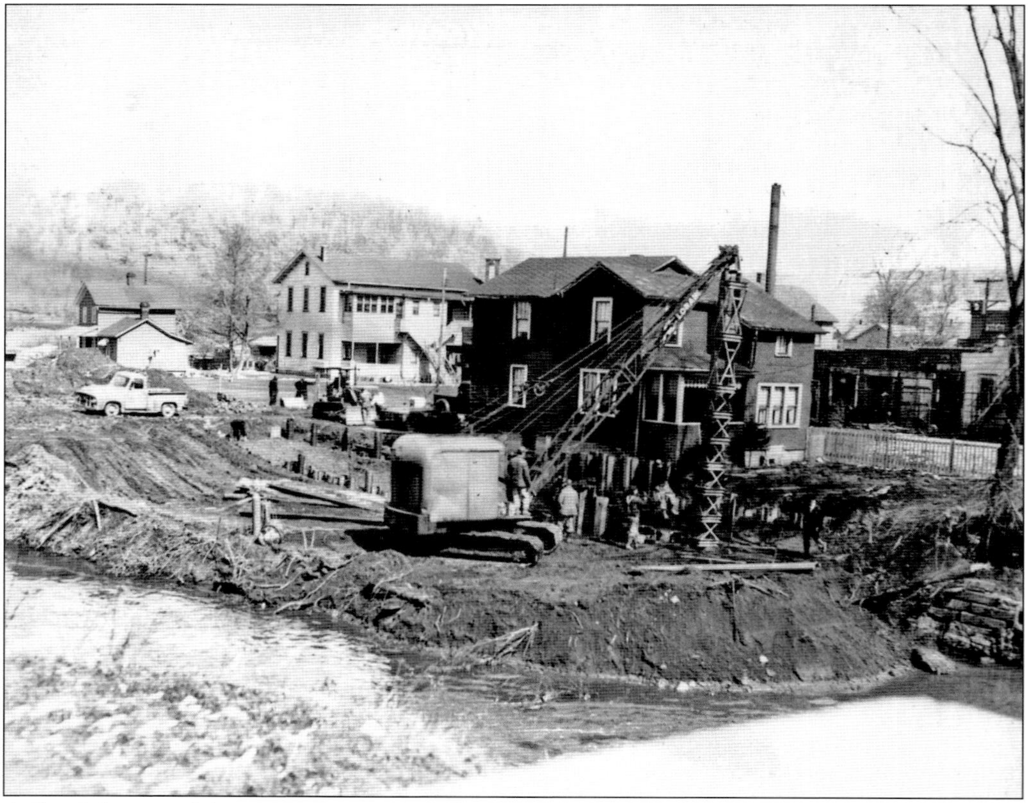

A flood the size of the one in 1936 is enough to get the ball rolling for flood prevention strategies. Unfortunately, the Great Depression and World War II delayed any attempts of completing such expensive projects. This photograph was taken from the Main Street Bridge over Little Toby Creek, facing northeast, as a pile driver sets steel supports for what will become a concrete wall in the 1950s.

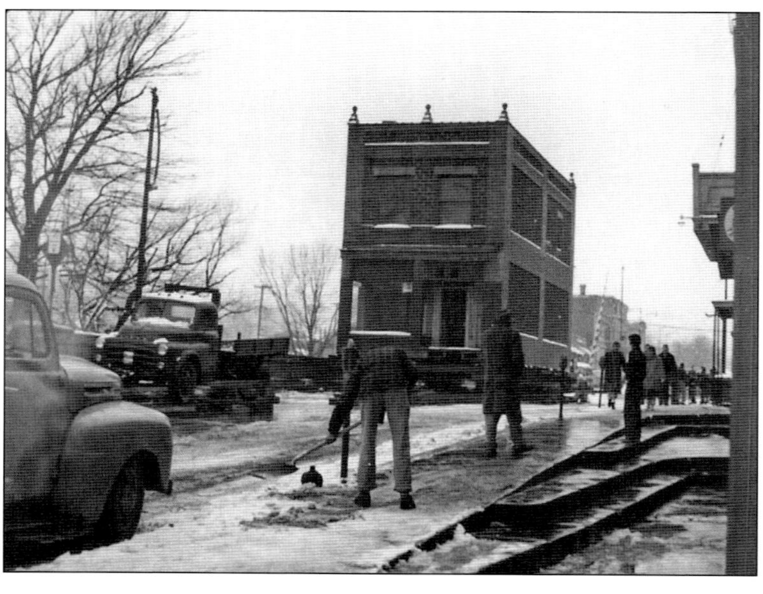

Construction of the flood control system required the moving of a few buildings, namely this one, as it passes over the Main Street Bridge over Little Toby Creek. It looks as though the weather did not cooperate, as a man shovels a slushy mixture of snow and ice into the street. The structure would be placed on the south side of Main Street across from Oak Street.

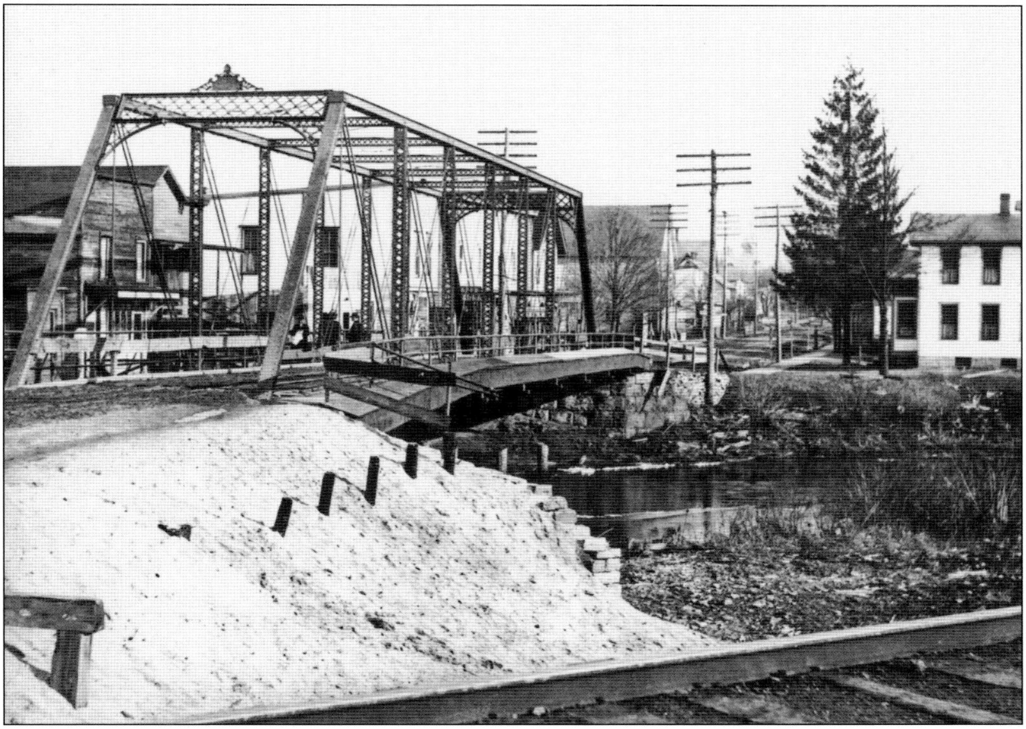

The Main Street Bridge over Little Toby Creek in Brockway has been replaced several times. The bridge shown above was probably the second bridge built in 1888, and was replaced by a concrete bridge in the 1920s. The third bridge was in rough shape by the time the 1996 flood hit, and it required replacement soon after the flood.

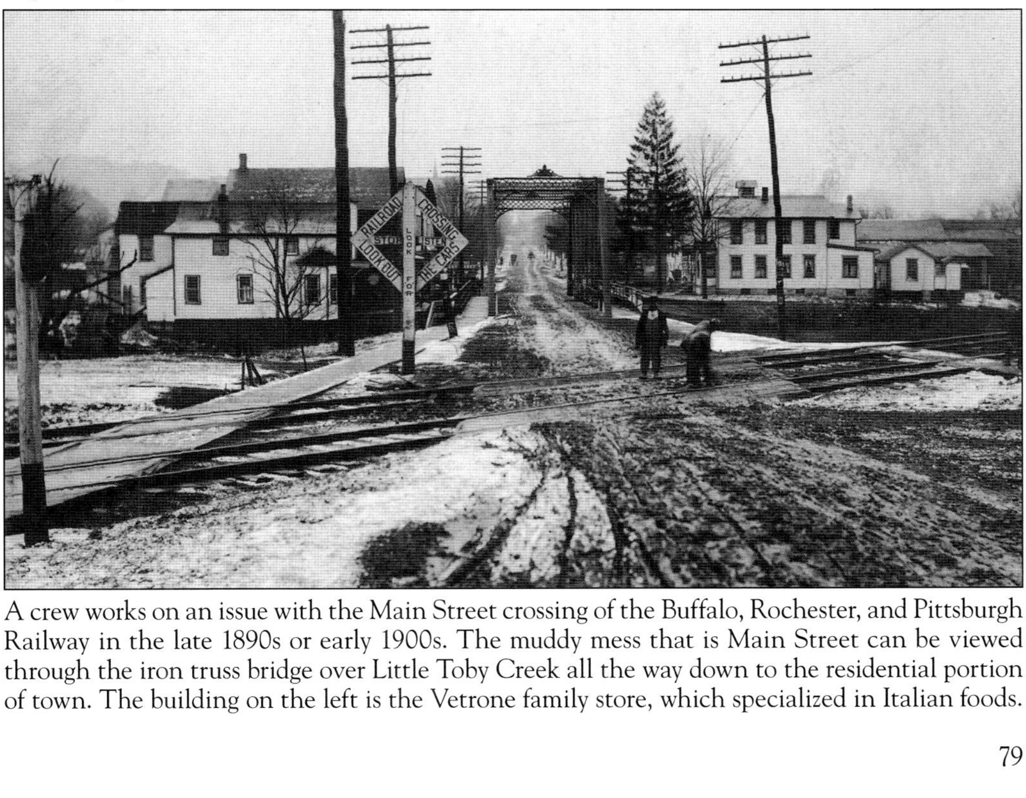

A crew works on an issue with the Main Street crossing of the Buffalo, Rochester, and Pittsburgh Railway in the late 1890s or early 1900s. The muddy mess that is Main Street can be viewed through the iron truss bridge over Little Toby Creek all the way down to the residential portion of town. The building on the left is the Vetrone family store, which specialized in Italian foods.

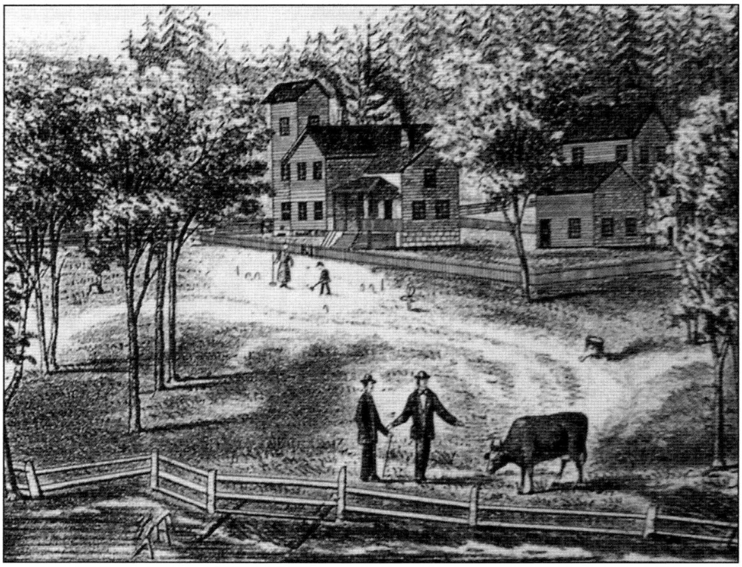

A. J. Thompson's residence, featured in this sketch from Caldwell's 1878 atlas of Jefferson County, was on the southwest side of Little Toby Creek, just upstream of the Main Street Bridge. A. J. Thompson built the first dam and water-powered sawmill at the village of Blue Rock in 1856. He also partnered in the firm Thompson and McClelland, listed as druggists in the 1878 Caldwell atlas.

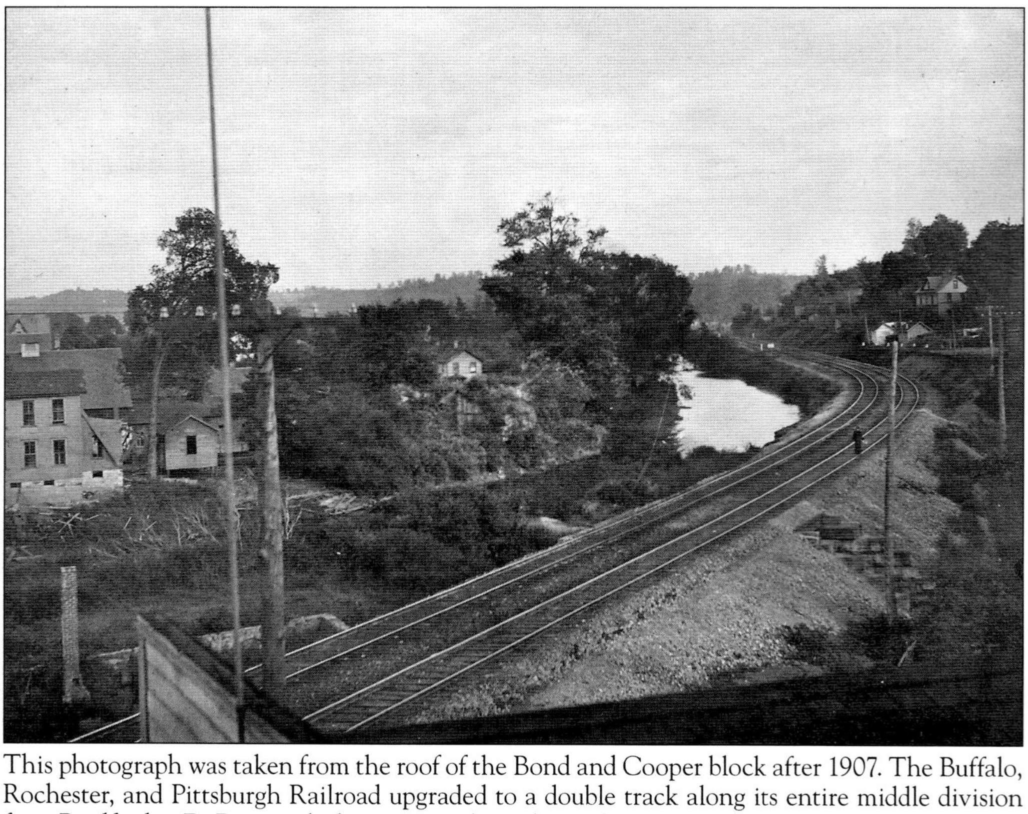

This photograph was taken from the roof of the Bond and Cooper block after 1907. The Buffalo, Rochester, and Pittsburgh Railroad upgraded to a double track along its entire middle division from Bradford to DuBois, with the segment through Brockwayville being completed around 1907. The large home on the right of the tracks on the hill may be the home of H. U. Niver, as marked on the 1878 Caldwell atlas.

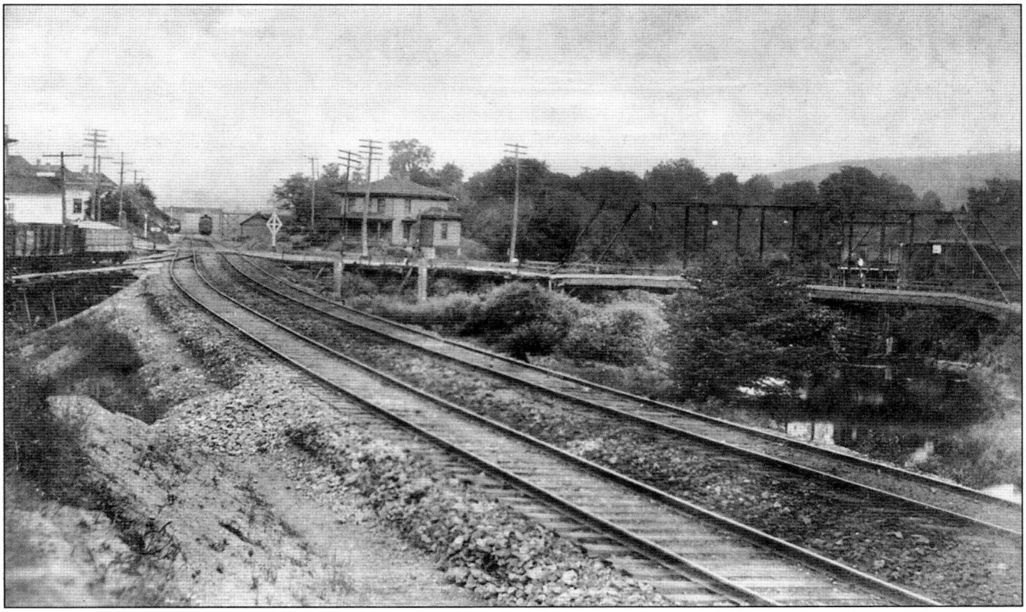

The Main Street Bridge over Little Toby Creek is featured in this 1906 photograph. The Buffalo, Rochester, and Pittsburgh Railway turns north to follow Little Toby Creek. The siding to the left was used to haul mine spoils to fill the Pittsburg, Shawmut, and Northern Railroad grade over the Arch Street tunnel. The house in the center belonged to Wellman Brothers and was the home of the station agent.

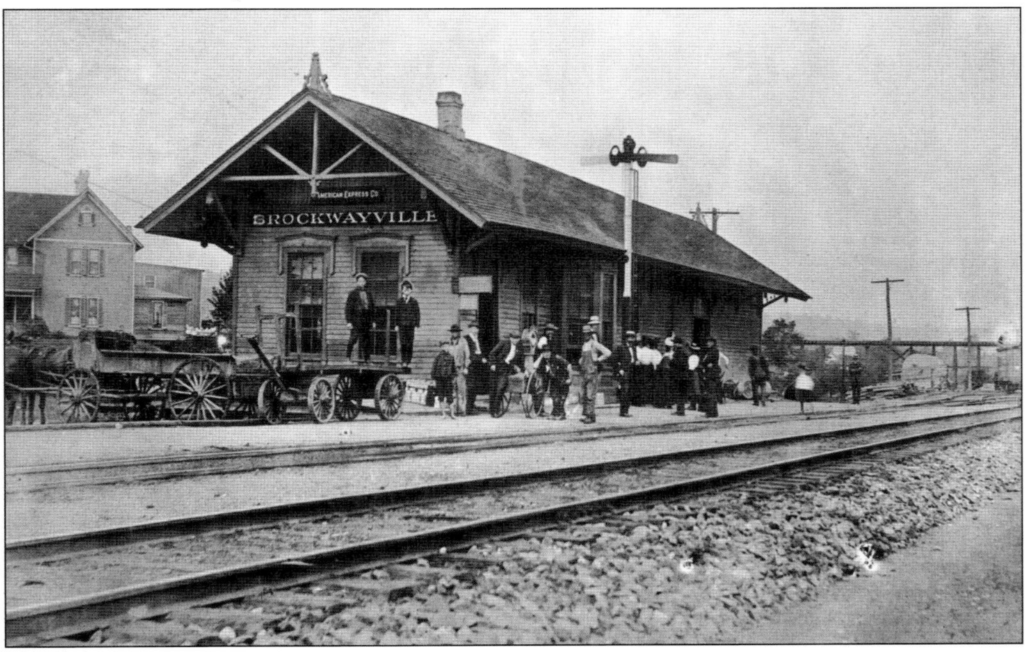

Some folks pause for the photographer on the platform of the original 1883 wooden structure of the Buffalo, Rochester, and Pittsburgh Railway station at Brockwayville. In the distance behind the station can be seen the trestle that was used to carry coal out of the West Clarion Mines of the Erie Railroad–owned Northwest Mining and Exchange Company who were mining the valley to the southwest of town.

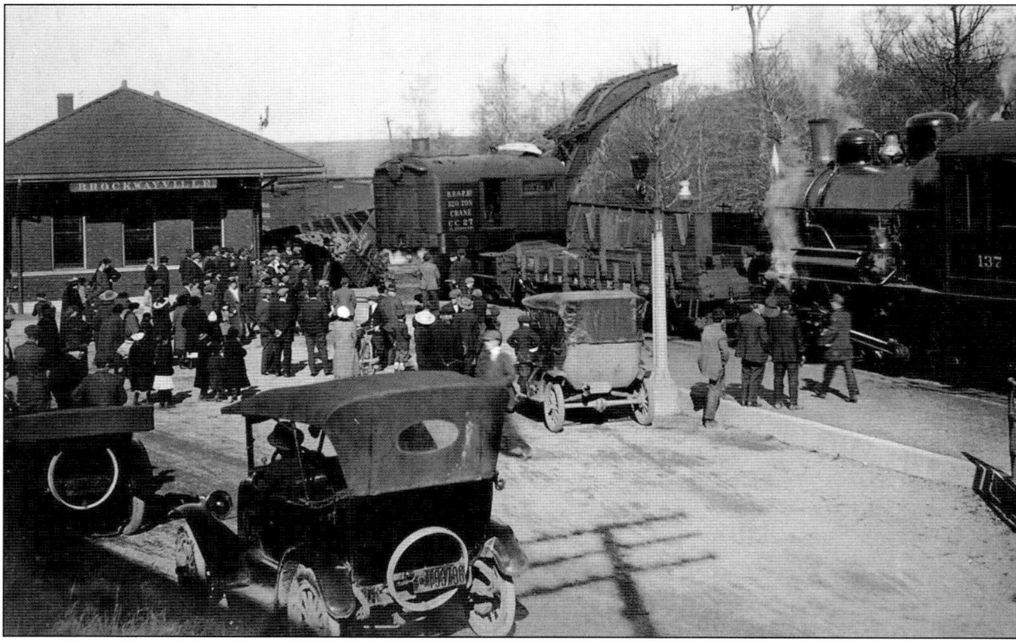

A November 1916 wreck at the Buffalo, Rochester, and Pittsburgh Railway station in Brockwayville almost claimed the life of one of the station workers, when a gondola of pig iron clipped the center of the building. A steam work crane, pushed to the station by locomotive No. 137, works on cleaning up the mess so that rail traffic can get moving again.

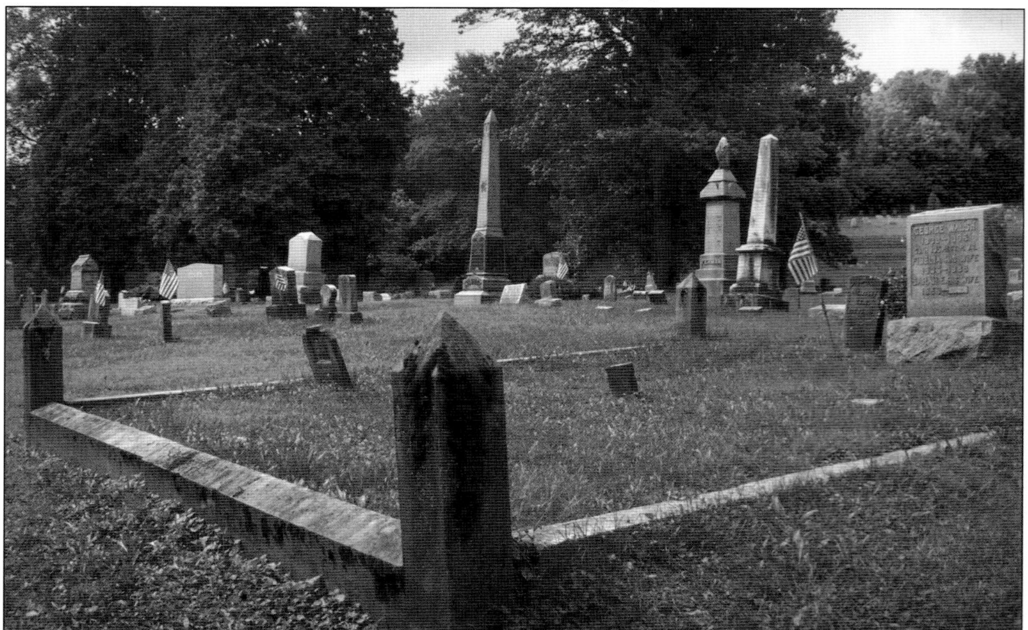

In 1866, twenty-five prominent citizens of Brockwayville subscribed $25 each to establish a cemetery in the hollow to the south of town formed by Curry Run. The list included Dr. Asaph M. Clarke, who donated the 10 acres, Dr. W. Niver, W. Wellman, Peter Galusha, Norman Lane, and A. J. Thompson. The first person buried in Wildwood Cemetery was Mrs. Fannie P. Johnson who died on August 26, 1868.

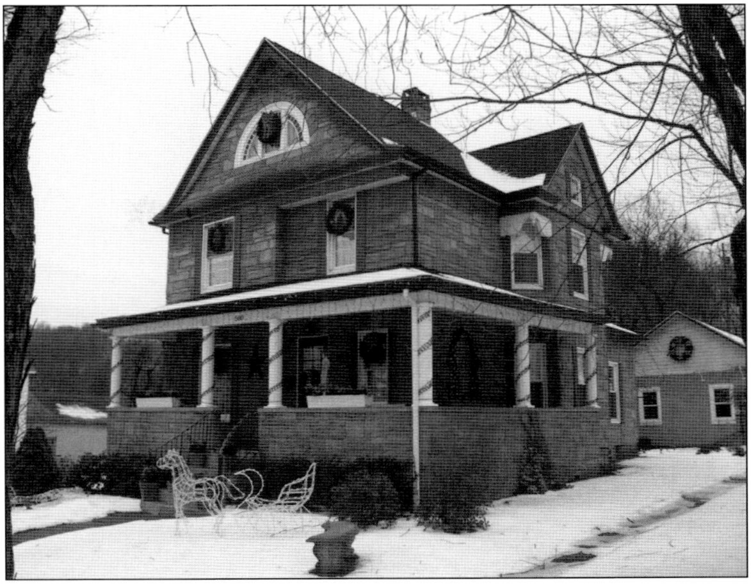

The difficulty with including individual houses is that not all of the beautiful houses in Brockway could be featured. This home is on the southwest corner of Broad Street and Fifth Avenue. There are several homes on Broad Street that date to the mid-1800s, this assumption being made based on a few photographs and architecture. A Baptist church once stood a few blocks to the right of this house.

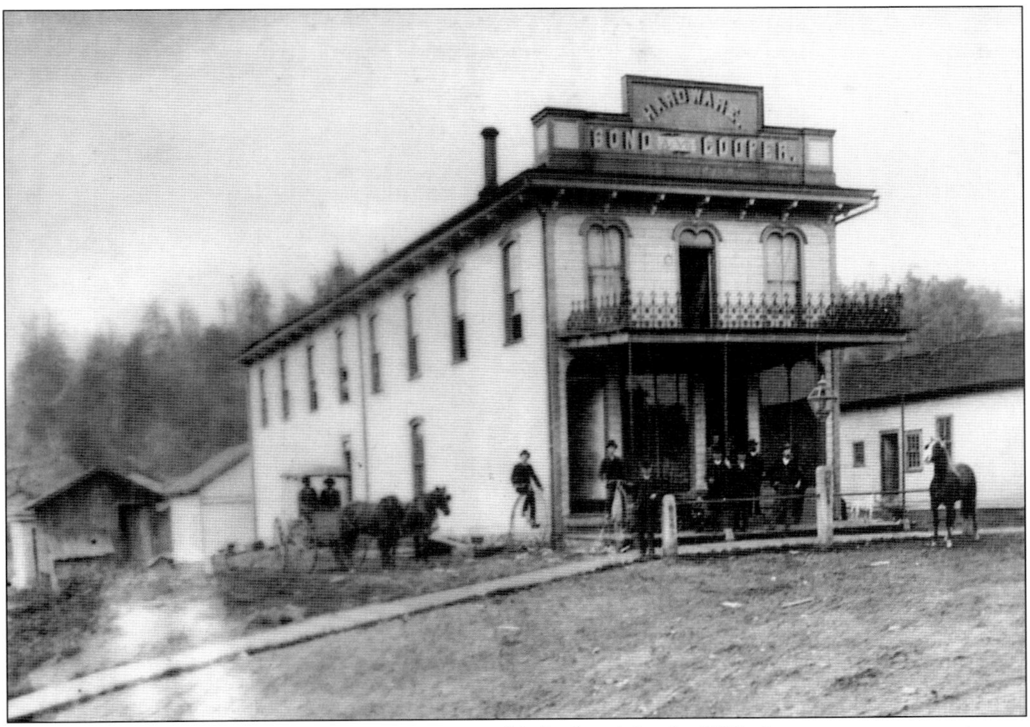

The Bond and Cooper hardware store was established in March 1882, dating its construction to before any railroad entered the town. Interesting features of this photograph are the surrey with the fringe, the two gentlemen on high-wheeled bicycles, and the old gas street lamp in the center post that supported the bar used to tie one's horse.

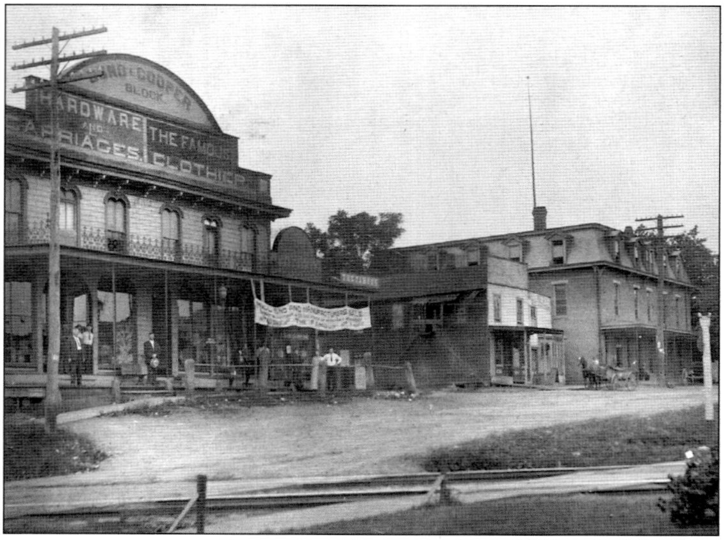

The Bond and Cooper block received considerable enlargement in 1889 to include the original hardware store on the left and the Famous clothing store on the right. The brick structure on the right end of the block was started in 1853 as Brockwayville's first hotel, the Aquagga House. It was known as the Railroad House for many years before 1885, when it became the Logan House.

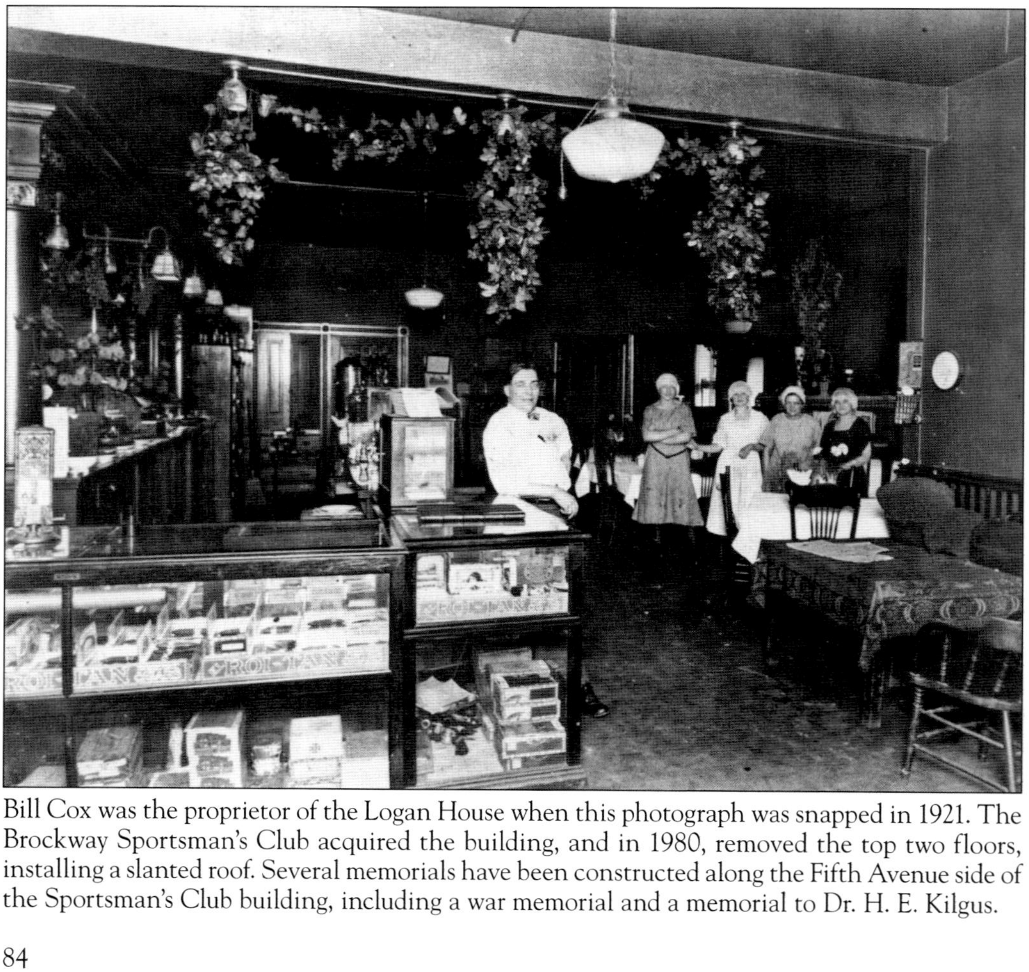

Bill Cox was the proprietor of the Logan House when this photograph was snapped in 1921. The Brockway Sportsman's Club acquired the building, and in 1980, removed the top two floors, installing a slanted roof. Several memorials have been constructed along the Fifth Avenue side of the Sportsman's Club building, including a war memorial and a memorial to Dr. H. E. Kilgus.

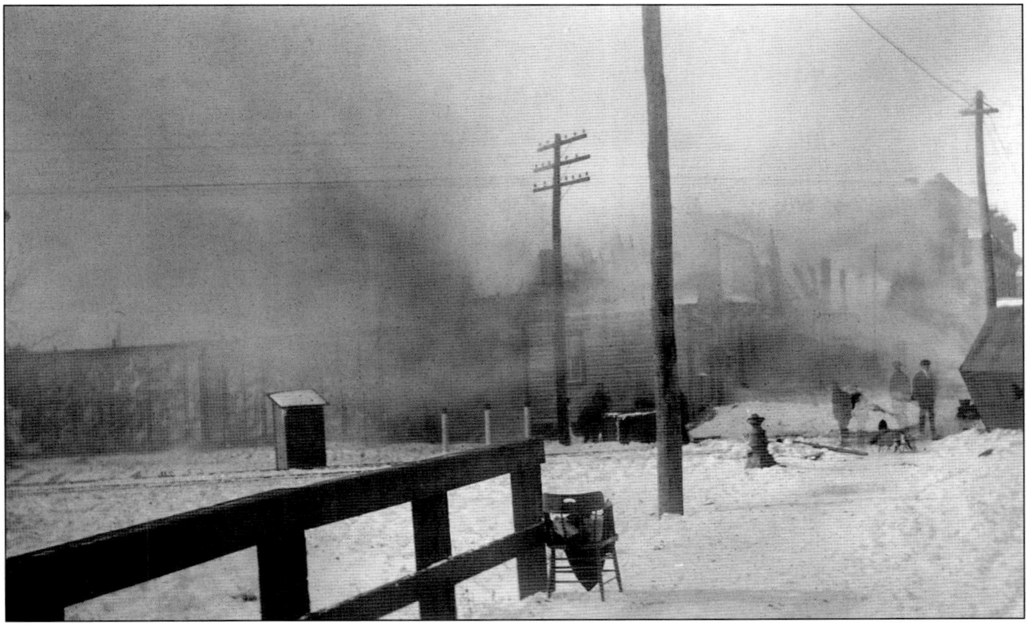

The Bond and Cooper block and several adjacent buildings went up in blazes on the night of January 17, 1923. The cause of the fire was the attempt to thaw frozen water pipes in the basement with a blowtorch. Firemen were able to protect the Cox Garage and the Logan House, but paint and blasting powder in the hardware doomed the chances of saving the structure.

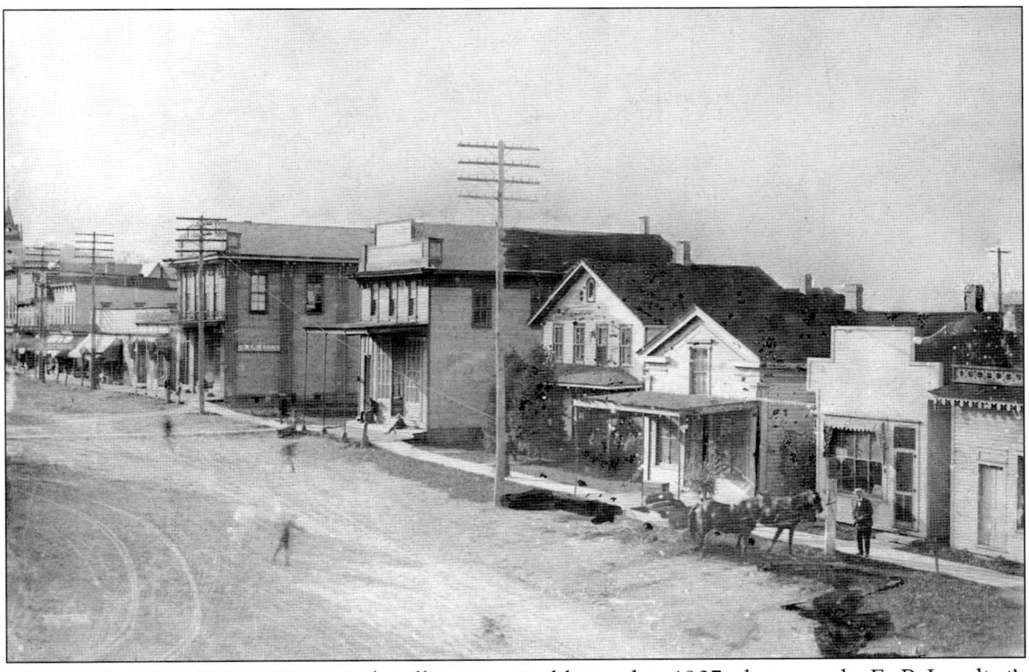

The north side of Main Street is hardly recognizable in this 1907 photograph. E. P. Landini's Shoe Repairing and Shoe Shine store is on the right. The next building was originally the Wellman Brothers store in the 1860s and became the Citizens Bank and Trust Company. Next was the Daniel Groves residence and store, constructed in 1881. The next building was Robert W. Moorhead's store, built 1854.

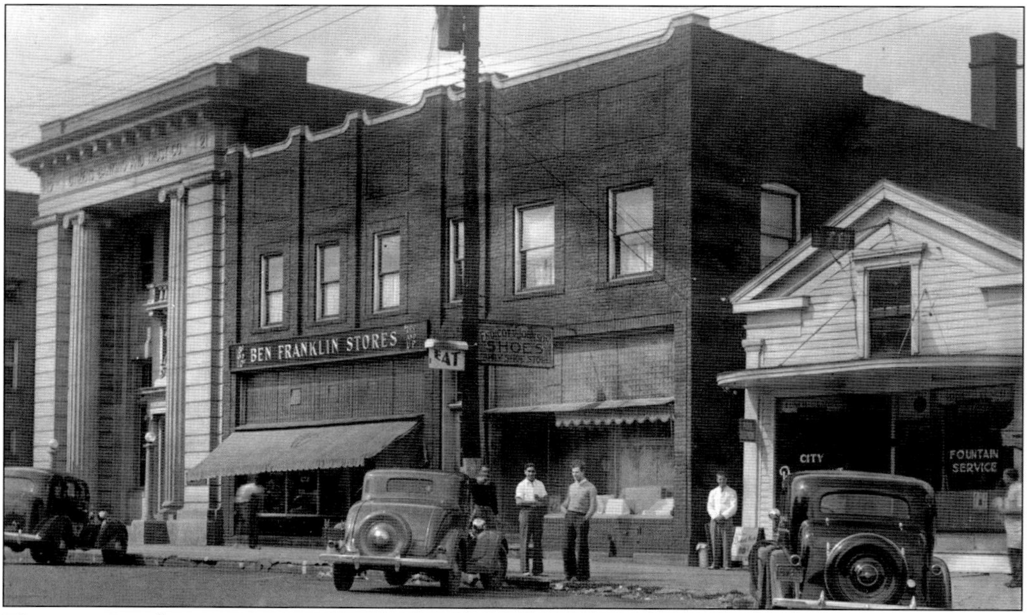

The new Brockway Citizens Bank and Trust Company building occupies the site of the D. D. Groves store, which was moved east, encased in brick, and expanded. In this photograph, the Ben Franklin Store and the Endicott and Johnson Family Shoe Store occupy the building. The old Citizens Bank and Trust Company building is occupied by the City Restaurant.

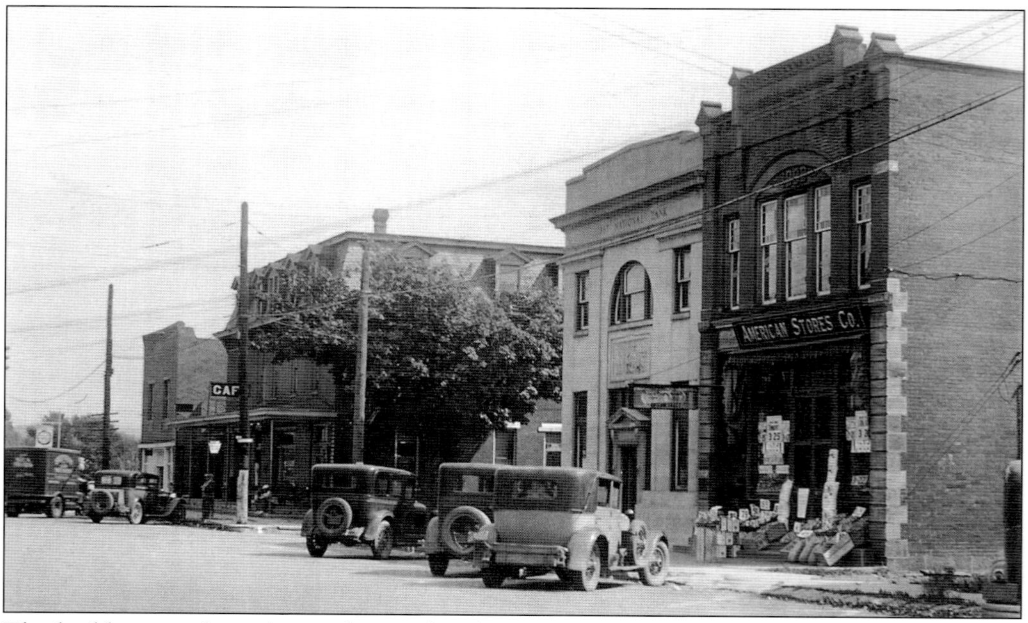

The building on the right on the south side of Main Street was the first bank in town, the Brockwayville Bank, constructed in 1888. The Brockwayville Bank became the First National Bank and moved one building to the east, but it failed during the Depression. The Logan House stands on the far side of Fifth Avenue, and the buildings beyond it replaced the Bond and Cooper block after the disastrous fire.

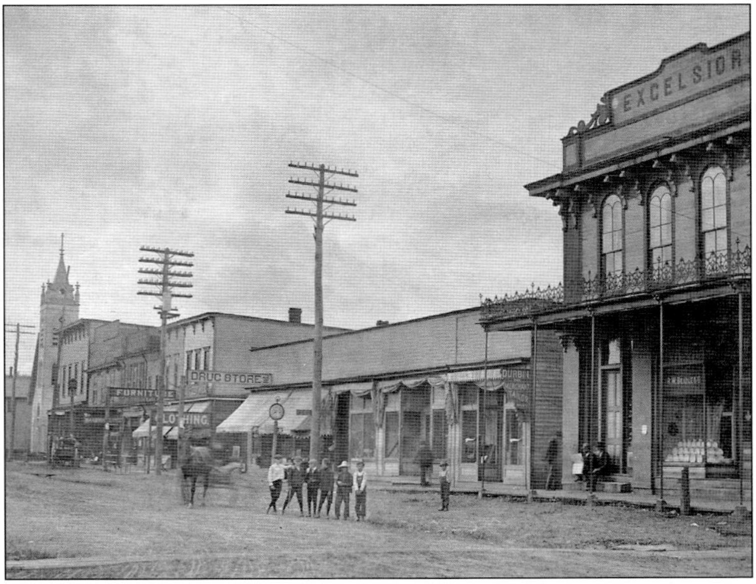

The Excelsior building was purchased from Robert W. Moorhead by Barrett T. Chapin in 1878, then by William G. McCain in 1888, and then by Robert W. Beadle in 1898. The rest of the block includes Durbin's Tailor shop, Briggs the tailor, the Bunyan and Tobin hardware, the E. B. Covill jewelry store, the post office, George W. Sibley's general store, and the Brockway Drug Store.

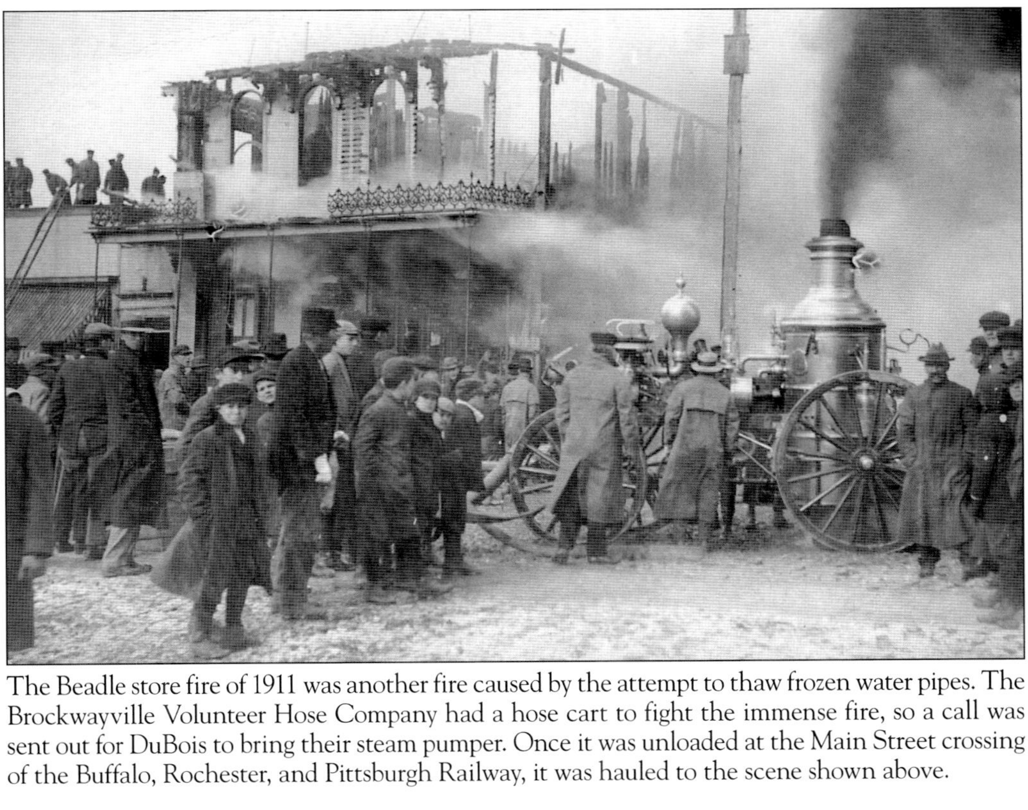

The Beadle store fire of 1911 was another fire caused by the attempt to thaw frozen water pipes. The Brockwayville Volunteer Hose Company had a hose cart to fight the immense fire, so a call was sent out for DuBois to bring their steam pumper. Once it was unloaded at the Main Street crossing of the Buffalo, Rochester, and Pittsburgh Railway, it was hauled to the scene shown above.

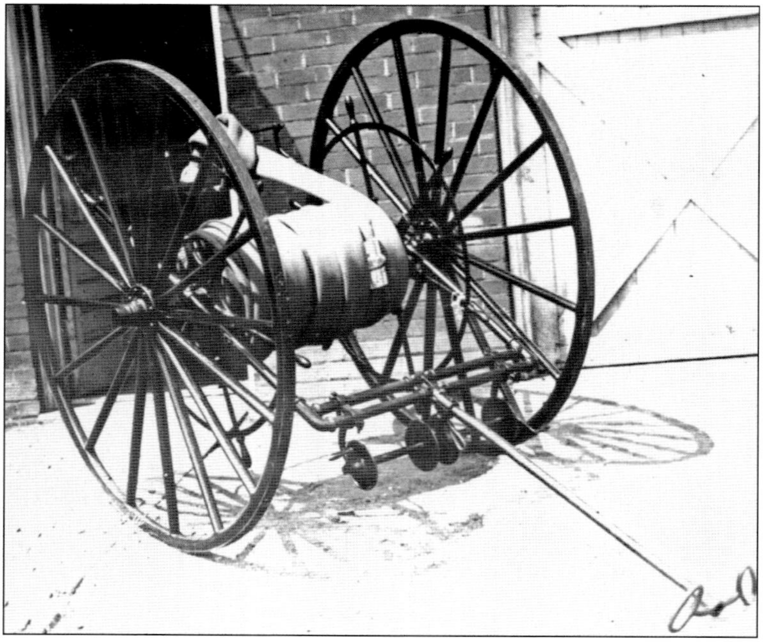

In 1898, the town purchased this two-wheel hose cart and 500 feet of hose to fight local blazes. When the Brockwayville Volunteer Hose Company was chartered in 1904, the little cart was the only piece of equipment they had until 1919. The cart and hose company saw plenty of action, from fighting small fires throughout the region, to fighting the big fires in town in 1909, 1910, and 1911.

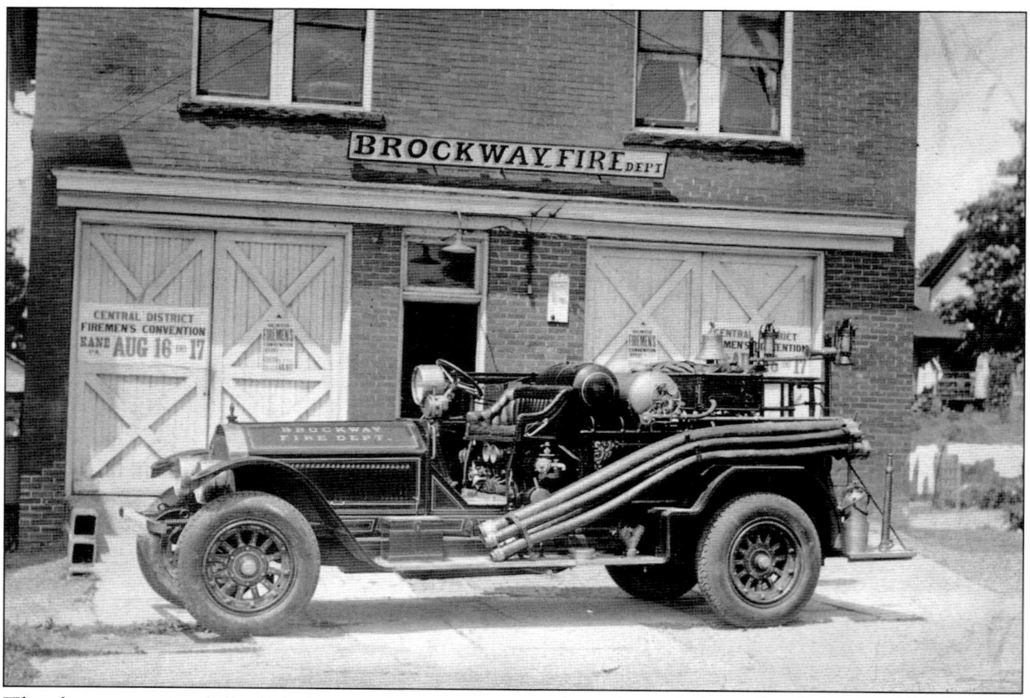

The first motorized firefighting equipment was purchased in 1919 in the form of an American LaFrance body mounted on a Model T Ford chassis with hose and chemical equipment. The truck in the photograph was the second one purchased by the Brockway Fire Department, an American LaFrance Fire Engine, in 1926 for $10,800.

Labor Day of 1921 was the day that Brockwayville celebrated electrification. The power plant of the Brockway Light, Heat, and Power Company on Evergreen (Railroad) Street was finished and ready to be put into service. The Brockwayville Volunteer Hose Company sponsored the celebration and is shown here decked out in formal uniform. Chief Edward J. Durbin, the first fire chief, is in the white uniform.

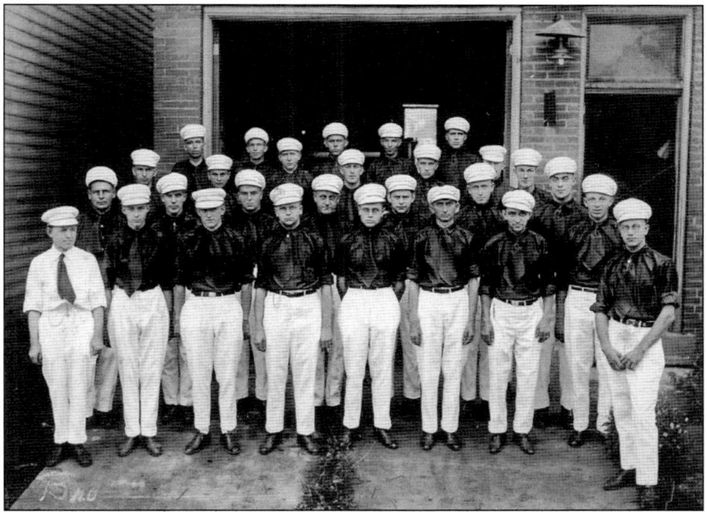

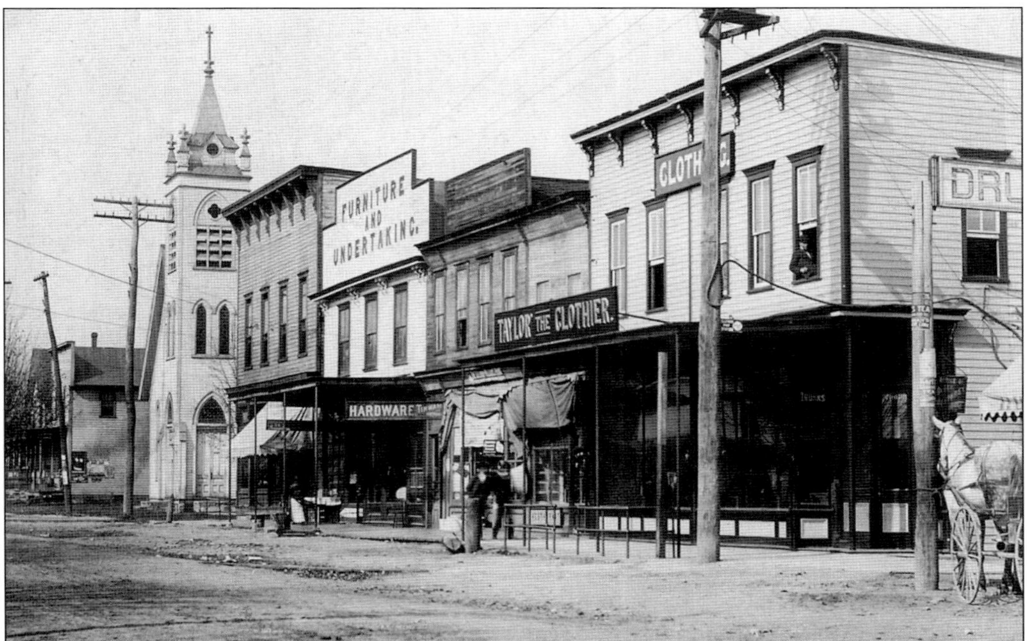

Pictured here was the west end of the business block on the north side of Main Street. The building on the right is the Taylor the Clothier store, followed by a restaurant, a hardware and tinware store, the Brockwayville Record office, and the J. S. Kearney grocery store in the last building, which was constructed to lodge the Independent Order of Odd Fellows.

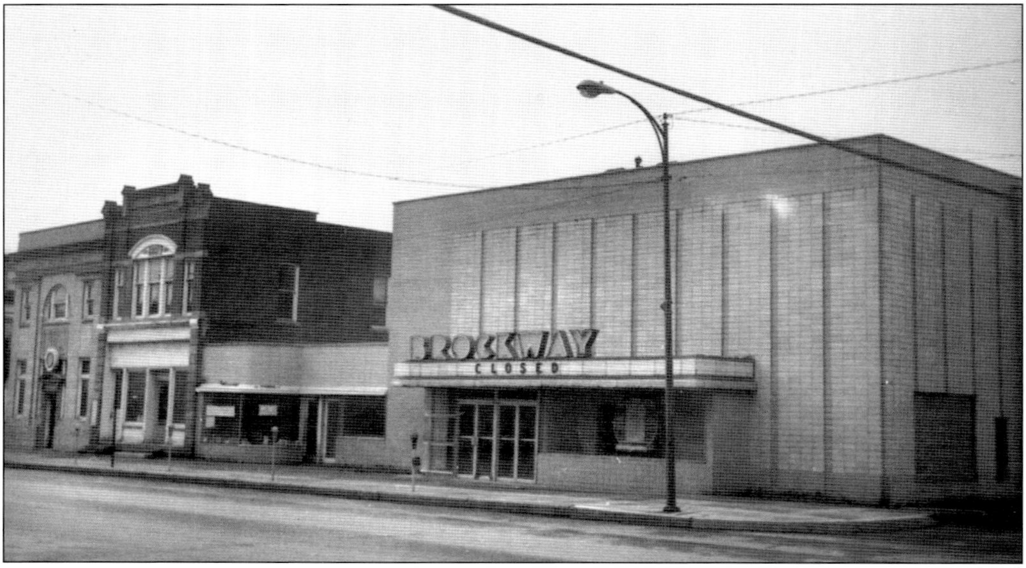

The south side of Main Street saw few changes since the bank buildings (on the left) were constructed. The one exception was the Brockway Theater, constructed in 1941 with the latest in projection technology. It would meet the same fate as the bank buildings in 1972, when the whole block was leveled to construct the new Brockway Citizens Bank, which would become the Savings and Trust Bank.

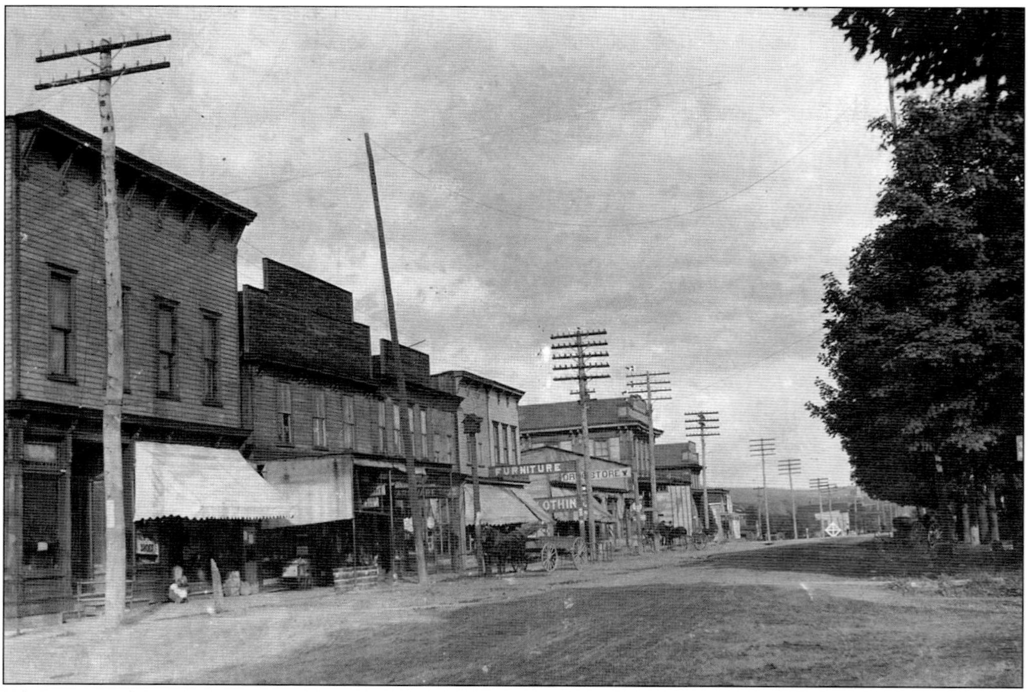

The entire business portion of Brockwayville—on the north side of Main Street between the Methodist church and the Buffalo, Rochester, and Pittsburgh Railway—is featured in this pre-1910 photograph. The lodge of the Independent Order of Odd Fellows on the left had a bowling alley and a poolroom in the basement. A few small fires were extinguished in this section in early March 1910.

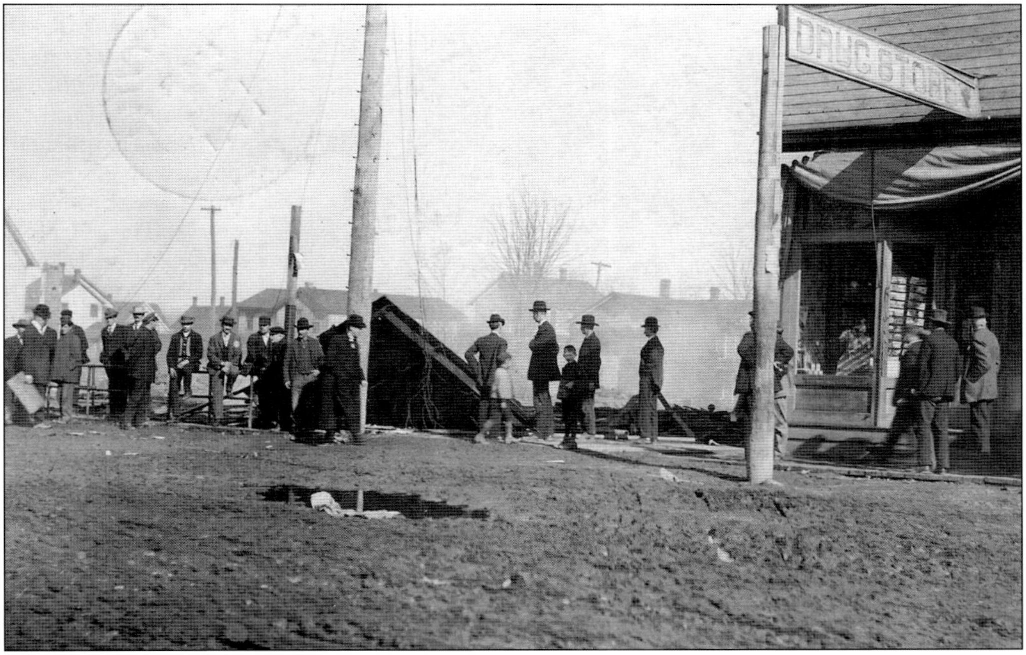

Just weeks after the small blazes of early March 1910 were extinguished, a huge fire leveled the block from the Odd Fellows hall to the Brockway Drug Store. The photograph above was taken on the morning of March 25, 1910, just west of the Brockway Drug Store. The fire took only about two hours to destroy the block, and it destroyed $50,000 worth of property.

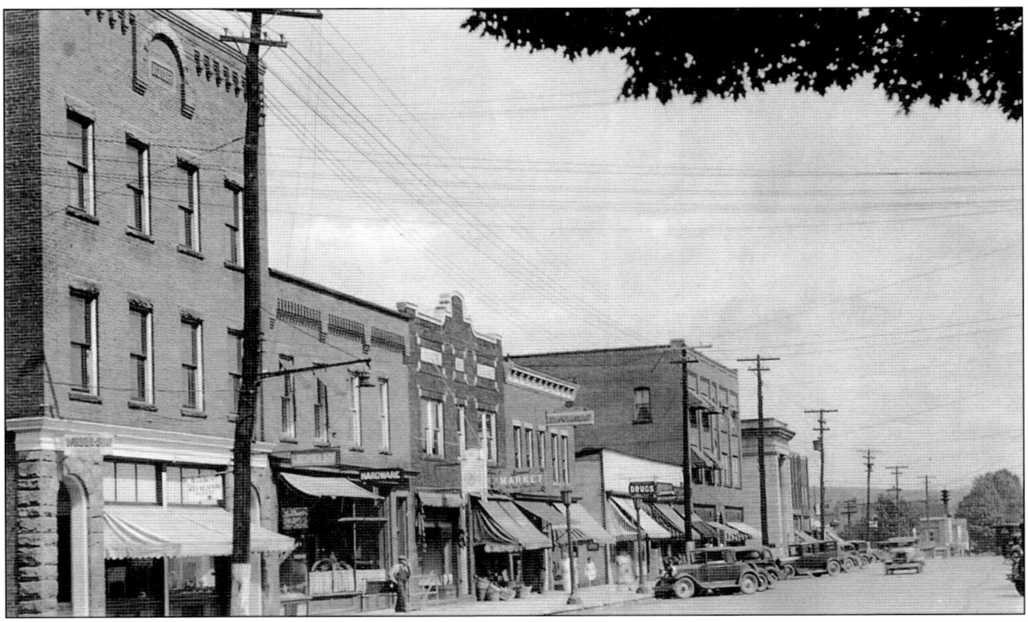

By 1921, most of the business portion of Brockwayville on the north side of Main Street between the Methodist church and the Buffalo, Rochester, and Pittsburgh Railway had been destroyed by fire and rebuilt with red brick structures. The Brockwayville Citizens Bank and Trust Company had been completed on the northeast corner of Fifth and Main Streets. The "north side" of today has changed very little since the 1920s.

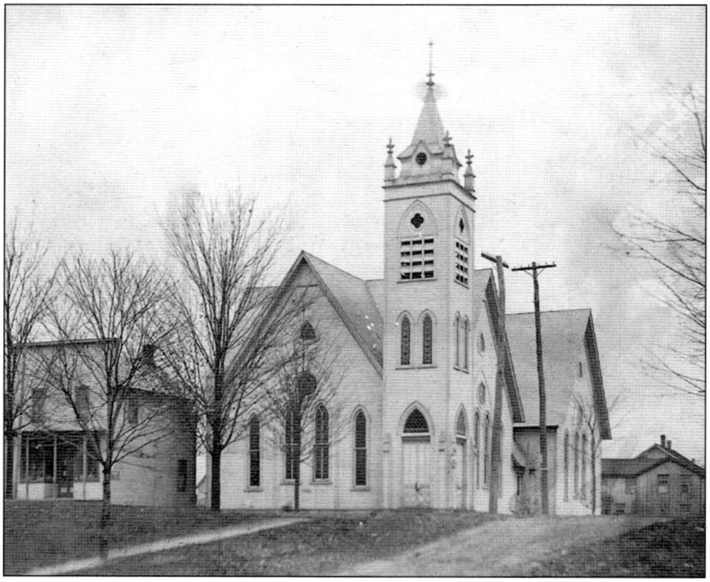

The Frost schoolhouse on the hill southwest of Brockwayville was the first meeting place for Methodists. The original structure, which is now known as "the chapel," was constructed between 1862 and 1865. The structure in the photograph was completed in 1889, with "the chapel" moved back Fourth Avenue. The entire structure of the Moorhead United Methodist Church was encased in brick in 1930, and an educational wing added in 1967.

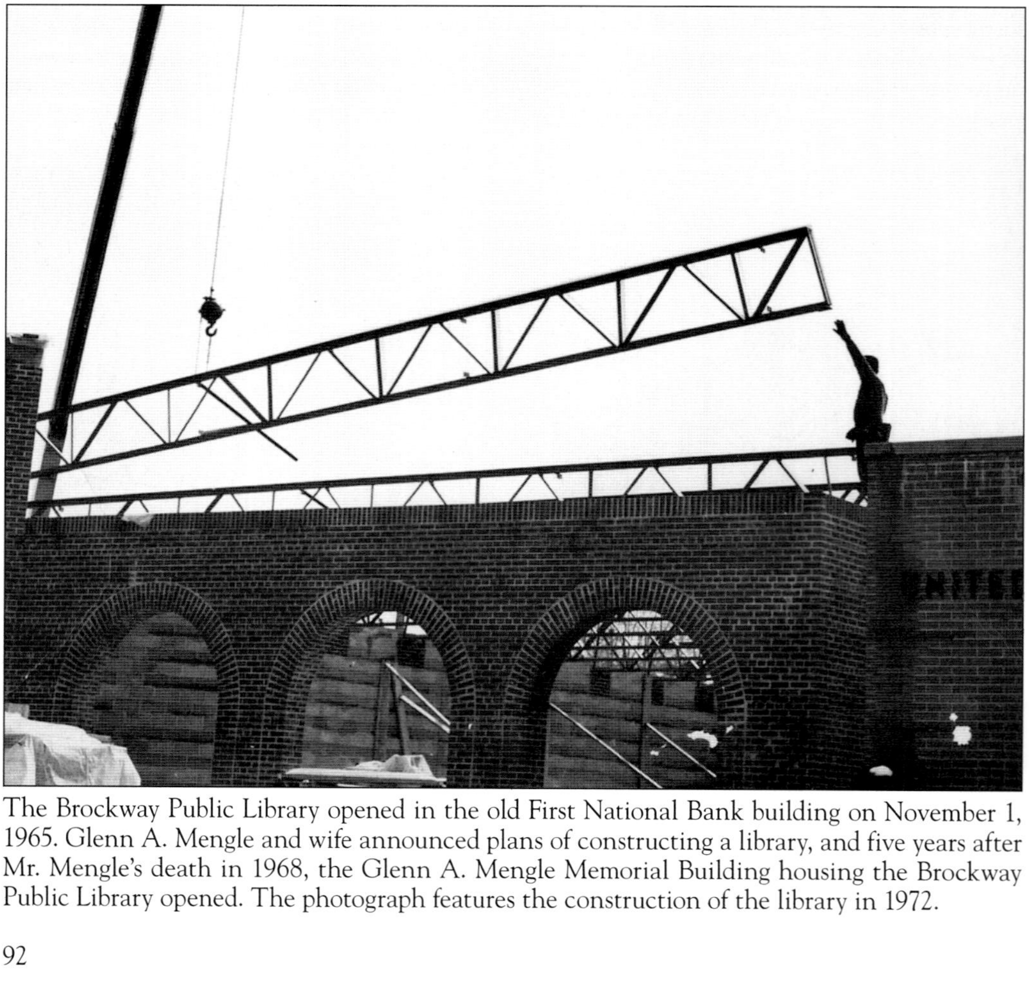

The Brockway Public Library opened in the old First National Bank building on November 1, 1965. Glenn A. Mengle and wife announced plans of constructing a library, and five years after Mr. Mengle's death in 1968, the Glenn A. Mengle Memorial Building housing the Brockway Public Library opened. The photograph features the construction of the library in 1972.

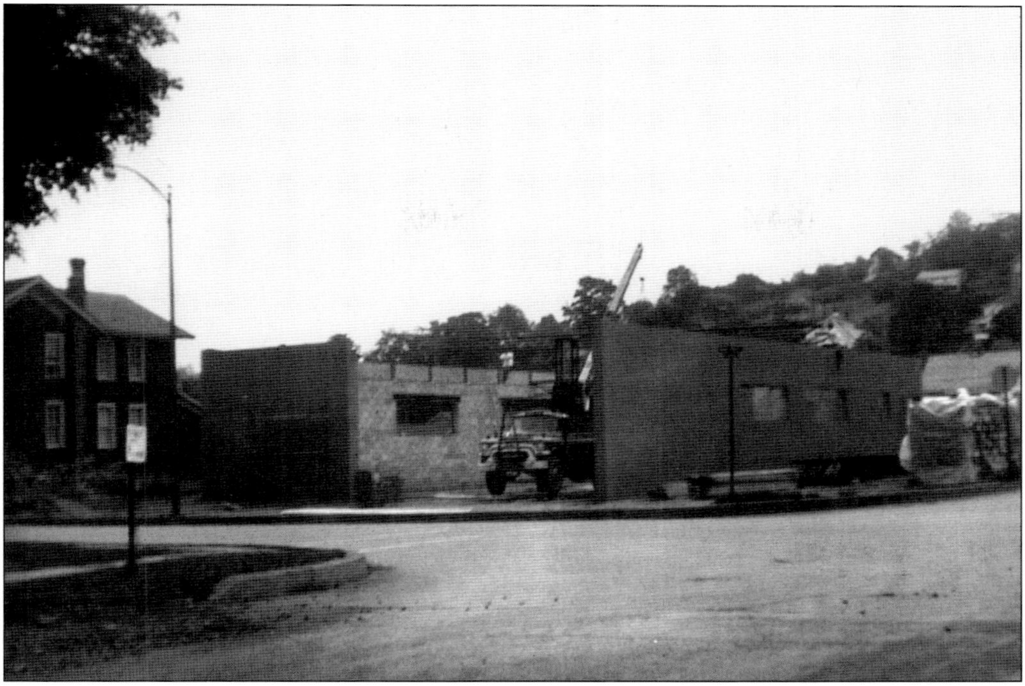

The Brockway Post Office occupied the old First National Bank building for a number of years. In the early 1960s, plans were drawn up to construct a new post office building on the southeast corner of Third Avenue and Main Street. The photograph features the construction of the new post office. The house to the left would be demolished for the Mengle Memorial Library.

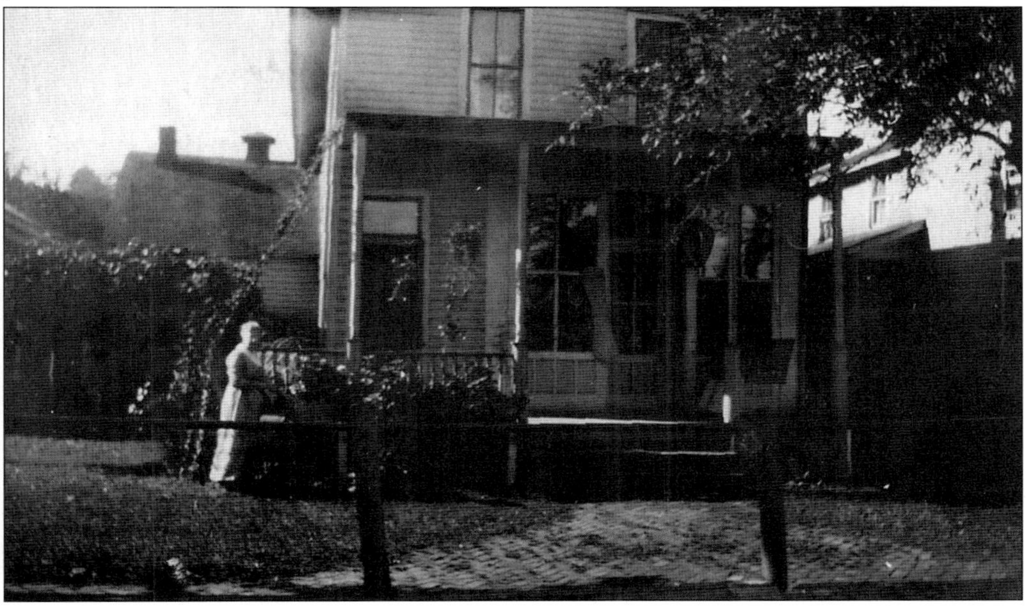

Thomas Ralston opened his harness and hardware shop prior to 1881 on the southwest corner of Main Street and Third Avenue. Thomas's son William continued the business in the same building, shown in this photograph taken in the early 1900s. The Ralston family continues to run the business from the same place today and has been in the grocery business for a number of years.

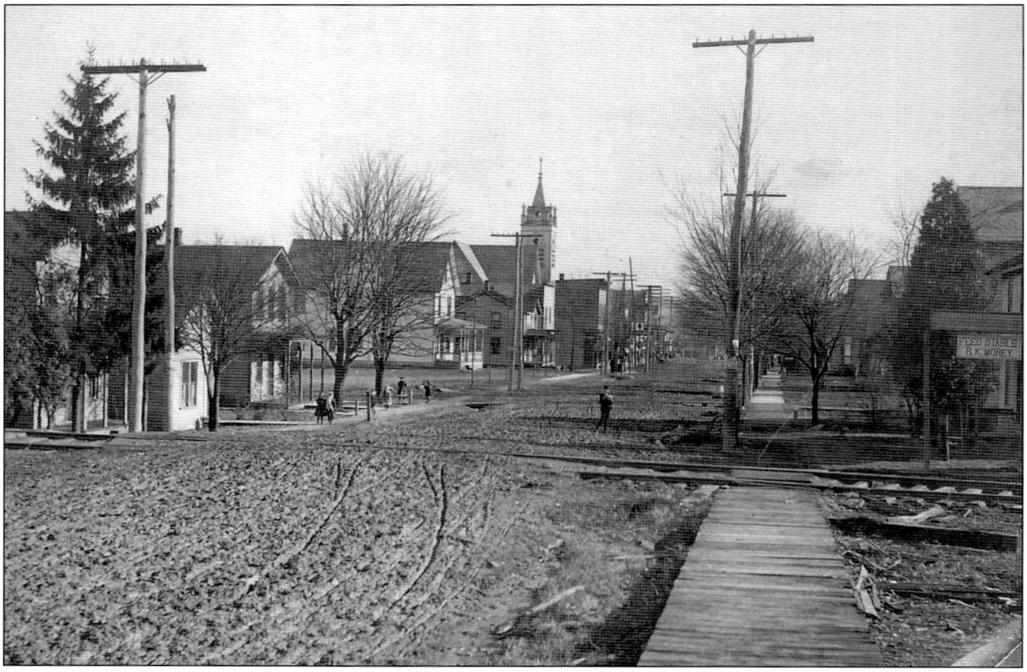

The railroad tracks leading to the West Clarion Mines up the valley to the right of the photograph are the feature of this final view of Main Street, looking east from Brookville Hill, in the late 1890s or early 1900s. One of the buildings on the left is the McLaughlin and Brothers blacksmith shop, while the feed stable of R. K. Morey is on the extreme right.

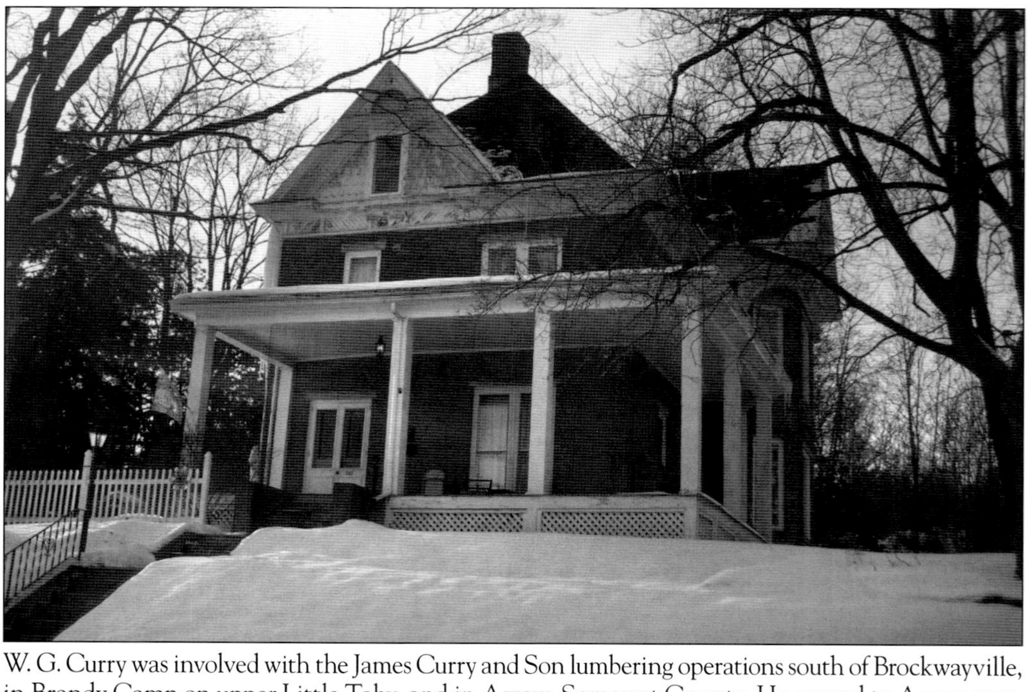

W. G. Curry was involved with the James Curry and Son lumbering operations south of Brockwayville, in Brandy Camp on upper Little Toby, and in Arrow, Somerset County. He moved to Arrow soon after James Curry's death in 1899 to help the company establish itself in its new location. He moved back to Brockwayville and lived in this brick home at the foot of Brookville Hill.

The Snyder Township High School was built in 1913–1914 way above the town on Brookville Hill, the hill that creates the western boundary of Brockwayville. The Snyder Township High School held classes in its rooms from 1914 to 1939. The school had a baseball field constructed beside it, and to the author's knowledge it is still in use. The building is now the Snyder Township Municipal Building.

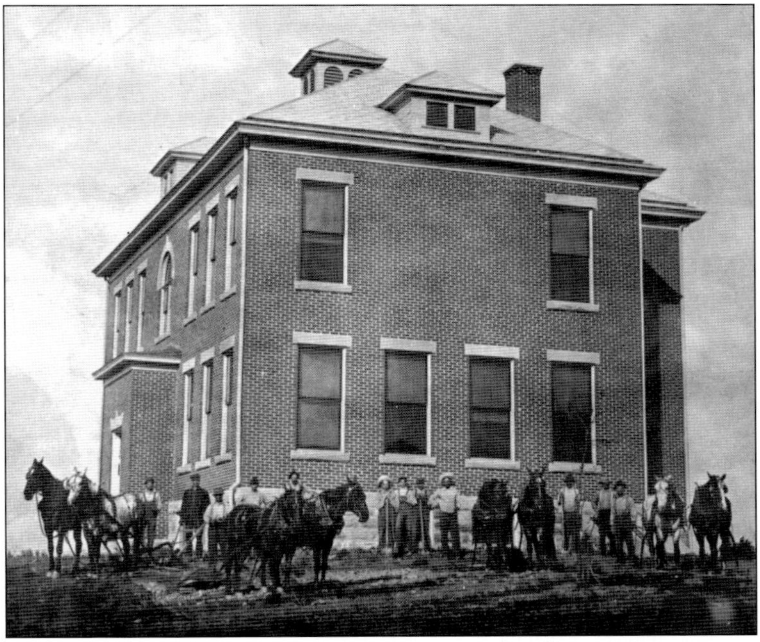

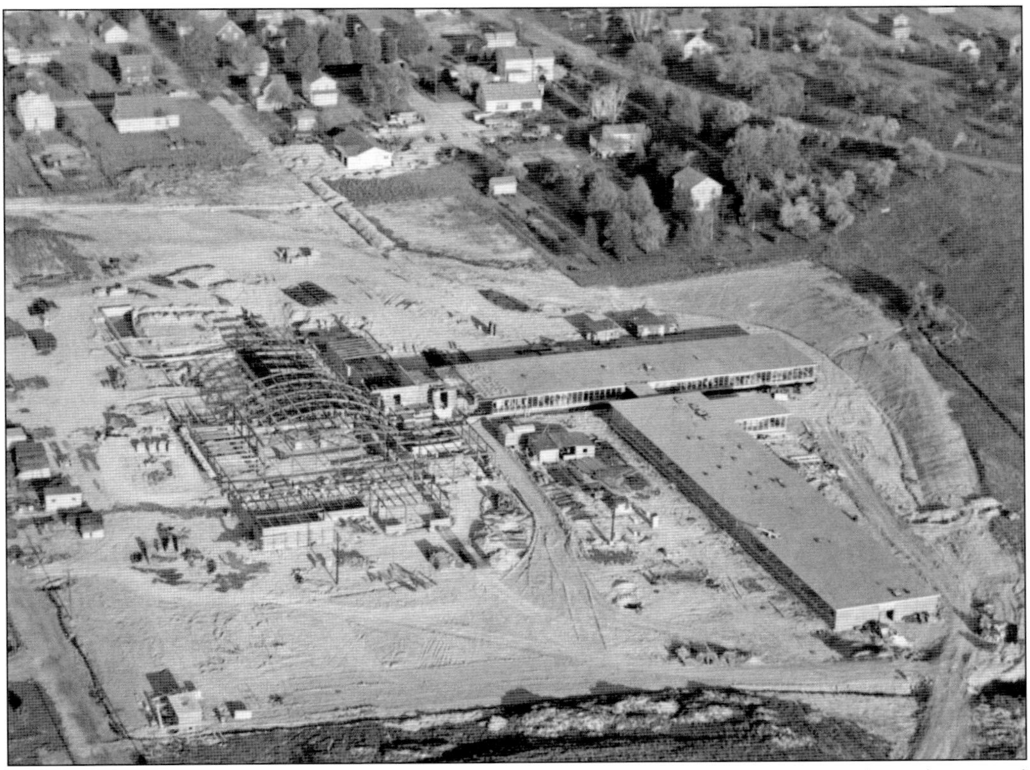

The new Brockway High School on North Street was under construction when this aerial photograph was taken in 1957. The school cost $1,486,566, and it was dedicated on September 7, 1958. A new elementary school costing $1,540,000 was constructed to the immediate west of the new high school in 1968. By 1978, all of the schoolchildren from Main Street and Ninth Avenue were moved to the new elementary school.

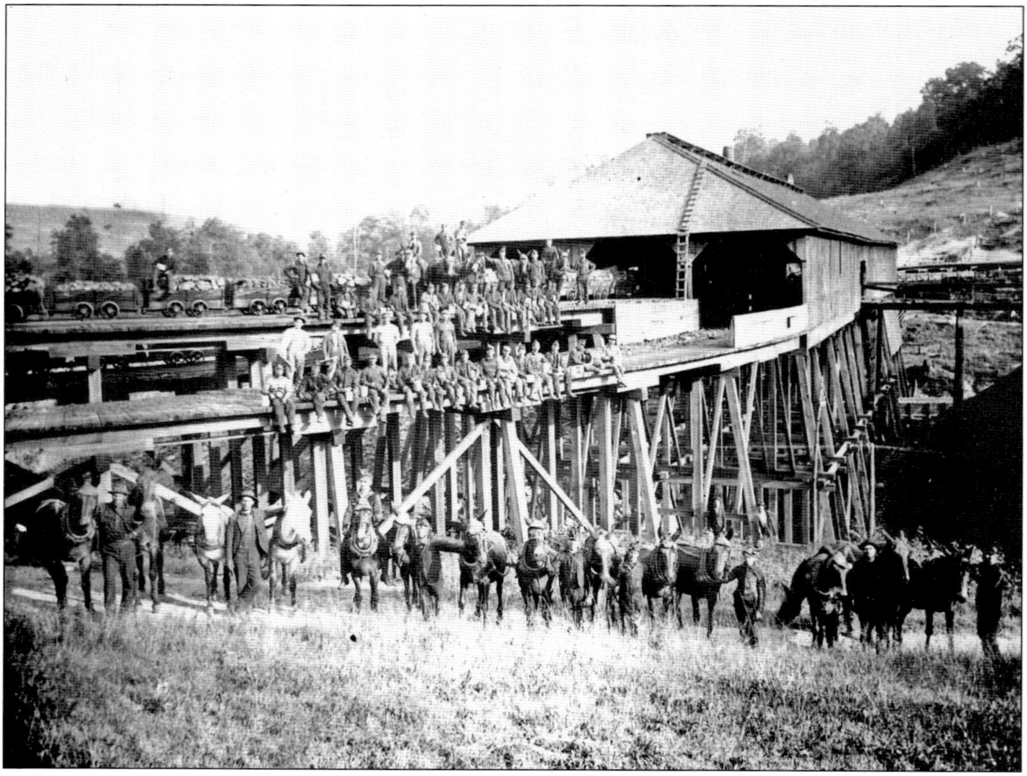

The Northwest Mining and Exchange Company announced the opening of a new mine in the hollow southwest of Brockwayville on July 30, 1897. The mine was called the West Clarion Mine, because the new mine was west of the Clarion mines at Crenshaw, which then became known as the East Clarion Mines. The photograph is of the mine tipple and crew when mules still hauled the coal out.

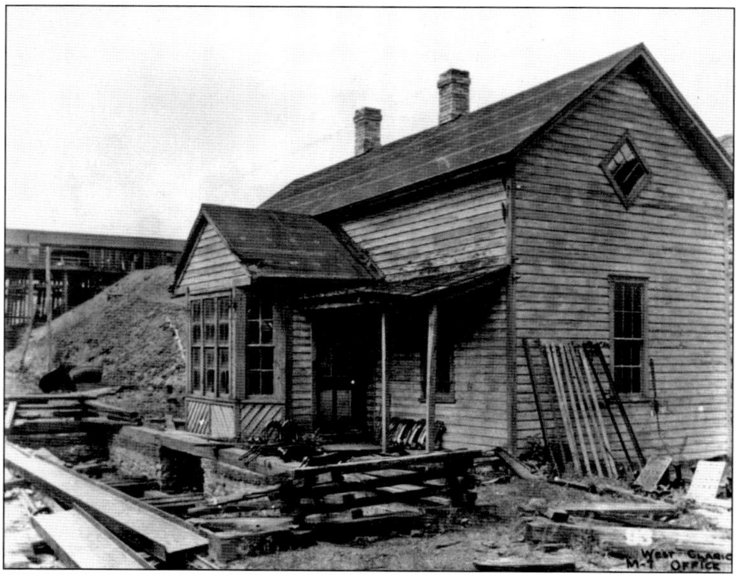

The West Clarion Mines received electricity from the Northwest Mining and Exchange Company's powerhouse at Helens Mills in 1913. Electrification reduced the need for picking the coal by hand and eliminated the need to use mules to haul the coal out of the mine. By 1898, the mine used eight electric cutting machines, cutting 100 tons of coal each day per machine.

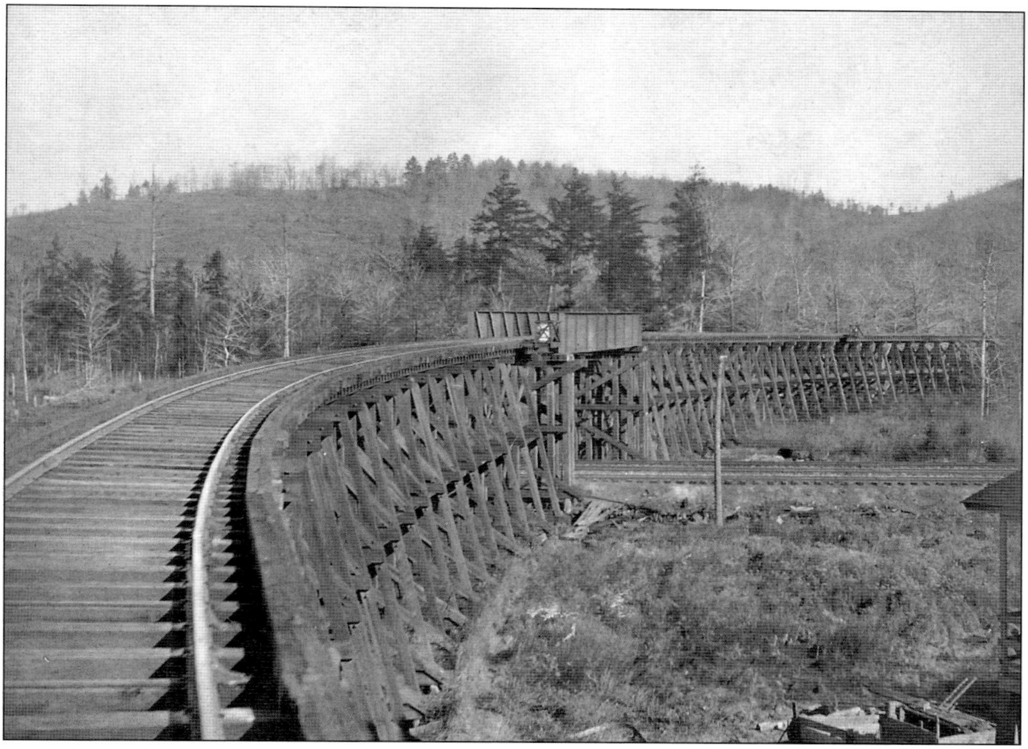

Because of the distance between the West Clarion Mine and the railroads, a new trestle had to be built north from the base of the western hillside of Brockwayville. It spanned over the Buffalo, Rochester and Pittsburgh Railway north of the depot, and across Little Toby Creek near the present football field. A connection was made with the BR&P Railway before it bridged Little Toby Creek.

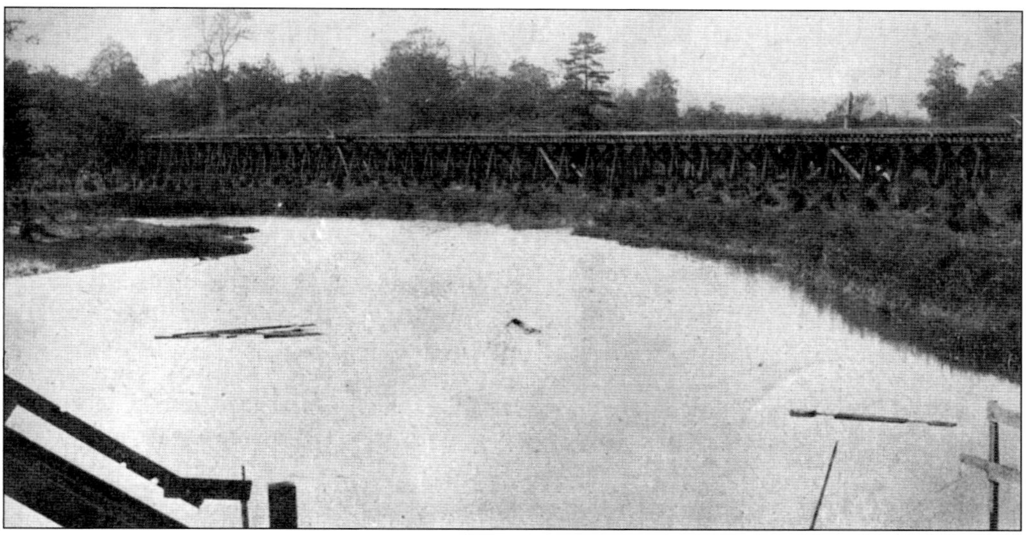

The West Clarion Mine trestle is shown here just to the east of the bridge over Little Toby Creek. The photograph was taken from Fred Olmstead's icehouse along Seventh Avenue across the old bayou created by a meandering Little Toby Creek. The trestle was eventually filled in with West Clarion Mine spoils. The Varischetti football field currently occupies the site.

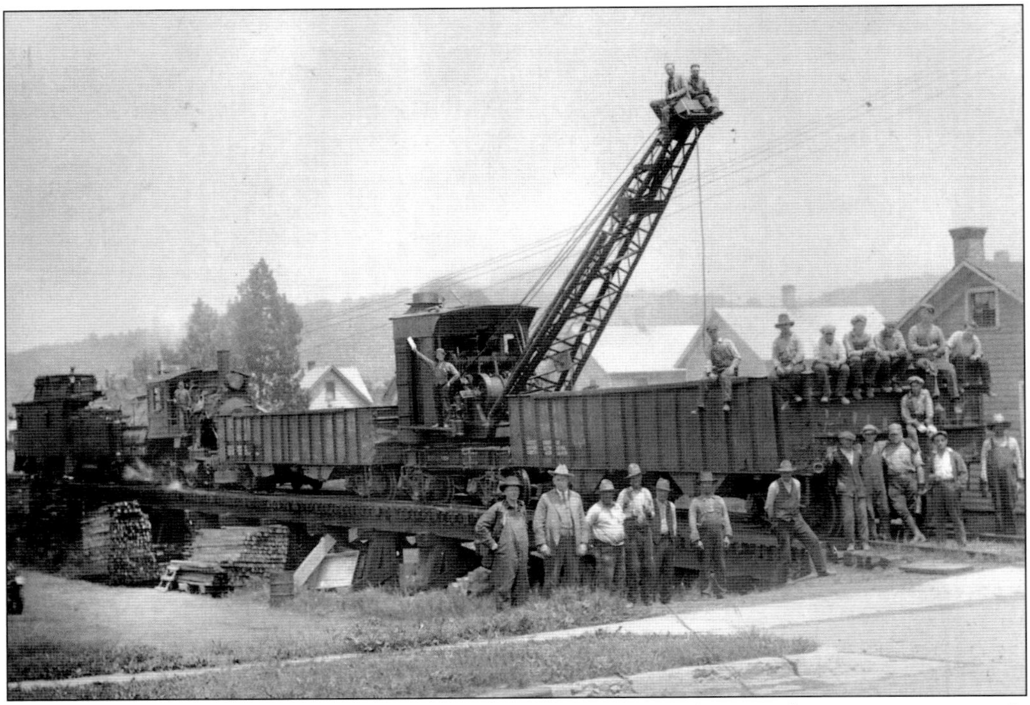

When the Granville mines opened to the southeast in 1917, an underground connection was made with West Clarion. How this connection occurred topographically is mind boggling, but it was decided to take all the coal out at the modern Granville mines. When the West Clarion Mine was closed in 1922, the long trestle that extended from the foot of Brookville Hill was removed by the crew in the photograph.

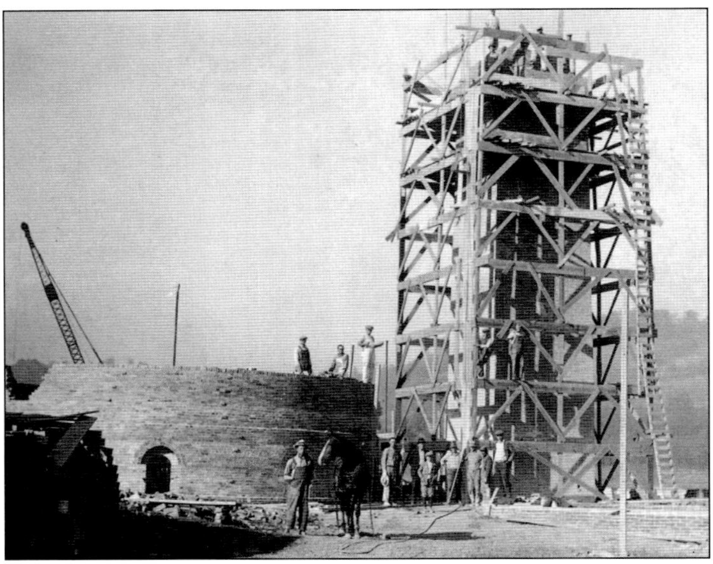

Dr. Asaph M. Clarke encouraged the commercial use of the clay deposits around town, but it took Dr. H. E. Kilgus to get the ball rolling. Upon moving to Brockway in 1925, he purchased the Chapin house, formerly the McCain house, at the southeast corner of Main Street and Tenth Avenue. He formed the Brockway Clay Company and constructed a modern clay manufacturing plant to the north of town.

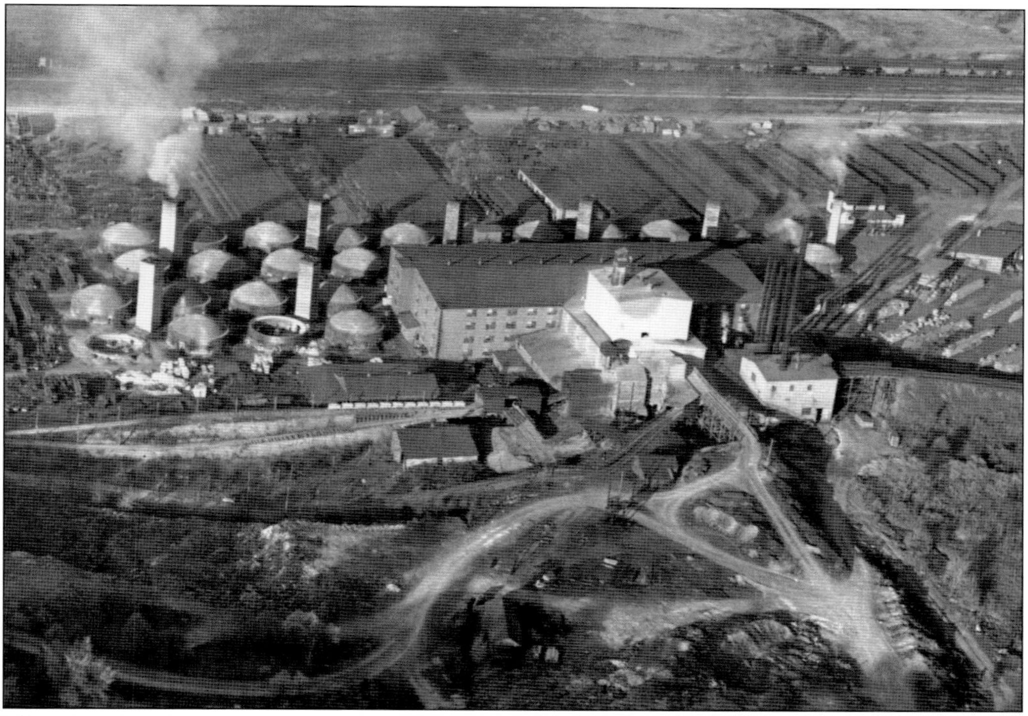

The plant hit the ground running, and demand for clay drainage pipe kept up throughout the Great Depression and World War II. The photograph features the Brockway Clay Company at what appears to be its heyday. B&O Railroad boxcars sit on the siding, waiting in a long line to be loaded with the product that was shipped all over the country.

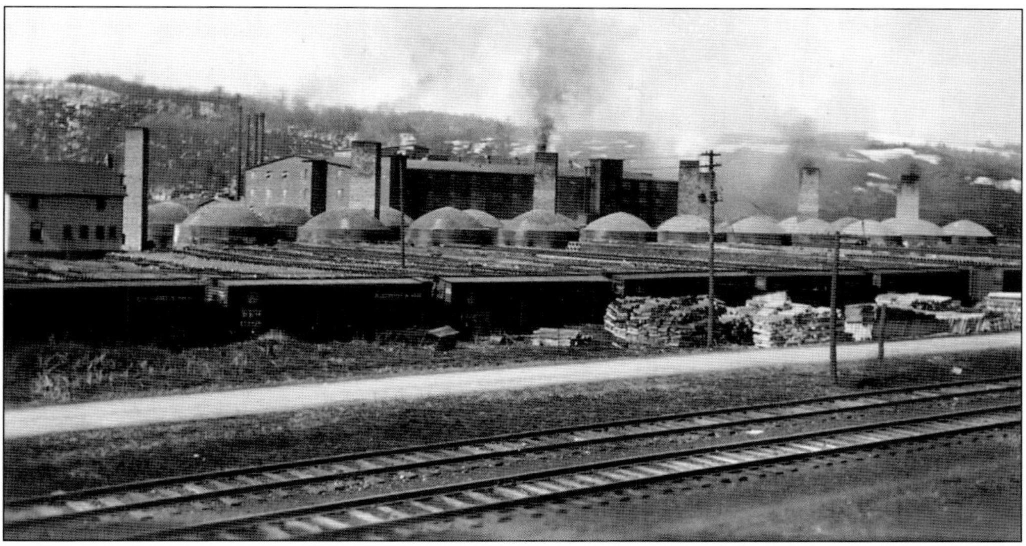

This photograph was taken from the northeast across the Baltimore and Ohio Railroad, formerly the Buffalo, Rochester, and Pittsburgh Railway. The first threat to the company was the passing of Dr. Kilgus in 1949, but his son Edward kept the business running, hitting peak production in the 1960s with over 270 employees. The company was still selling off inventory when the plant burned on May 21, 1999.

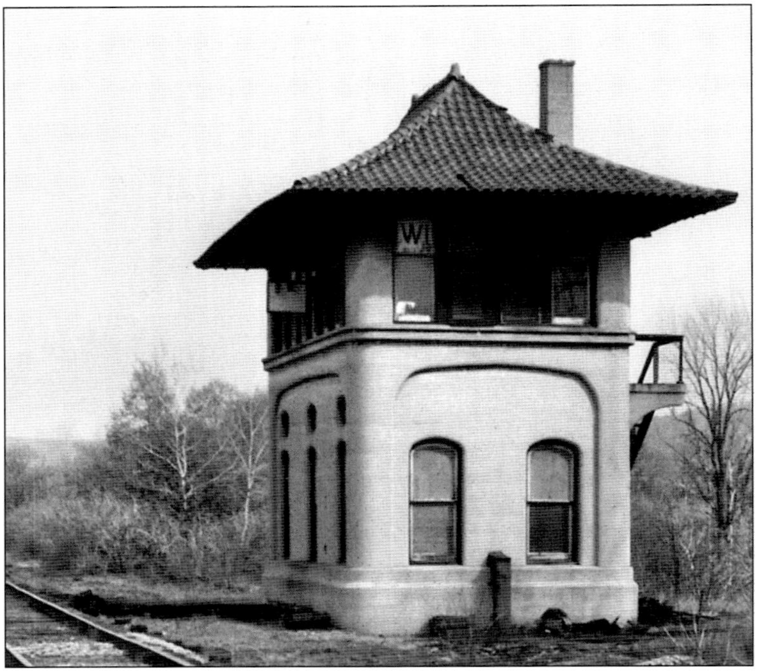

The WI Tower along the Buffalo, Rochester, and Pittsburgh Railway was built across the tracks from the Brockway Clay Company in 1918. It functioned as an office for train orders and as a mechanical interlocker for the Erie Railroad connection to the south. Frank Bianco worked the telegraph at the WI Tower for many years, but the building was placed out of service in November 1970.

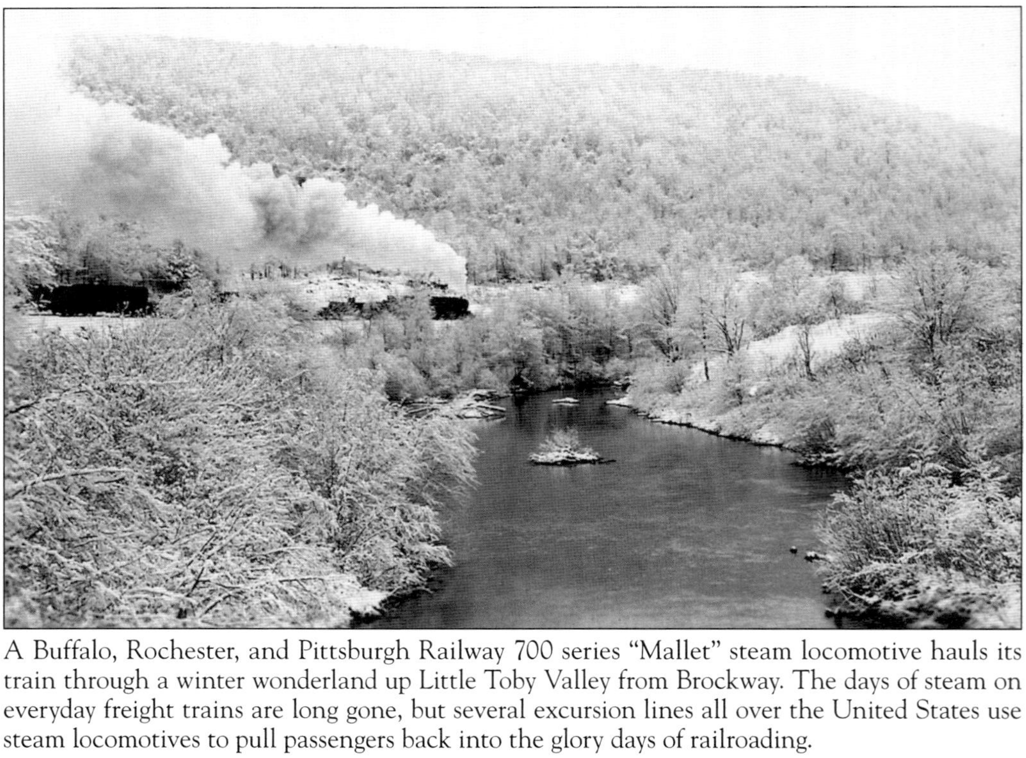

A Buffalo, Rochester, and Pittsburgh Railway 700 series "Mallet" steam locomotive hauls its train through a winter wonderland up Little Toby Valley from Brockway. The days of steam on everyday freight trains are long gone, but several excursion lines all over the United States use steam locomotives to pull passengers back into the glory days of railroading.

Three

Lower Toby Valley

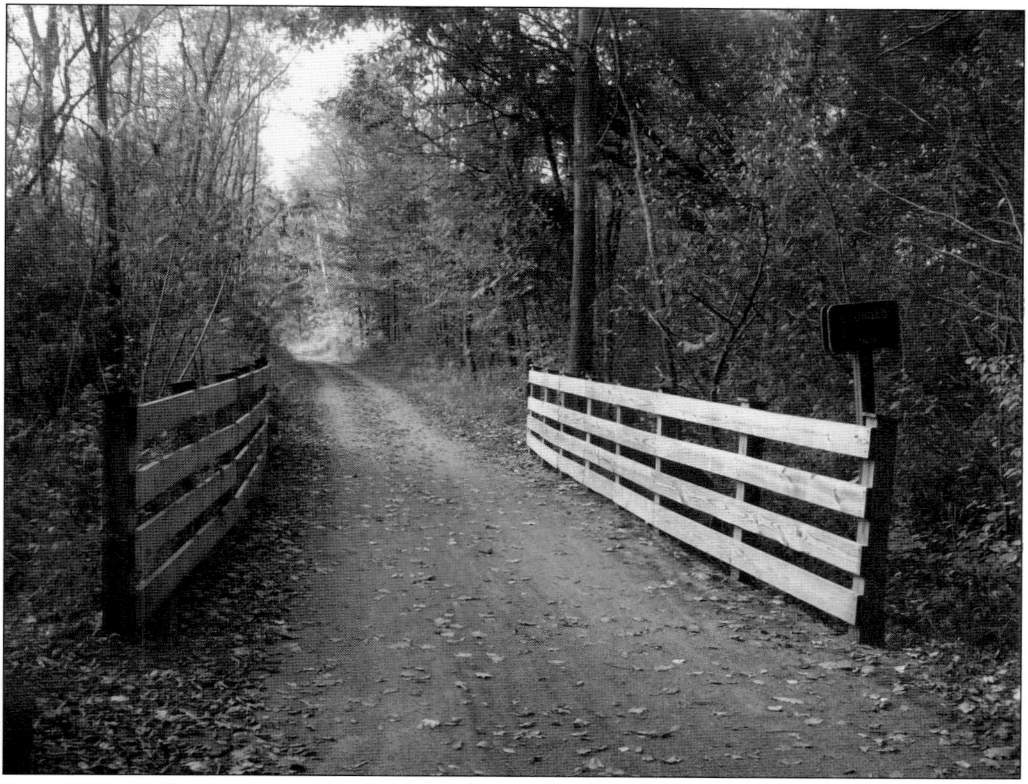

Lower Toby Valley focuses on the deep, winding valley that stretches north to the Clarion River. It also includes a few of the smaller settlements to the south and west of Brockway. Hugging the eastern bank of Little Toby Creek from Brockway to its mouth is the Clarion–Little Toby Rail Trail (shown above), a beautifully maintained 18-mile trail that serves hikers, bikers, and skiers from across the state.

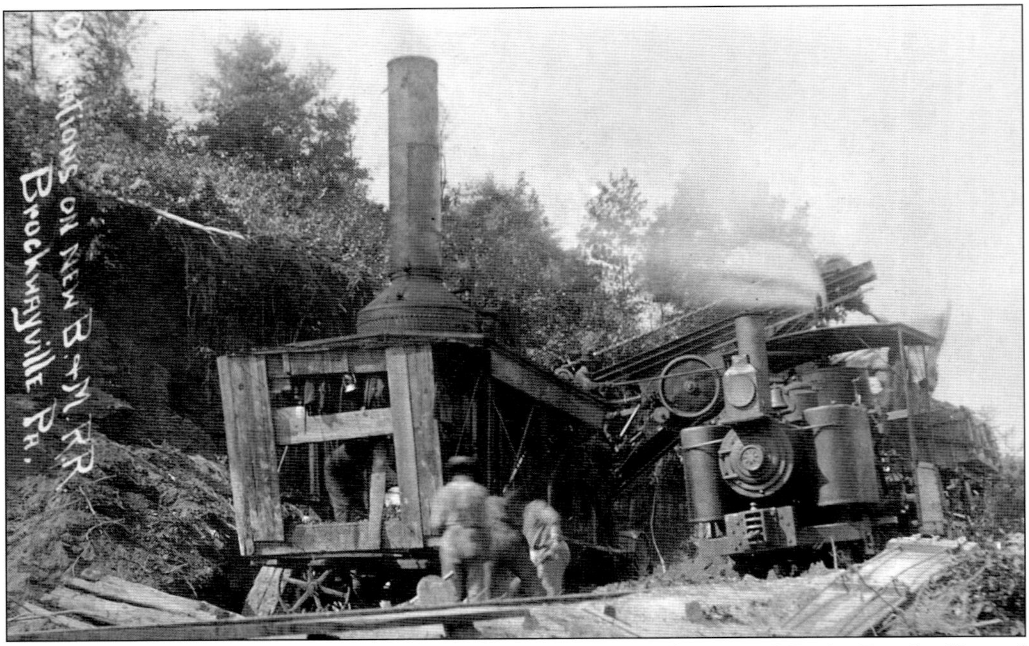

The label on this photograph calls this railroad operation the B&MRR, for Brookville and Mahoning Railroad, but it was renamed the Pittsburg and Shawmut Railroad to avoid confusion with the Boston and Maine Railroad. Construction on this segment began in 1903 with its southwestern terminus at Freeport on the Allegheny River. The P&S was leased by the Pittsburg, Shawmut, and Northern Railroad until 1916.

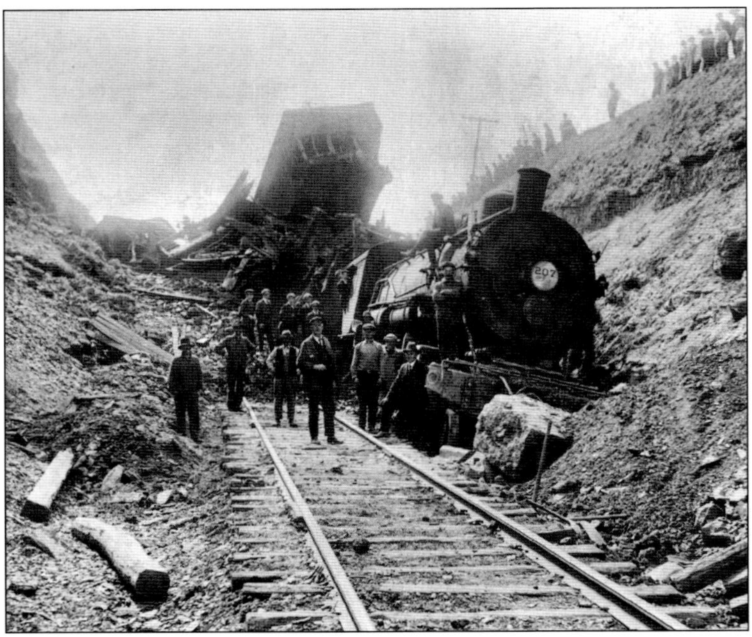

The Shawmut Line was known for "piling cars high in hard to reach places." This 1919 wreck was caused by mine subsidence in the cut just southwest of Brockwayville. The track-clearing crews and the repair shops were never short on work in the Brockway area, as almost every week a train wreck is reported in the Brockwayville Record.

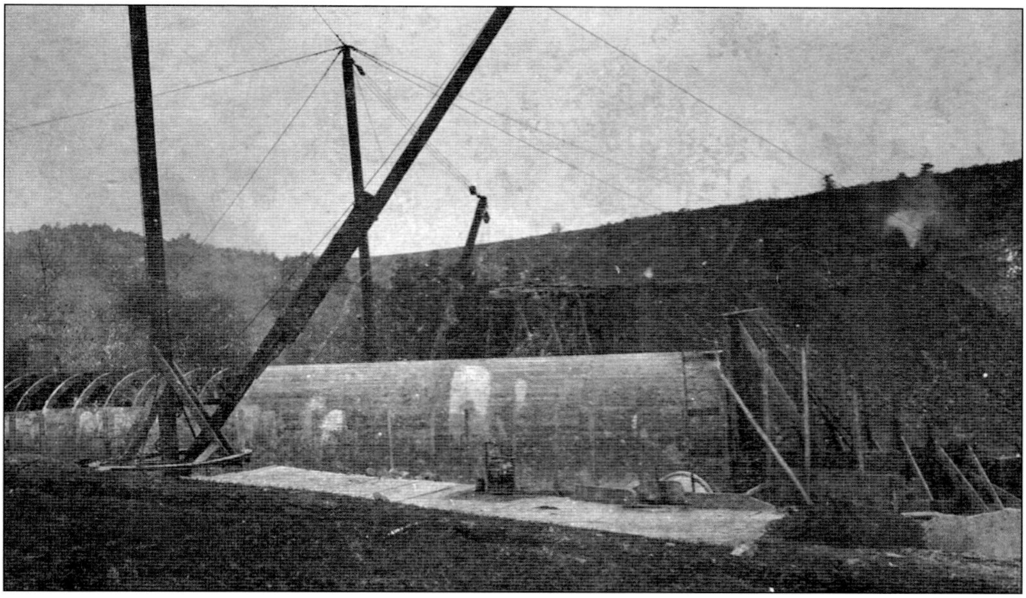

Construction of the Arch Street tunnel and fill is underway in this 1905 or 1906 photograph, approximately 1 mile south of Brockwayville. The fill started as what looked like a trestle made of square timbers but was then filled with stone once the concrete of the tunnel was set. A culvert was also built beside the tunnel to allow a small, unnamed stream to continue feeding Curry Run to the north.

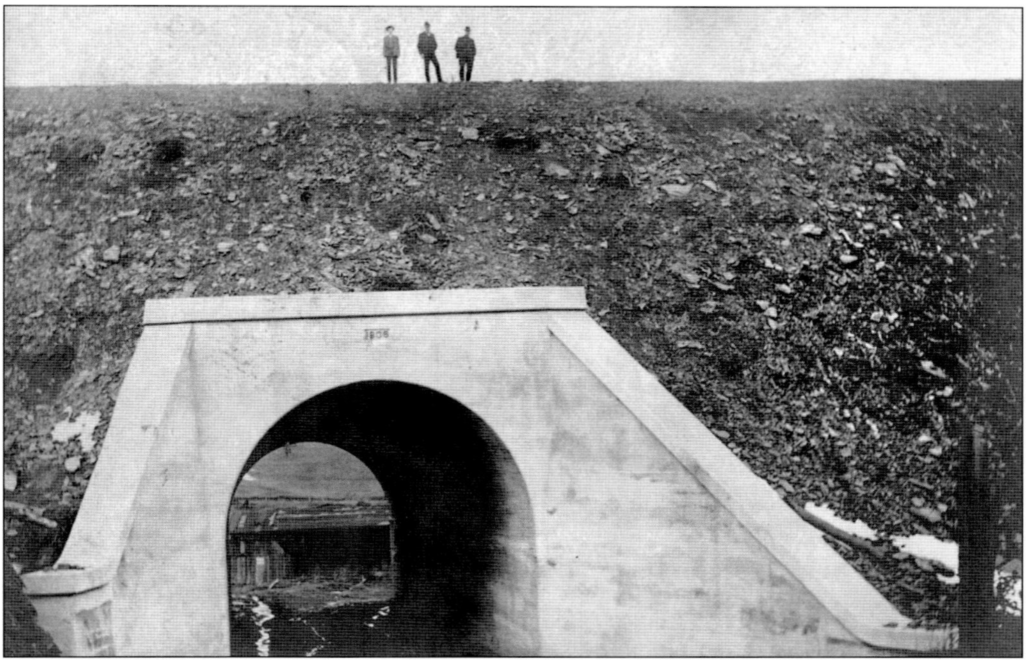

The Arch Street tunnel was completed in 1906. This photograph was taken on the road to the south of the tunnel, looking through the tunnel toward Curry Run. Curry Run flowed north into Little Toby Creek in Brockwayville. James Curry started his lumbering career on Curry Run in 1885. He also had lumbering operations near Brandy Camp on upper Little Toby Creek and at Arrow, Somerset County.

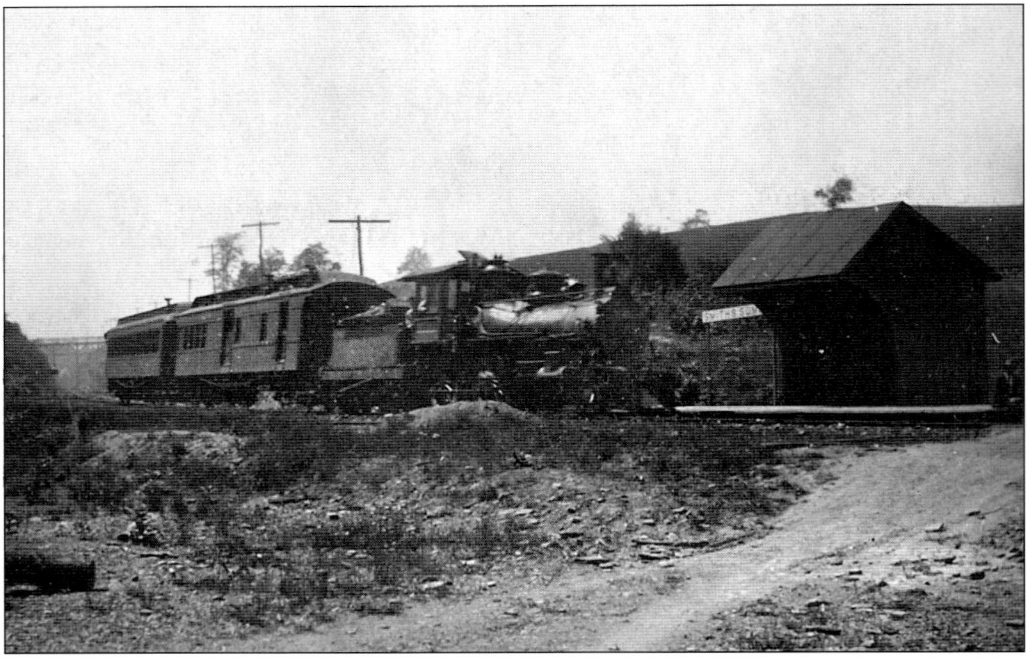

One of the highest points on the Pittsburg and Shawmut Railroad was Smith's Summit, just west of the Arch Street tunnel. The Shawmut had a small shelter here for passengers. This photograph shows an early Shawmut passenger train with the old bridge across the cut to the west of the shelter. The bridge was torn down, leaving a suspiciously sharp curve on Horizon Drive.

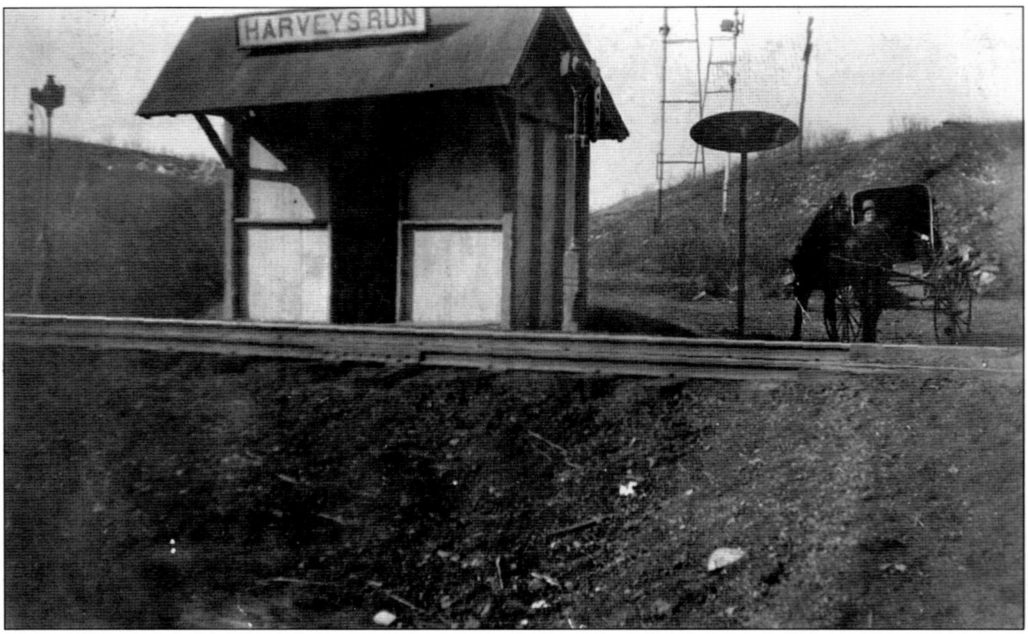

The Harveys Run shelter was located where the original 1883 grade of the BR&P Railway was built between Brockwayville and DuBois. The old grade is now occupied by a road named Old Grade that runs west of Harveys Run, but then the grade traveled north into the Beechtree area, and east along Rattlesnake Run to Lanes Mills. All of these curves were removed around 1908.

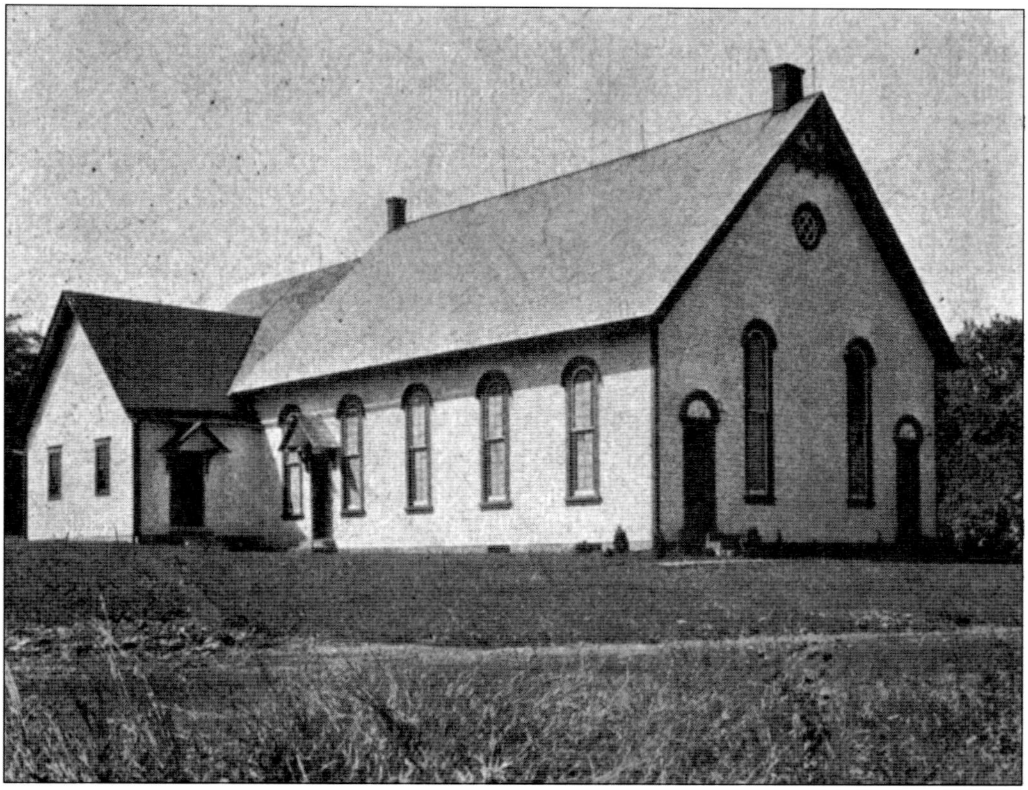

The Beechwoods Presbyterian Church was built in 1849 and became the center of religious, social, and political activities of the Scotch-Irish community that had been established in 1824 by Alexander Osborne and company. The Scotch-Irish of Beechwoods remained a close-knit group even through the arrival and departure of European miners in the neighboring mining towns of Beechtree and Coal Glen.

The Beechwoods high school was constructed in 1905 beside the Presbyterian Church. A vocational wing was added in 1916, and it was one of the first vocational schools in the state. The state board of education was so impressed that Hon. Martin G. Brumbaugh, governor of Pennsylvania, attended the dedication ceremonies. With the consolidation of schools with Brockway, the building was no longer needed and abandoned in the late 1950s.

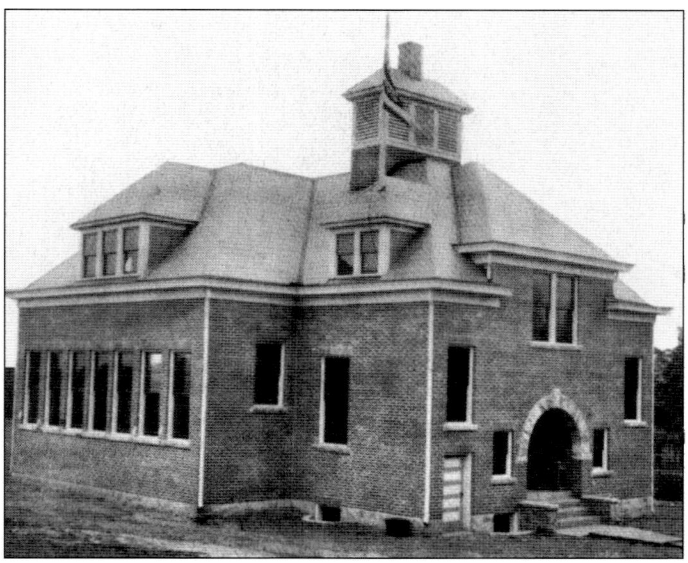

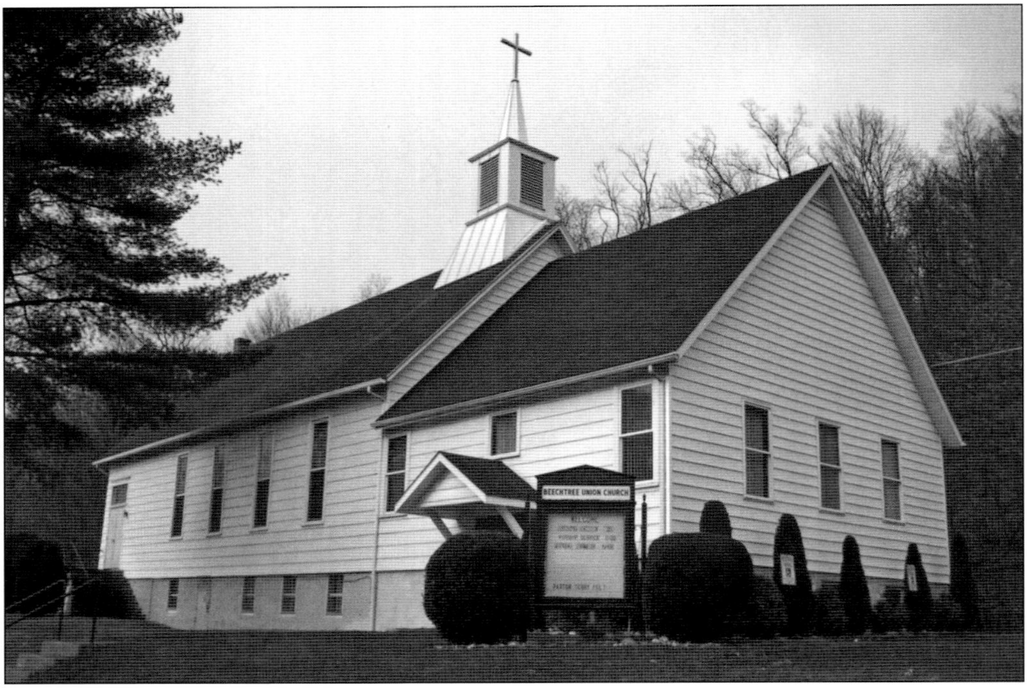

The village of Beechtree, with its church shown here, sprung up because of coal. The original purpose of the Buffalo, Rochester, and Pittsburgh Railway was to get to the coal owned by the Rochester and Pittsburgh Coal and Iron Company at Beechtree. The original mainline ran through Beechtree, with a spur to the mines, but it was moved east to straighten the route for heavier locomotives.

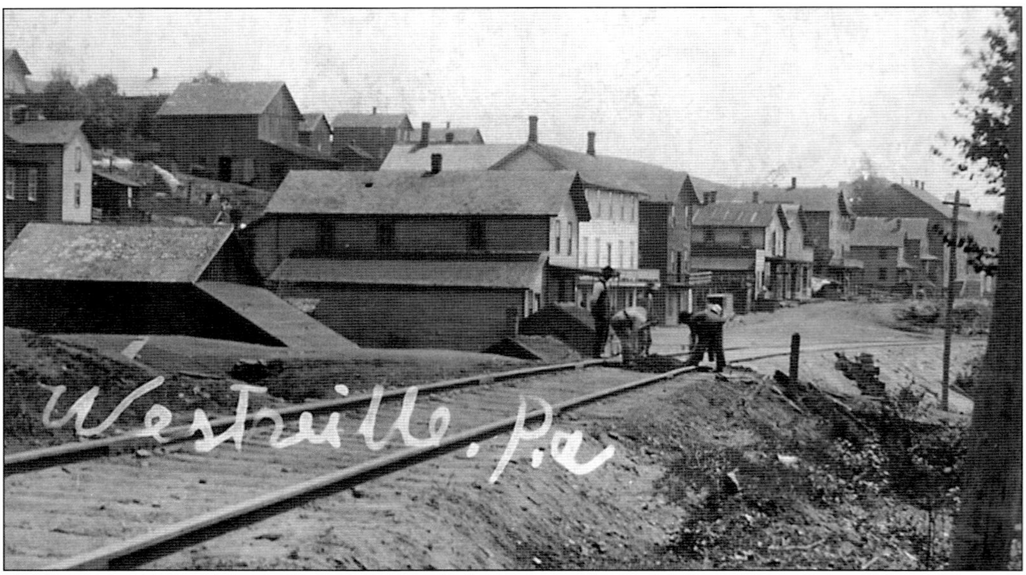

The establishment of Westville, originally called Craventown, is curious in the fact that no mines originally opened in the immediate vicinity of the village. It was halfway between the Beechtree mines and the Coal Glen mines, so a store and a hotel were constructed to serve both coal towns. The Westville store outlasted the company stores at Beechtree and Coal Glen by several decades.

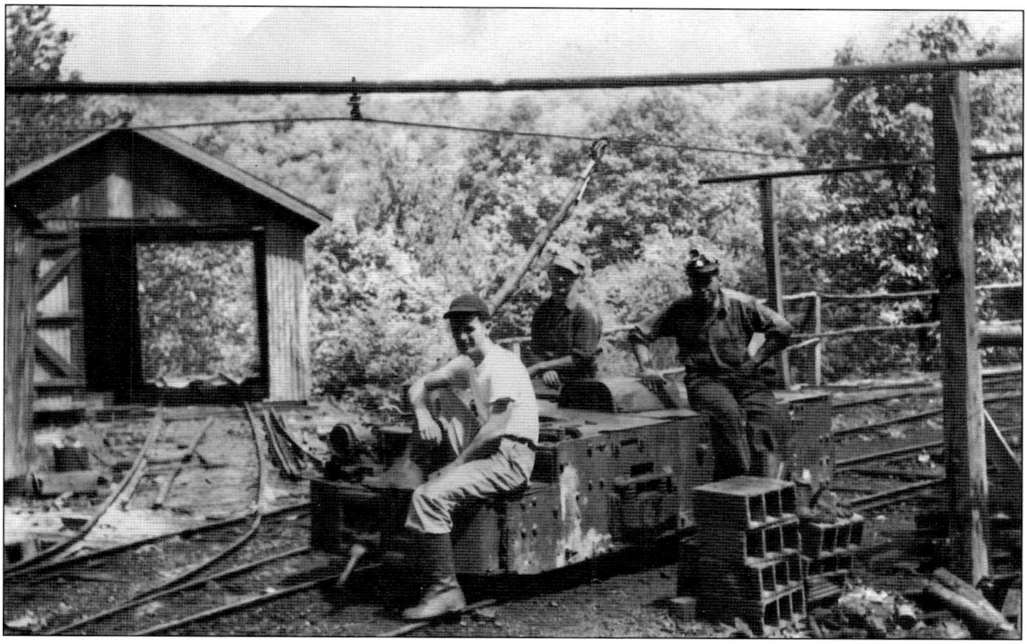

George Walwork, Joe Wells, and Rudolph Lundblad pose on the electric mine locomotive used in Lundblad's mine in Westville. The mine was opened in the late 1940s across the valley to the south of the town of Westville. Although the mine opened about 60 years after the original mines were opened in the valley at Beechtree, high-quality coal was still hauled out of the mine. (Beverley Lundblad Lindemuth.)

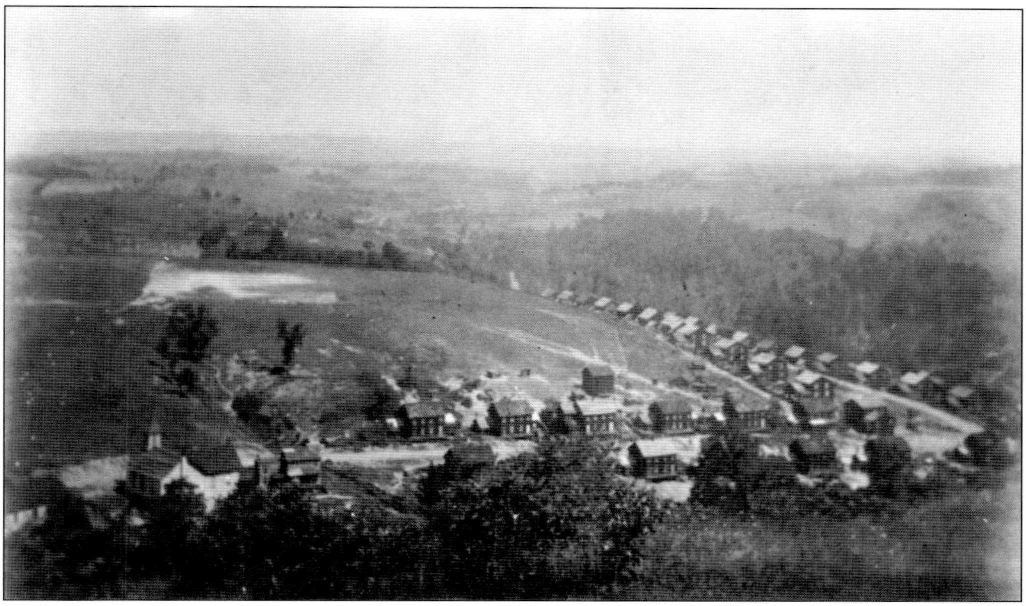

The mining town of Coal Glen is at the western terminus of the Beechtree branch of the Buffalo, Rochester, and Pittsburgh Railway. A few of the original homes are still occupied, but many of the homes and the church in the lower left of the photograph have been torn down. The boiler stack for the mine power plant still stands out of sight to the right in the photograph.

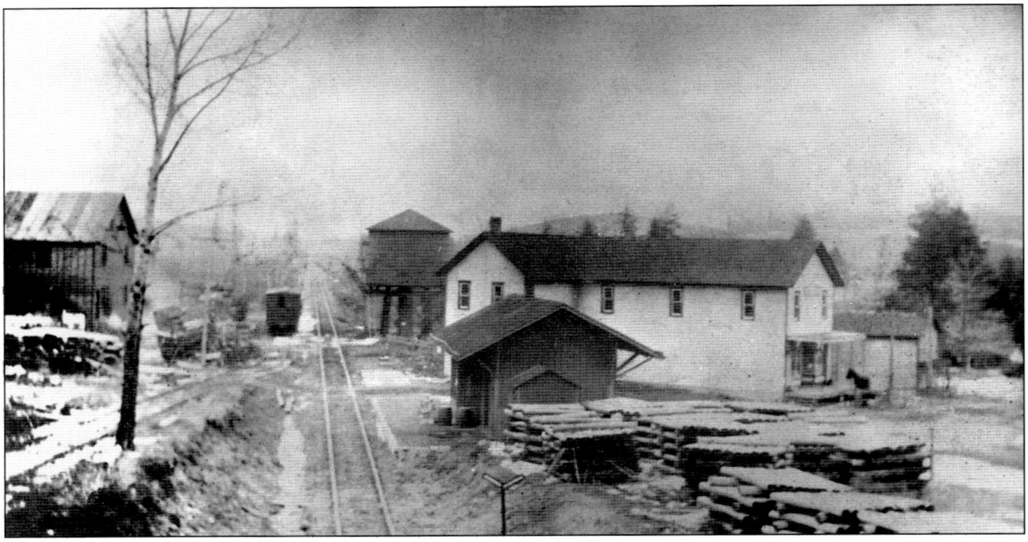

The village of Allens Mills is located several miles west of Brockwayville along the Pittsburg and Shawmut Railroad. In 1878, Allens Mills had a sawmill and a grist mill along Mill Creek, a cabinet shop, a grange hall, and a post office. This early 1900s photograph of Allens Mills shows a store and the Pittsburg and Shawmut Railroad depot.

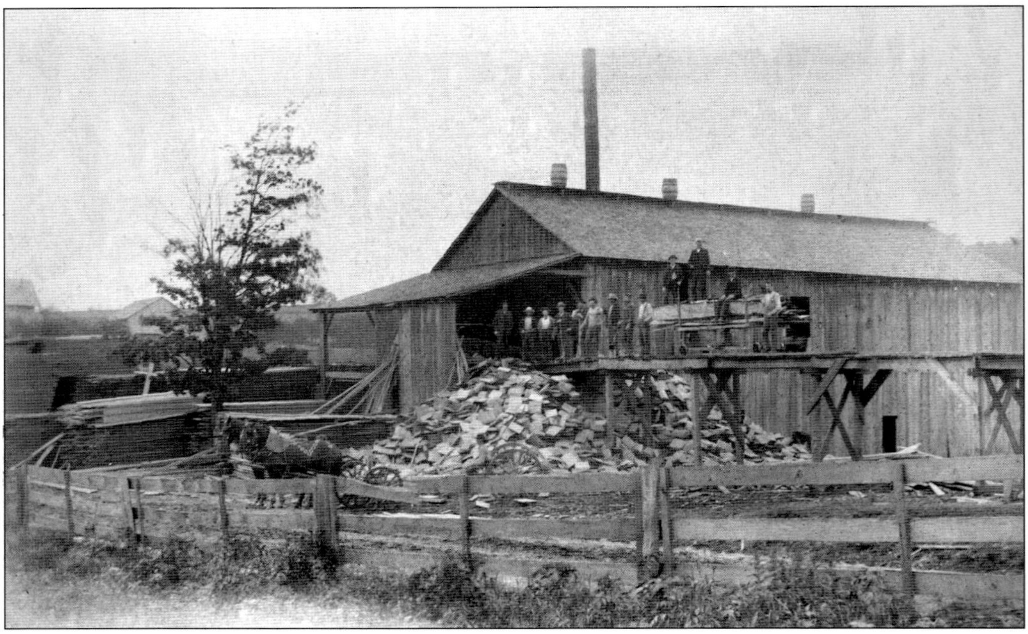

William Shaw and members of the Atwell family built a sawmill in the village of Sugar Hill, about 4 miles west of Brockwayville, in 1878. Jesse, Wallace, Burt, and John Atwell all worked the mill. E. C. Stewart was also a lumberman near Sugar Hill, and after extensive lumbering in that area, he was able to use Carrier's railroad to ship his mill equipment to Glen Hazel, Elk County.

The earliest known church in the village of Sugar Hill was the Protestant Episcopal church built on the Robinson farm hill in 1871, near the current Sugar Hill Cemetery. The photograph is of the Sugar Hill Presbyterian Church and manse, taken in the early 1900s. The structure was built in 1892, and today is still serving the Presbyterian faith of the surrounding community.

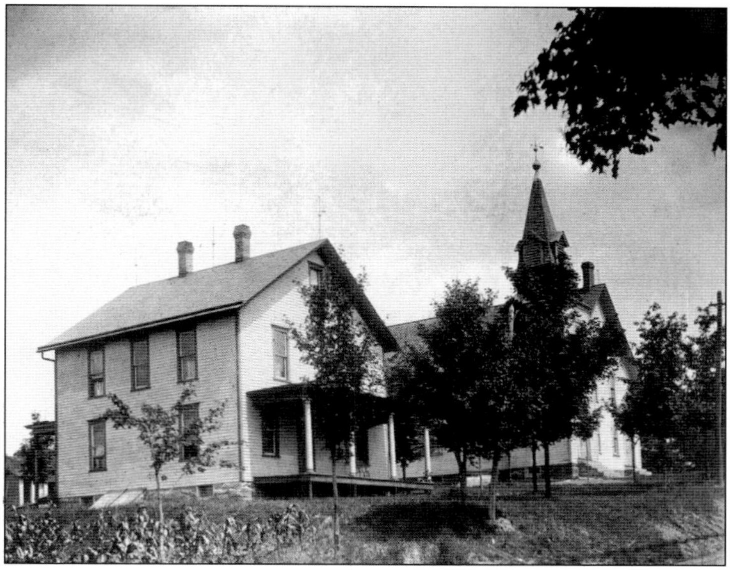

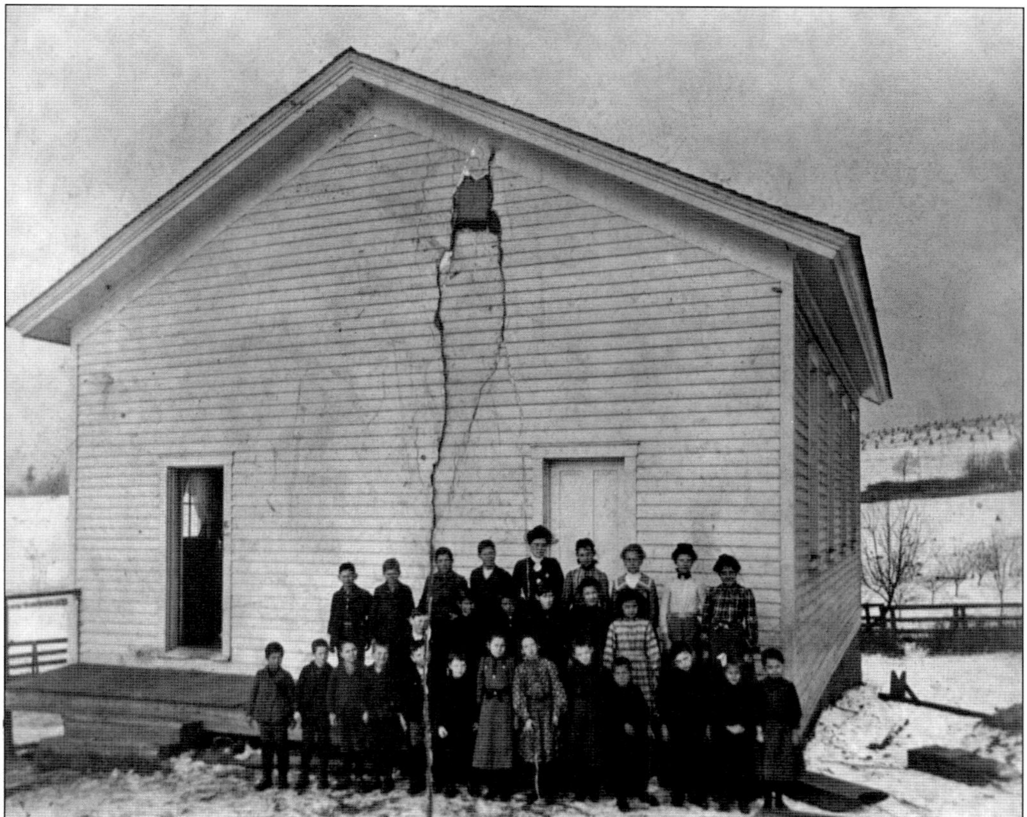

The Sugar Hill schoolhouse stood on the hillside immediately opposite of the intersection of Coal Tipple Road and Route 28. This photograph of the teacher and her class was taken between 1900 and 1904. A batch of tornados broke out over Sugar Hill in 1924, destroying the schoolhouse and several other homes and barns across the countryside.

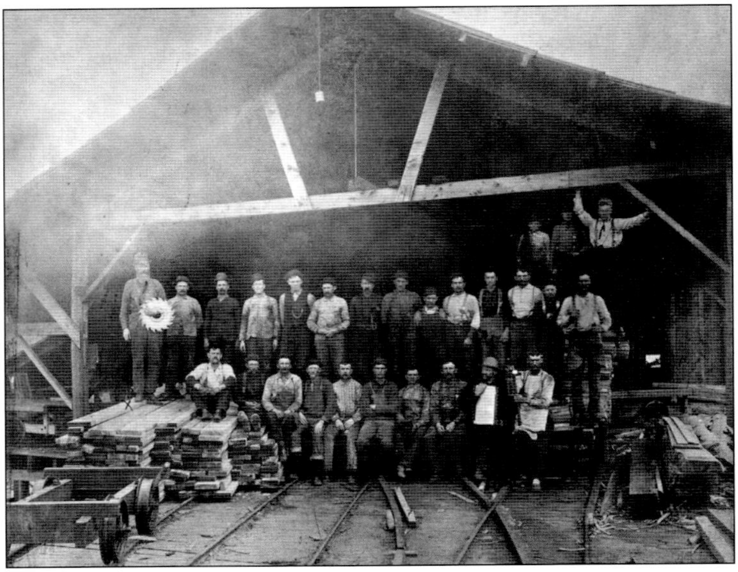

The first sawmill on Baghdad Run was built by John Alexander. It was later purchased by the firm of Buzard and McCain, who ran it for several years in the 1880s and 1890s. Reynolds L. Buzard and William G. McCain constructed mansions across from each other on Main Street in Brockwayville, and they still stand facing each other on the northeast and southeast corners of Main Street and Tenth Avenue.

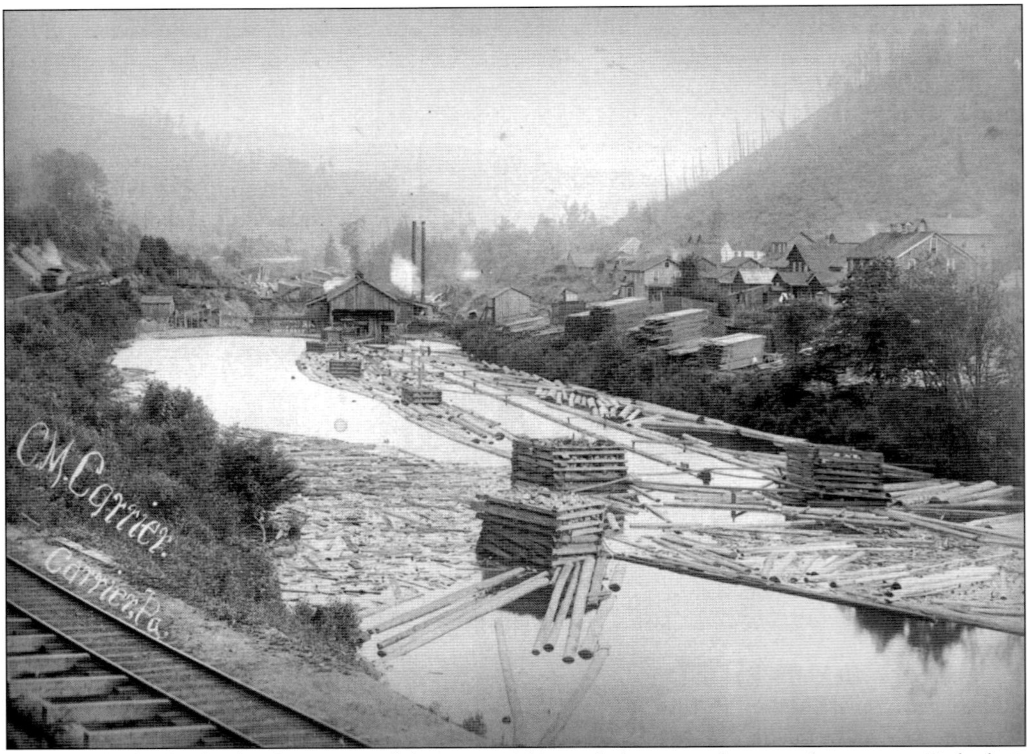

Peter Galusha built the first sawmill here in 1850, and the town became known as Galusha's Mills. Nick M. Brockway, a Civil War veteran and of the Forest Lumber Company, purchased the mill in 1878, when Galusha died, and changed the name of the town to Oyster. In 1890, Cassius M. Carrier purchased the mill, made extensive improvements (shown above), and changed the name of the town to Carrier.

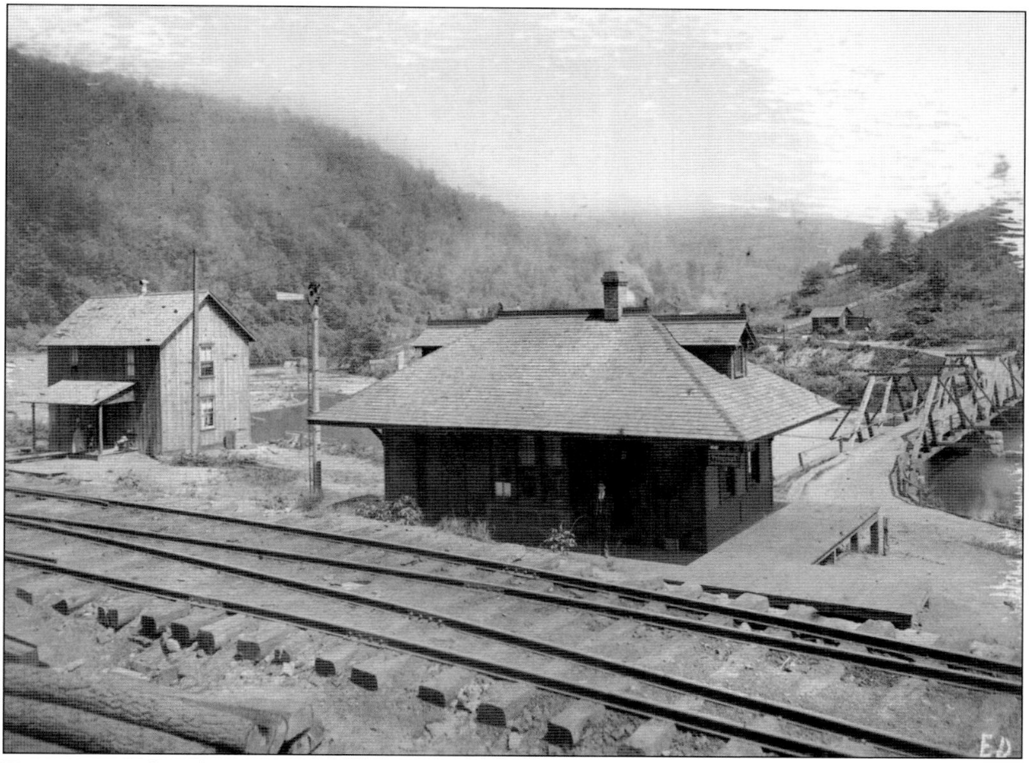

Two major railroads ran through Carrier; the Buffalo, Rochester, and Pittsburgh Railway, on the west bank, and the Ridgway and Clearfield branch of the Pennsylvania Railroad, on the east bank, allowing Carrier to ship lumber anywhere in the country. The depot shown above was the BR&P depot built in 1892. The bridge in the background was for the old county road that ran between Brockwayville and Ridgway.

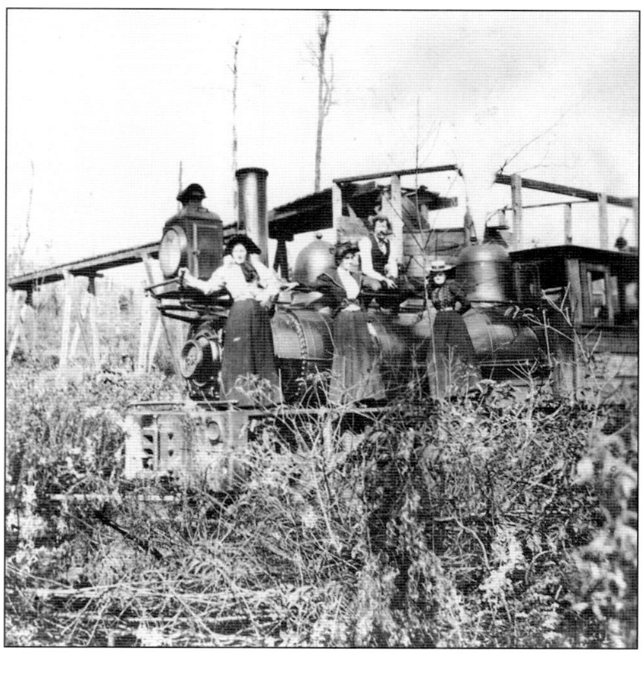

Cassius Carrier constructed a standard-gauge logging railroad up the Forest Hill to the west, winding it around the knob to the south, and back north for many miles throughout his timberlands. It had multiple branches that reached into the North Fork Creek watershed. He reportedly ran two 2-truck Shay locomotives and a 2-truck Climax locomotive to bring the logs down the winding grade to the millpond.

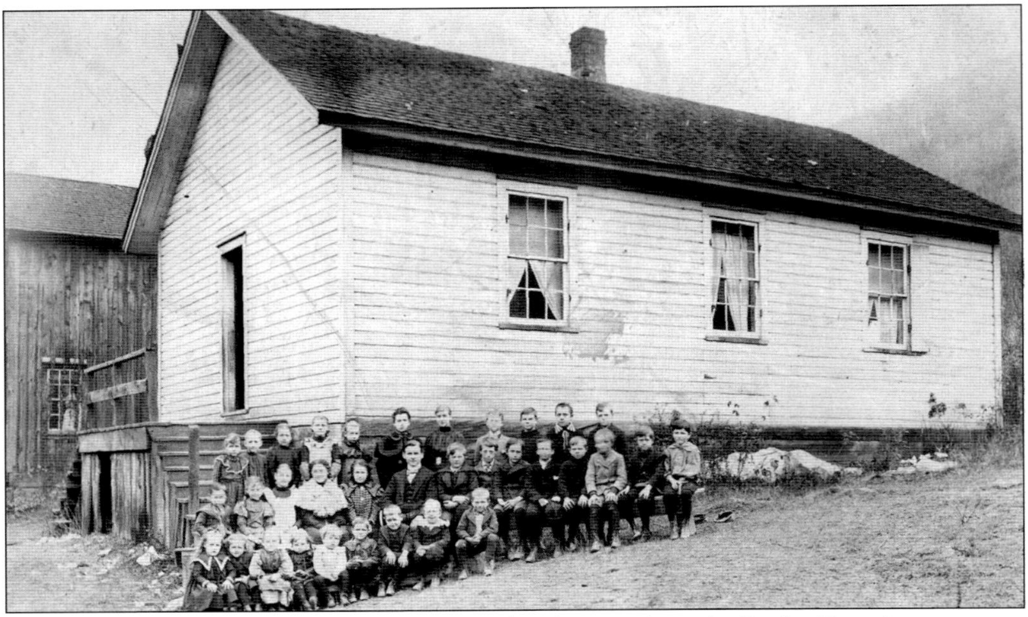

Prof. Benjamin Longwell, seated in the center of his class, taught at the Snyder Township one-room schoolhouse at Carrier for many years. This photograph was taken in 1898 or 1899, just as Cassius M. Carrier was finishing his decade of highly successful lumbering at the town. Longwell taught at the Carrier school for several years before the town was deserted because of lack of timber.

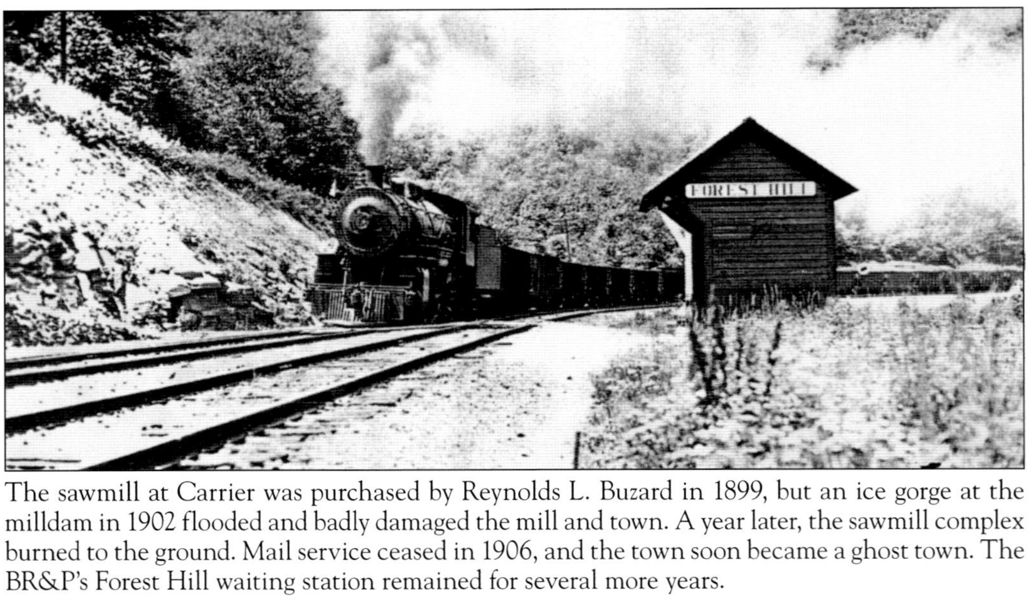

The sawmill at Carrier was purchased by Reynolds L. Buzard in 1899, but an ice gorge at the milldam in 1902 flooded and badly damaged the mill and town. A year later, the sawmill complex burned to the ground. Mail service ceased in 1906, and the town soon became a ghost town. The BR&P's Forest Hill waiting station remained for several more years.

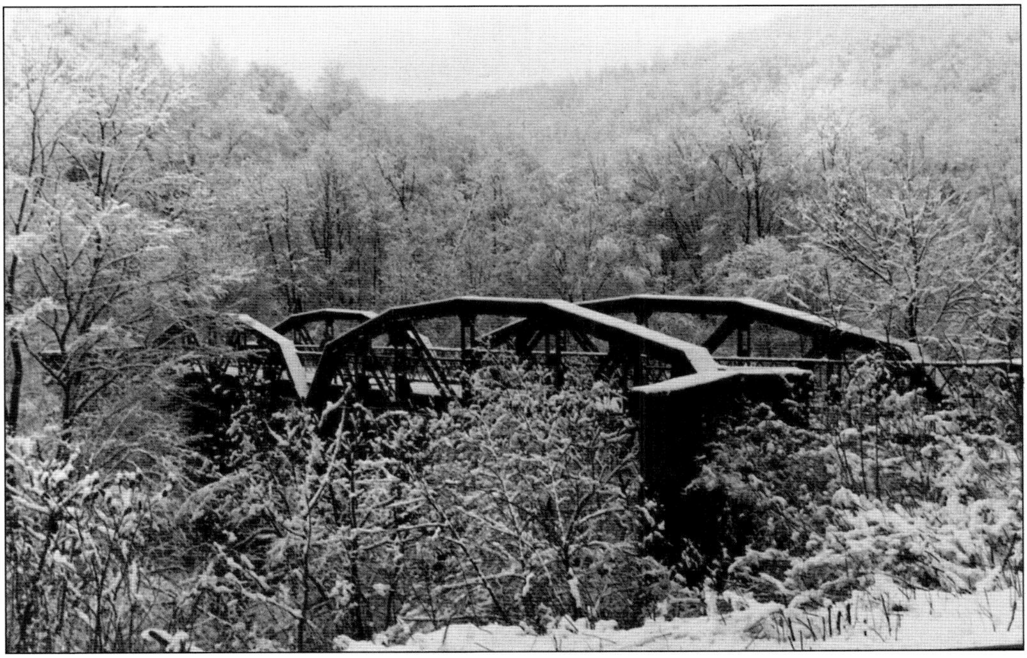

The county road continued to be used until U.S. Route 219 was constructed to the east up over Boot Jack hill into Ridgway. The steel bridge at Carrier, shown above, lasted until World War II, when every piece of extra metal in the country was scrapped for war materials. The stone piers still stand today, the middle one being an interesting obstruction to paddlers of Little Toby.

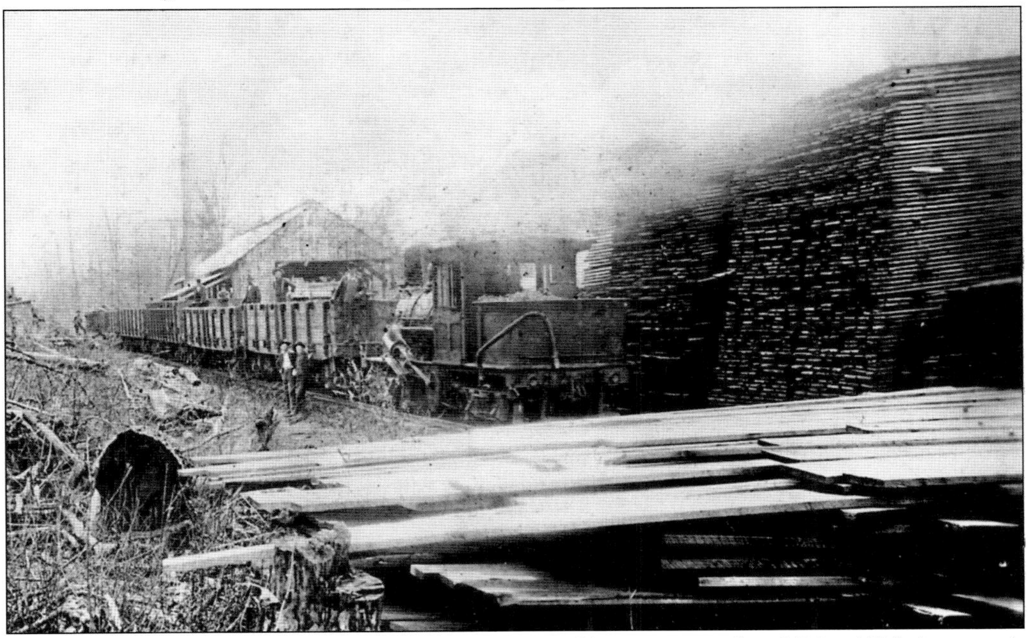

Henry Perry Dull's sawmills along Lucas Run were served by Carrier's railroad. This 1896 photograph shows Carrier's Climax locomotive with a train to be loaded with Dull's finished lumber. After Buzard purchased Carrier's Mill and Carrier removed his railroad, Buzard used a narrow-gauge wood-railed tram road to haul his lumber along Lucas Run back to Forest Hill, then a log slide to get the logs to the millpond.

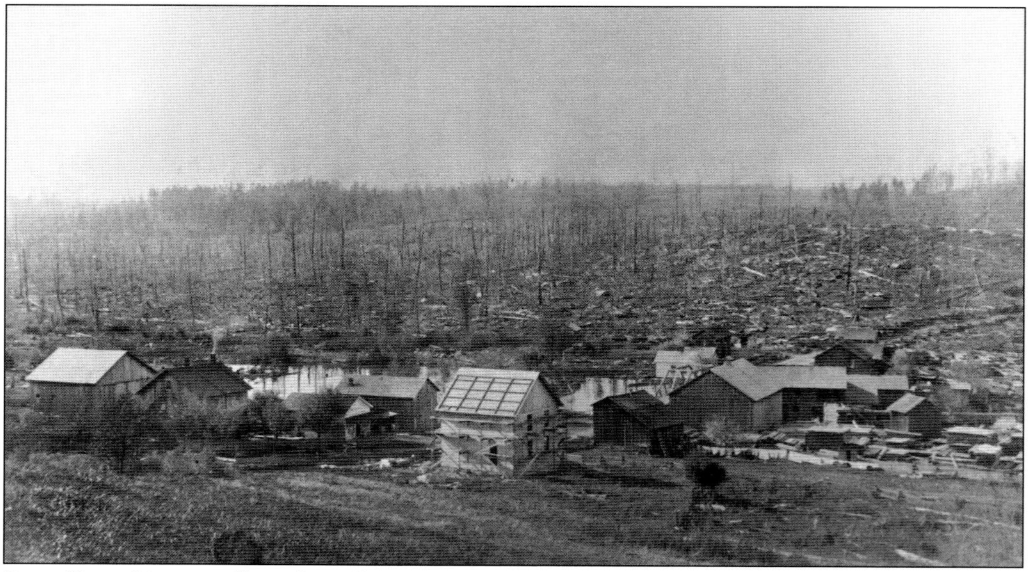

Peter Hetrick's sawmill in the village of Blowtown along North Fork Creek was also served by Carrier's Lucas Run railroad. The lumber contracting firm of Deghan and McDonald owned a tract of over 1,000 acres near Blowtown, and their bark was shipped to local tanneries also by way of Carrier's railroad. Blowtown's neighbors were the villages of Munderf and Schoffner's Corners, the latter having a post office.

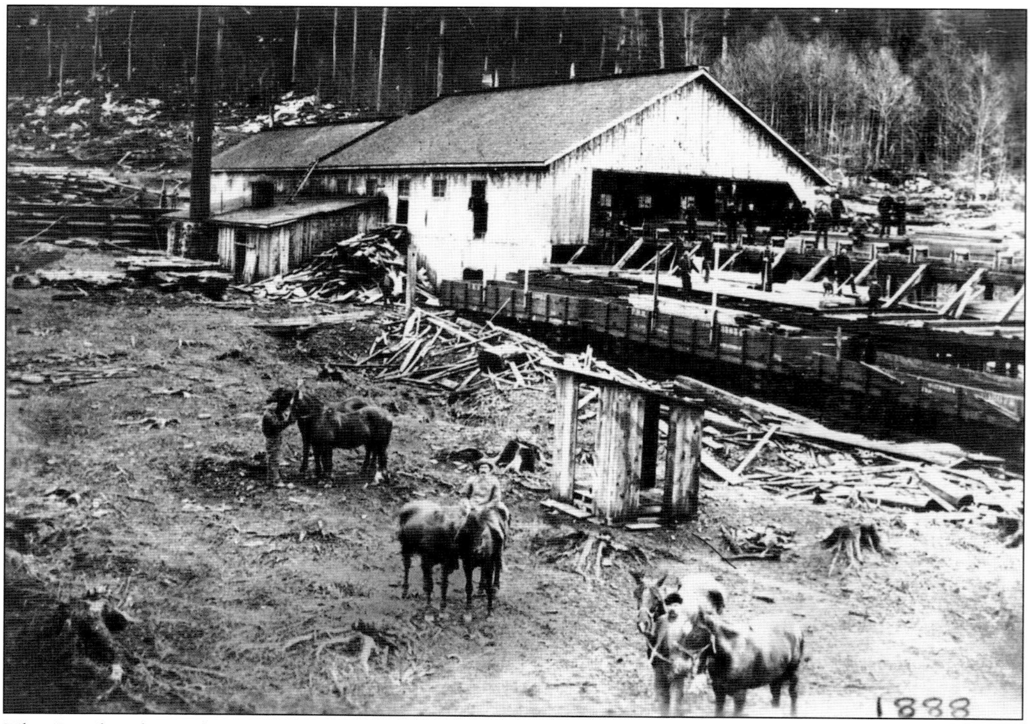

The Portland Lumber Company built a sawmill along Vineyard Run near its junction with Little Toby Creek in 1883. A small village sprung up with a few homes and a store and depot in same building. Logs were skidded or pulled through log slides by teams to the millpond. The company purchased a two-cylinder, 13-ton Shay in November 1888 to haul logs to the millpond.

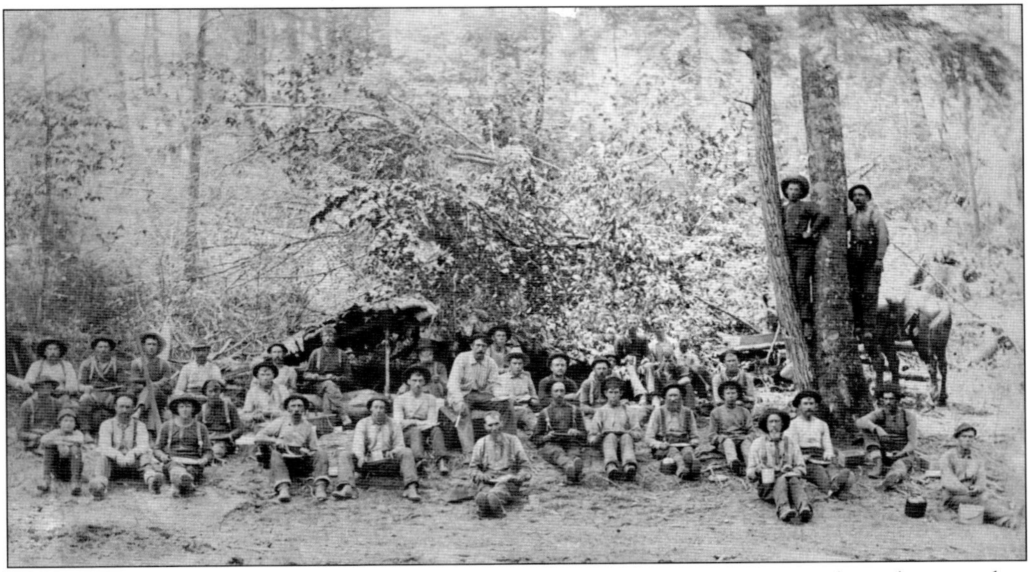

A woods crew of the Portland Lumber Company mill at Vineyard Run pauses for a photographer during a meal break. A team of horses is tied up to the tree on the right, but the feature of interest is the lean-to in the left center of the photograph. Perhaps the crew built lean-to camps if the cutting was far enough from the mill. (Elk County Historical Society.)

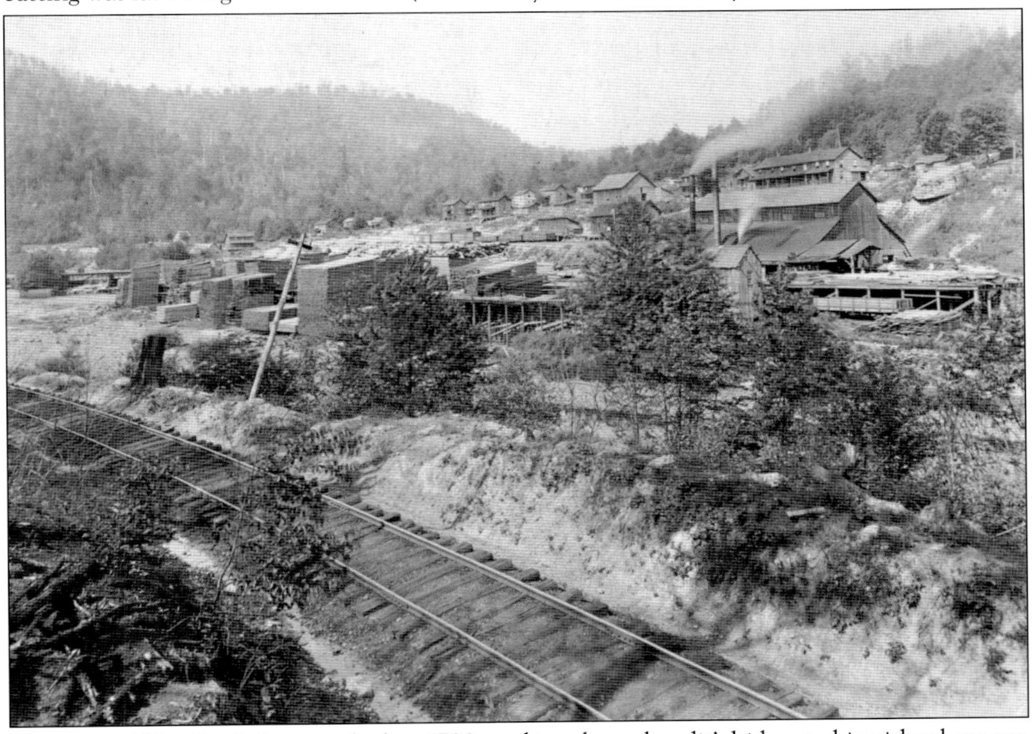

The story of Blue Rock dates to the late 1700s and involves a bandit's hideout, skirmishes between Native Americans and Europeans, and a love story between an early pioneer named Mr. Slade and a Native American maiden. A. J. Thompson of Brockwayville built a water-powered sawmill at Blue Rock in 1856. The mill was passed around several other lumbermen before falling into the possession of James L. Ellis in the 1860s.

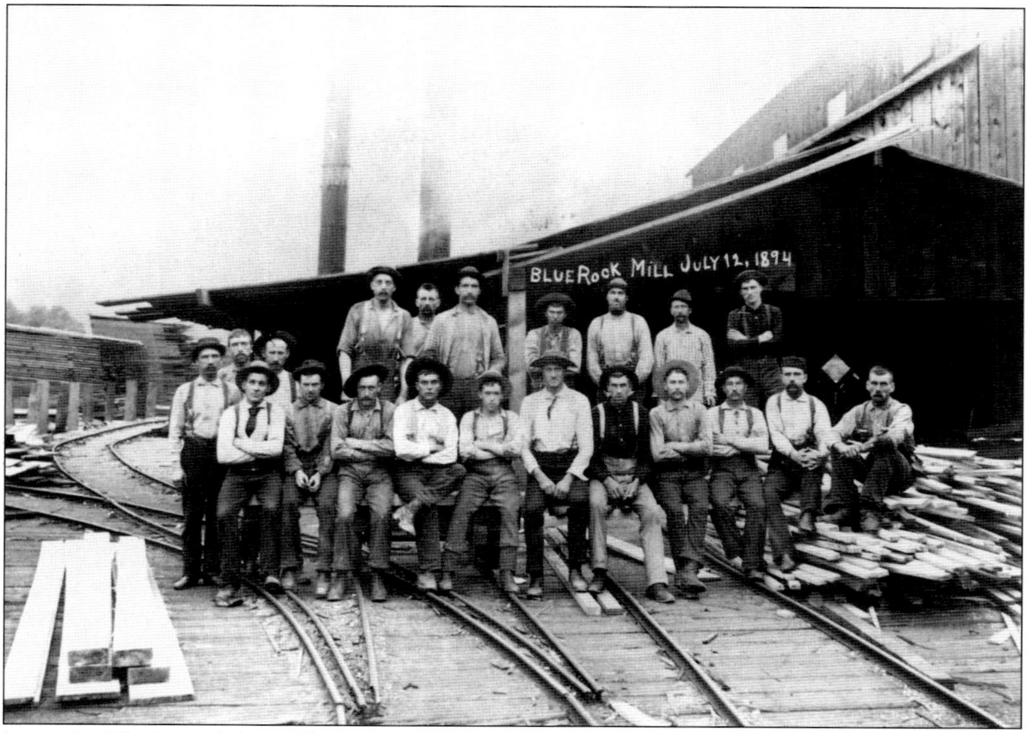

James L. Ellis leased the mill to Norman and William Lane of Lanes Mills from 1867 to 1873. Norman lost his leg in a log slide incident in 1871, the mill burned down while operating it beyond the lease date, and the Lanes were forbidden to engage in any lumbering business at Blue Rock after 1874. The name of the town was changed from Blue Rock to Ellmont in 1887.

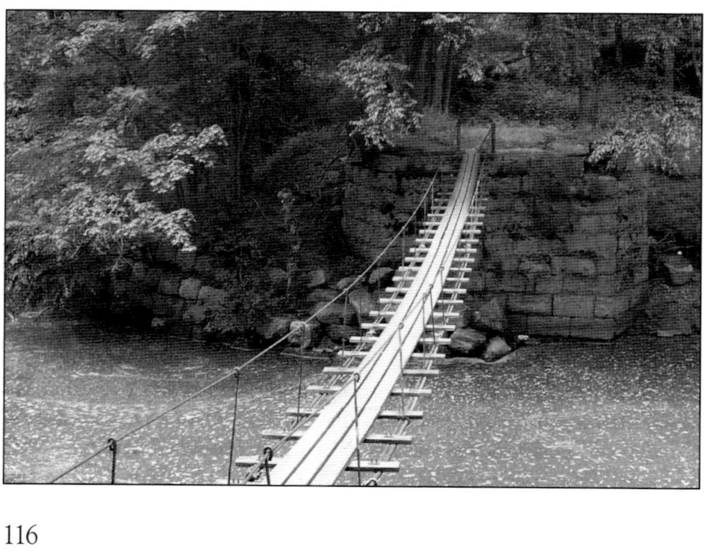

After the Lane possession, the mill was passed around many lumber firms before the timber around the mill was exhausted. In 1902, a new iron truss bridge was built over the old bracket dam for the county road between Brockwayville and Ridgway. It now holds a swinging bridge, and is a popular spot for fishing, swimming and picnicking at the 5-mile mark of the Clarion–Little Toby Rail Trail.

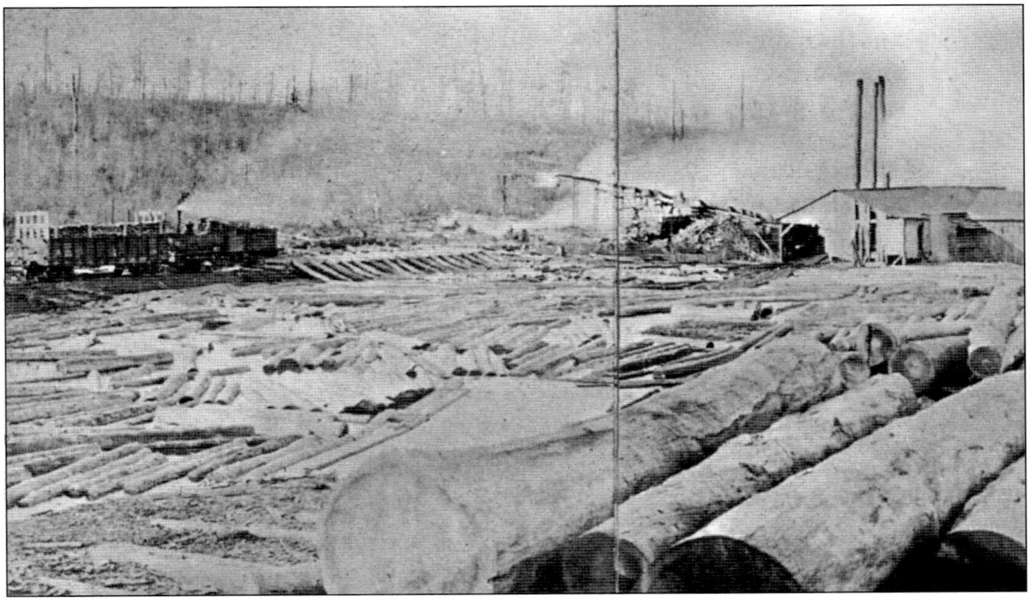

Thomas Raine of Summerville purchased a large tract of timber along Maxwell Run in Elk County in 1891. By 1892, Thomas's brother John joined and created the firm Raine and Raine. With the Raines' sawmill was the town of Rainetown, containing a blacksmith shop, a large company store, a big boardinghouse, 13 shacks called homes, and a school that was also used as a church.

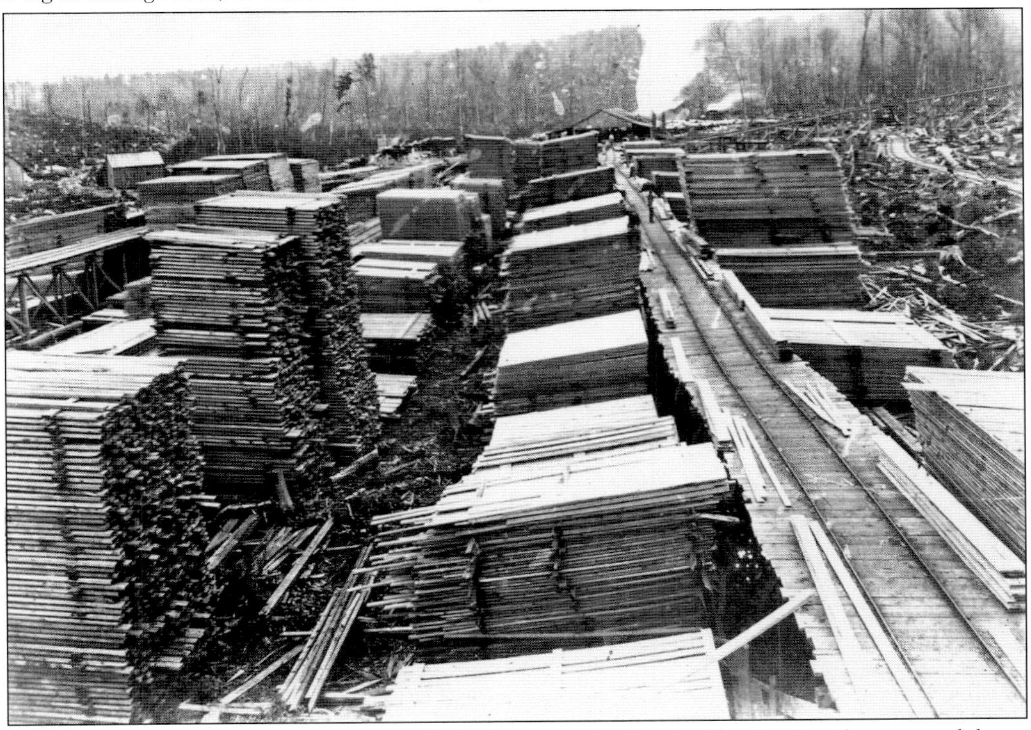

The Raine and Raine operation originally had to team the finished lumber 3 miles east and down a winding corduroy wagon road to the lumbering village of Empire along the Buffalo, Rochester, and Pittsburgh Railway on the west bank of Little Toby Creek. The Raines would purchase the existing lumbering operation at Empire, but to what extent they used it is uncertain.

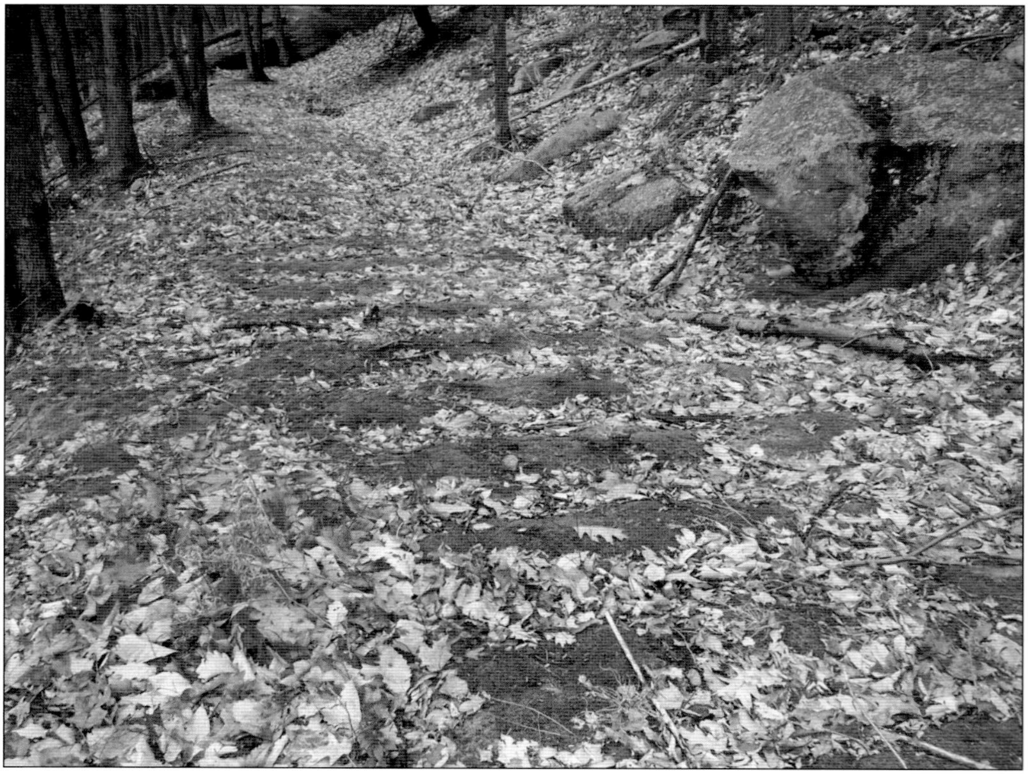

The extent of the Raines' logging railroad makes for extremely scenic hikes along Maxwell Run to the west and east down the hill into Little Toby Valley. The Civilian Conservation Corps converted parts of the railroad to a road in the 1930s to help reach and replant deforested timber tracts. The depressions in the photograph indicate where the ties were laid along a switchback along the logging railroad.

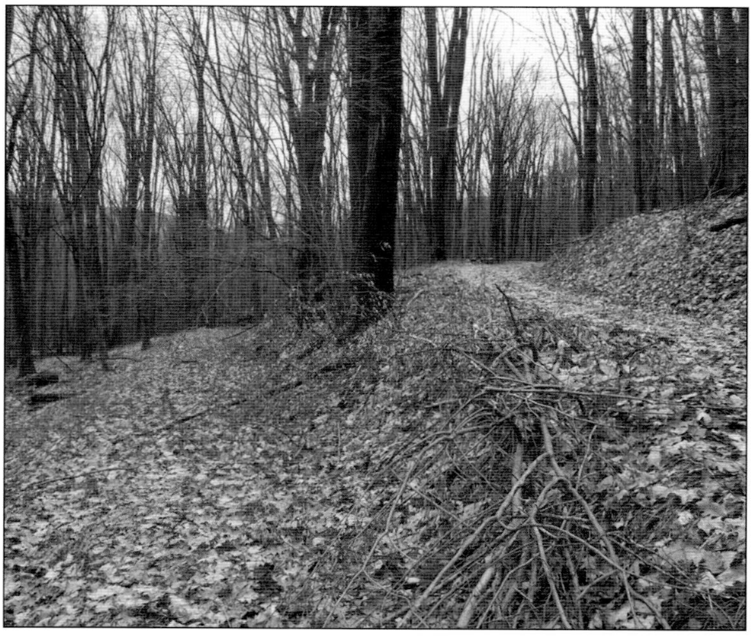

Raine and Raine's successes at Rainetown forced them to find a better way to get their finished lumber down the steep bluff to the railroad along Little Toby Creek. They constructed a standard gauge railroad from Rainetown down a double switchback and connected it with the Buffalo, Rochester, and Pittsburgh Railway. This 2008 photograph shows the lower grade and the upper grade of the first switchback.

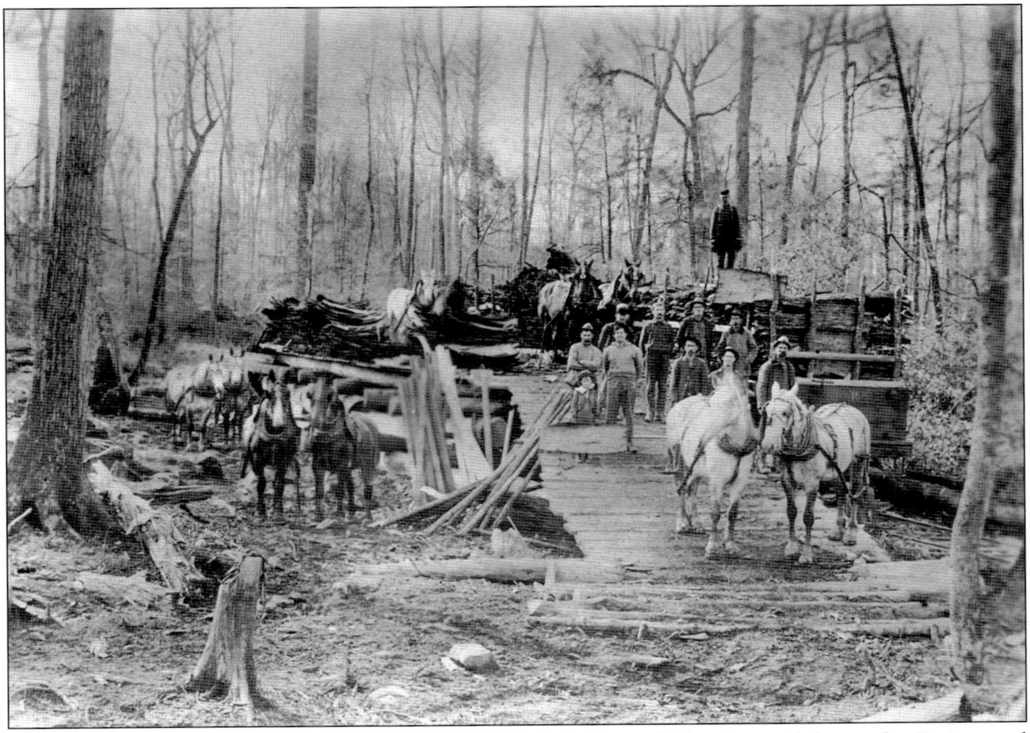

The bark from the estimated 25 million feet of hemlock would be shipped down the Raine and Raine switchback to the Buffalo, Rochester, and Pittsburgh Railway and on to the huge Eagle Valley Tannery in Ridgway. Rainetown had a series of tragic fires in the early 1900s, and with the Raines increasing interest in the Meadow River Lumber Company in Rainelle, West Virginia, the town was deserted by 1905.

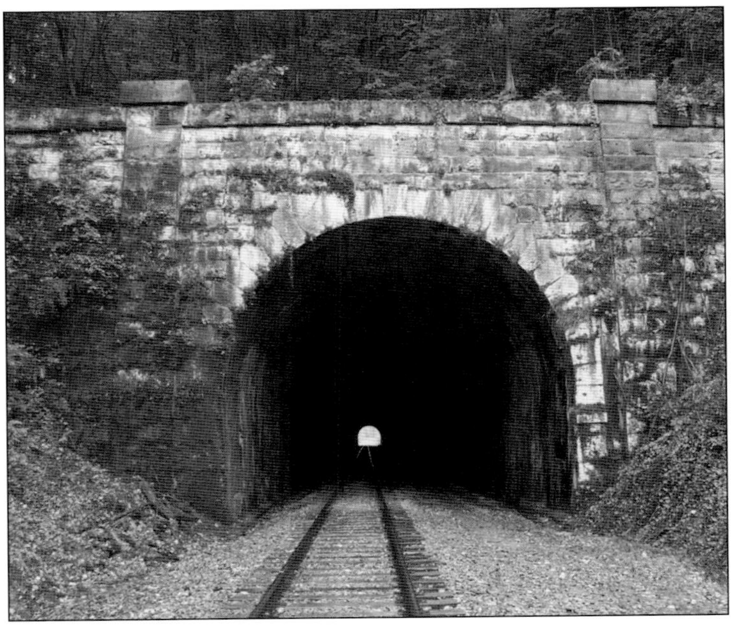

The Buffalo, Rochester, and Pittsburgh Railway's Empire Tunnel was constructed between 1907 and 1908 by the Eyre Shoemaker Construction Company. The tunnel eliminated a dangerously sharp curve around Elk Lick Bluff, in efforts to straighten and double-track the entire middle division of the BR&P Railway. It is speculated that the stone for the tunnel was quarried on the hill to the east and across Little Toby Creek.

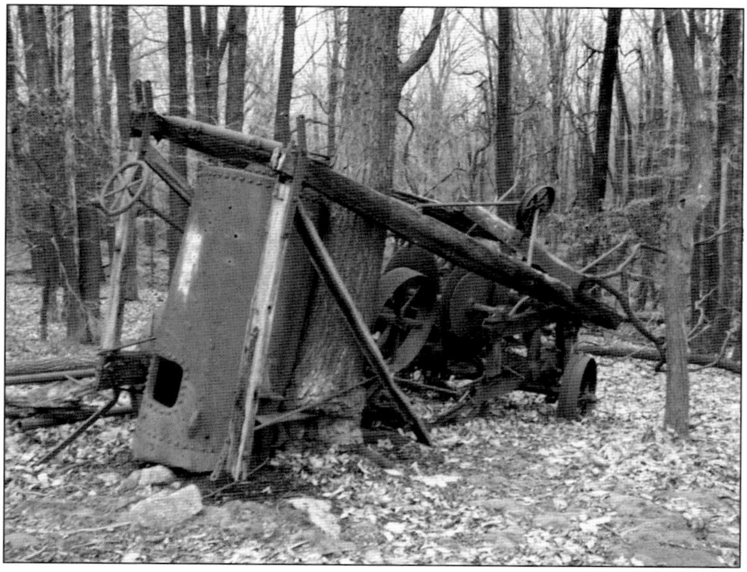

This awkward-looking old-time steam engine sat at the top of the old Garocii stone quarry on the hill to the east, opposite the Empire Tunnel. Stones from the quarry were hauled down a steep switchback to the Garocii stone crusher at the base of the hill. Again, it is speculated that the operation started around 1907, when cut stones were needed to build the Empire Tunnel. (David Keith.)

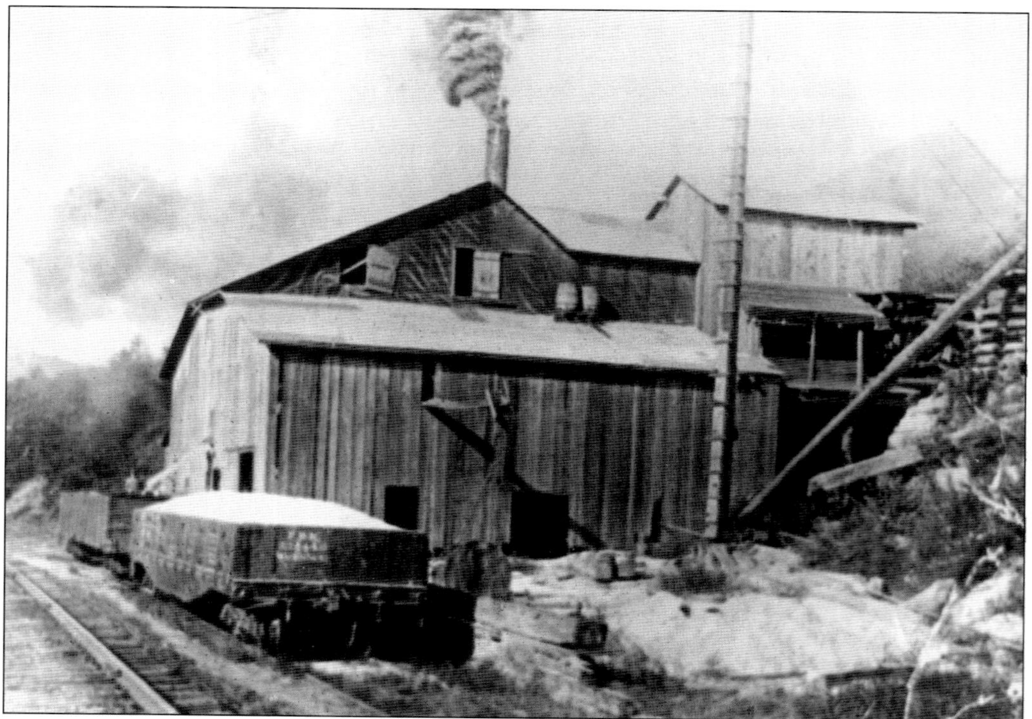

The Garocii stone crusher was owned by Joseph, Benjamin, and Andrew Urmann and operated under the name Ridgway Croyland Silica Sand Company of Ridgway. The foundation for the stone crusher building still stands along the Clarion–Little Toby Rail Trail. Multiple foundations surrounding the stone crusher indicate a sizeable workforce was employed at the industry. A historic sign indicates that the operation ceased in 1929.

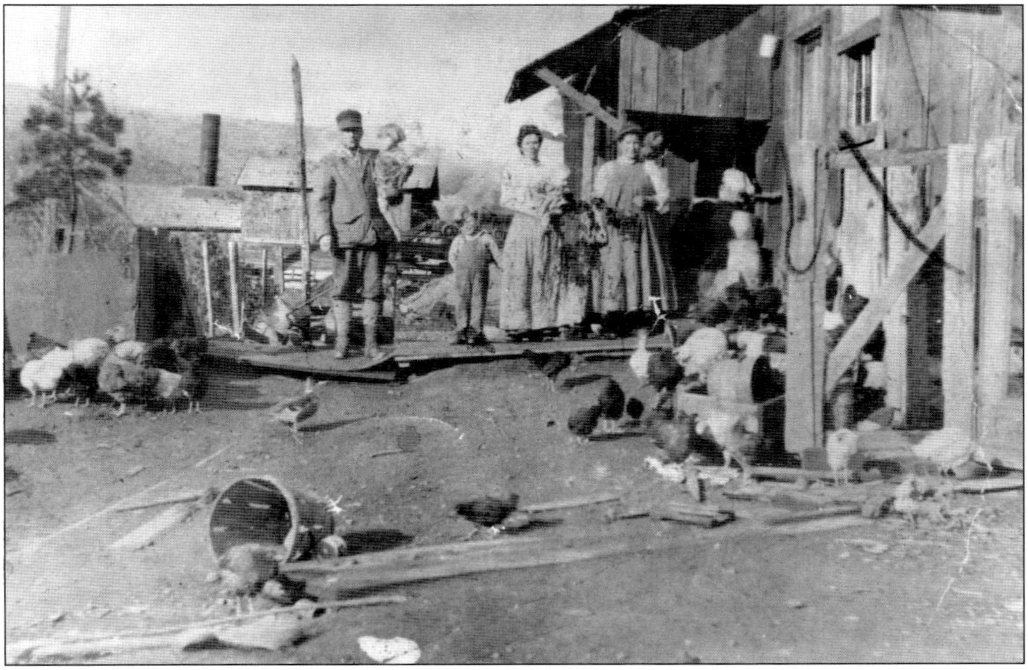

The Garda family was one of the families that called the village of Grove home. Grove's industries included the Garocii stone crusher, which can be seen in the left background behind the Garda family. Grove also had a small depot along the Ridgway and Clearfield Railroad. Another industry close to Grove was Shorts Mills, a lumbering operation about half a mile south of Grove along Coward Run.

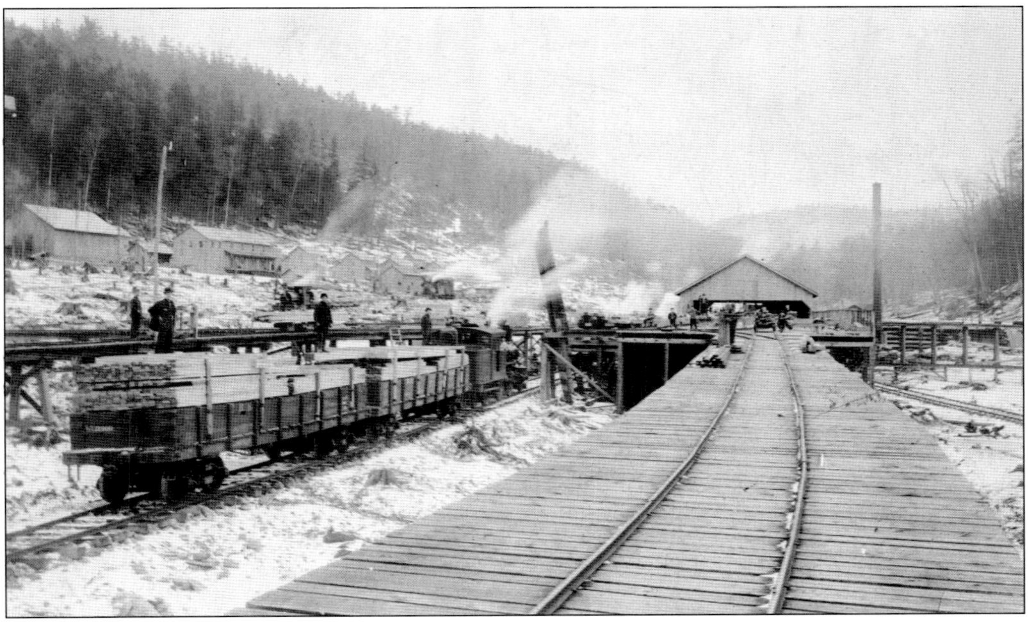

After the Portland Lumber Company finished cutting all its timber along Vineyard Run in 1895, it moved the mill equipment to a new location to the north and rebuilt the mill along Laurel Run. The site became known as Croyland, and several homes, a boardinghouse, and stables were constructed along the hillside above the mill. (Elk County Historical Society.)

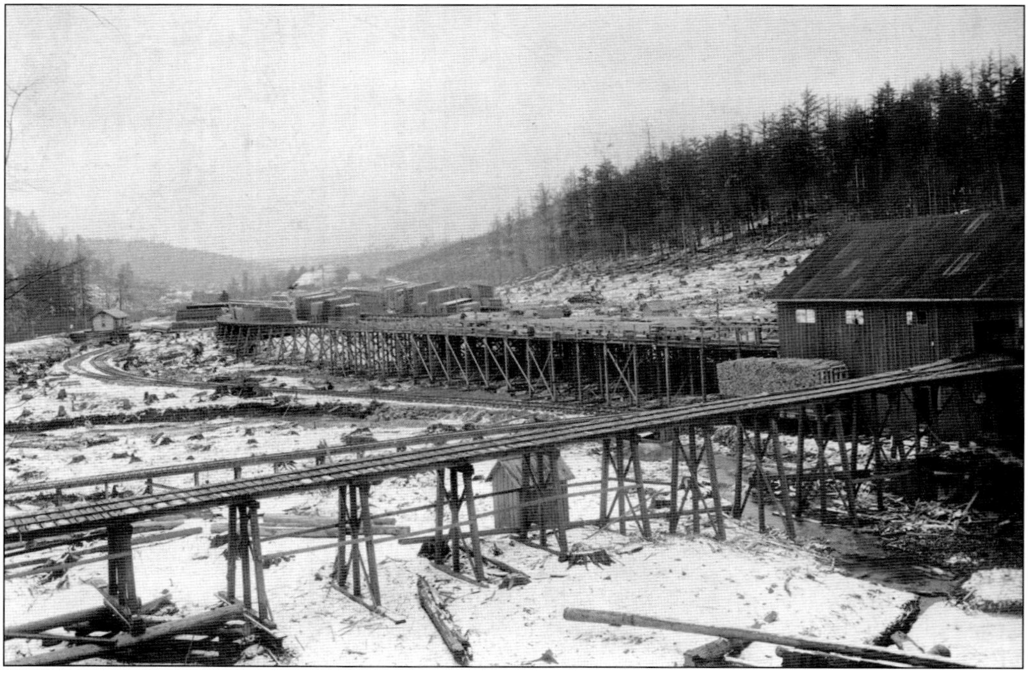

This view of the Portland Lumber Company Mill at Croyland looks northwest across the stacks of finished lumber. The small Ridgway and Clearfield Railroad depot is on the left. The mill at Croyland operated until late 1902, when the timber along Laurel and Belmouth Runs was exhausted. All remaining timber of the Portland Lumber Company would be cut at the huge sawmill at Portland Mills. (Elk County Historical Society.)

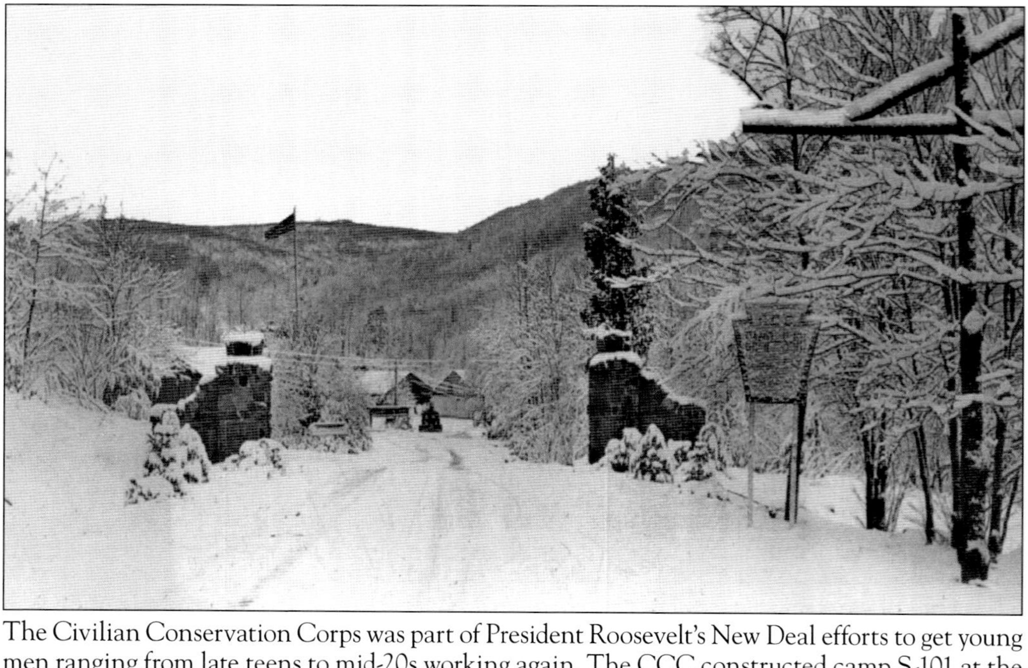

The Civilian Conservation Corps was part of President Roosevelt's New Deal efforts to get young men ranging from late teens to mid-20s working again. The CCC constructed camp S-101 at the junction of the R&C Railroad and the Clarion River Railway at Croyland in 1933. The stone entrance gates to the camp shown in the photograph are still standing.

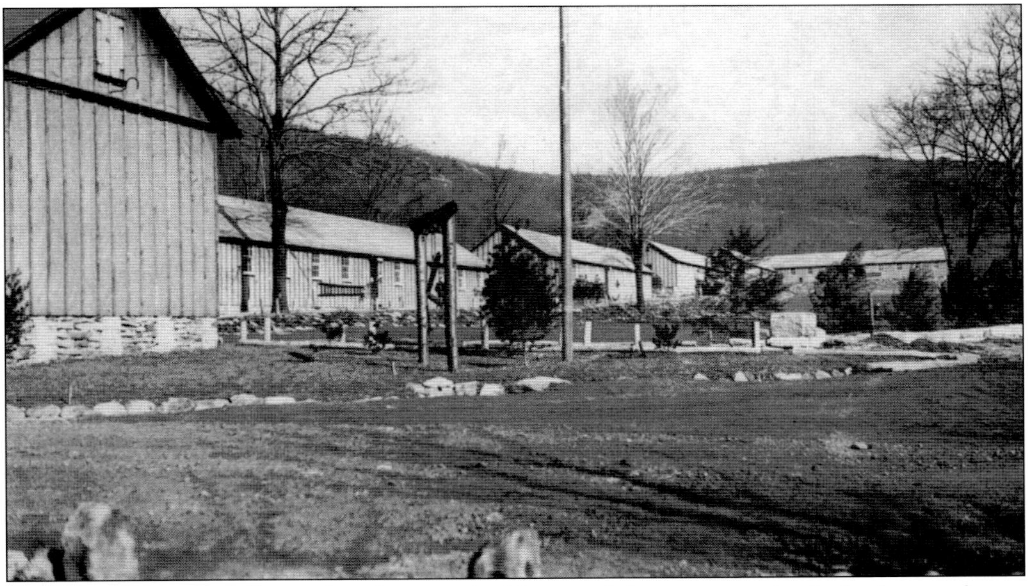

The building on the left was the education building, and the structures in the background were the barracks. The grounds in the middle were the parade grounds where roll call was made early in the morning. Enrollees would spend the rest of the day in the woods working on various conservation projects. At night, they would attend classes then wind down in the recreation hall behind the barracks.

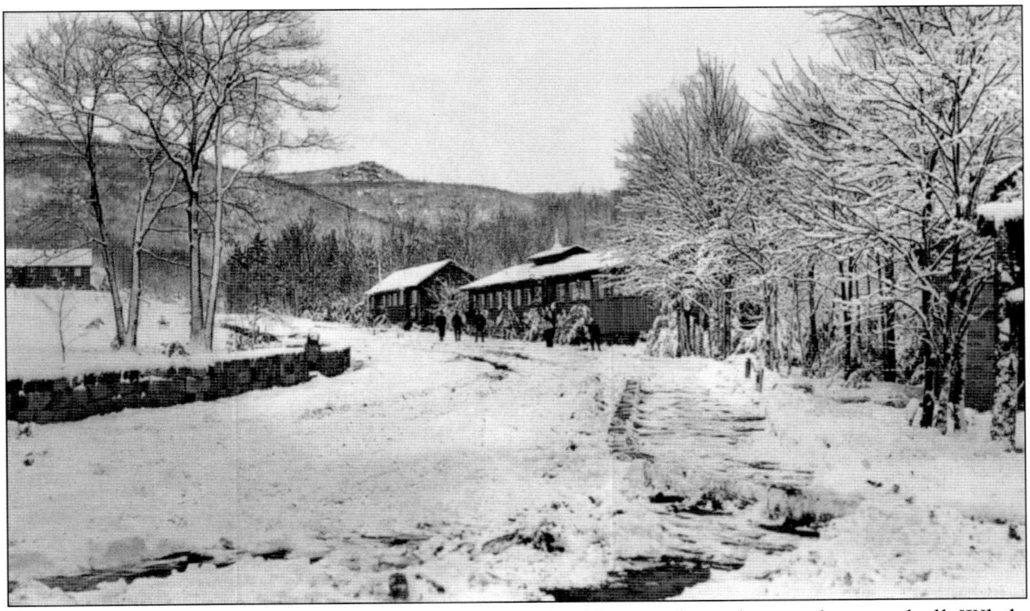

The left-center building was the infirmary, and the building to the right was the mess hall. While occupying camp, company No. 5446 constructed 25 miles of truck trails, 27 miles of foot trails, worked 2,000 acres of tree and plant disease control, completed 40 miles of roadside cleanup, planted 85,000 trees, and constructed 40 small dams and numerous feeding shelters for small game.

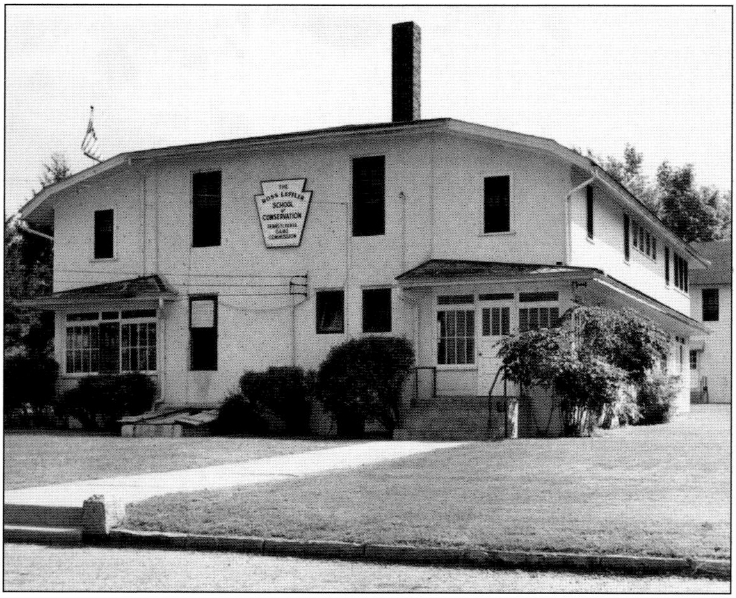

Other projects of the Croyland CCC boys included cleaning up the grounds of the Ross L. Loeffler School of Conservation, the first school dedicated to training Pennsylvania Game Commission officers. The school opened in 1936 and was highly successful, but after 50 years of priceless in-the-woods training 7 miles northwest of Brockway, the state decided to move the school to Harrisburg.

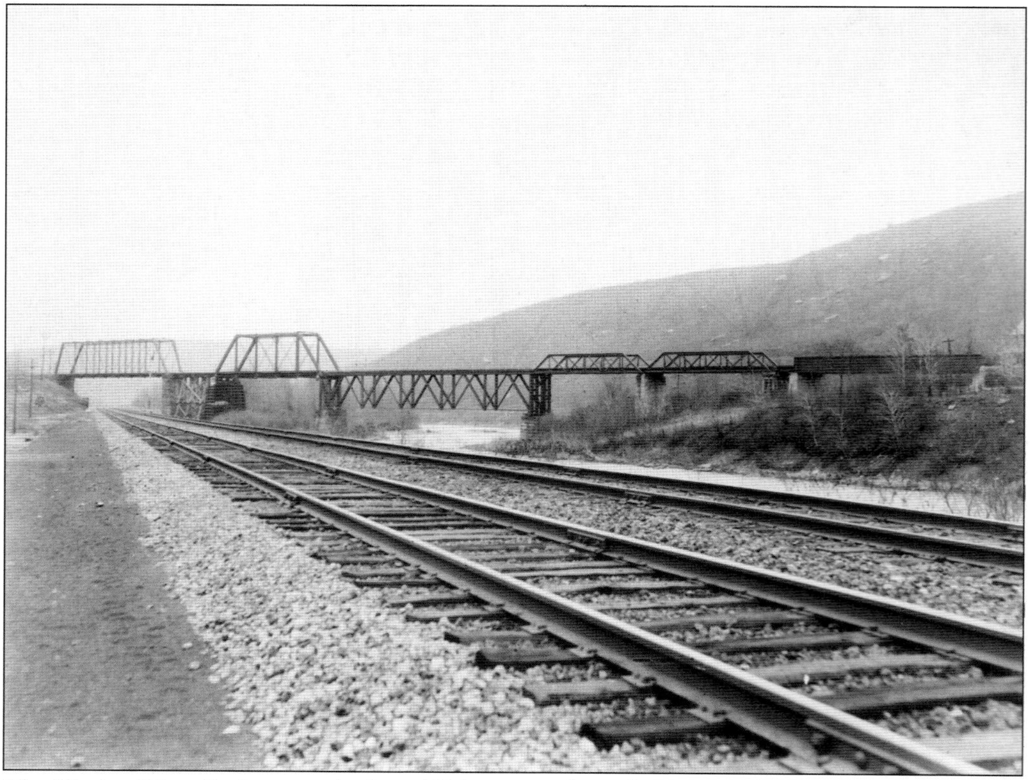

The Clarion River Railway was built in 1890 to serve the industries north along Little Toby Creek and down the Clarion River. It was built from Croyland and almost immediately crossed the Ridgway and Clearfield Railroad, Little Toby Creek, and the Buffalo, Rochester, and Pittsburgh Railway on this long trestle. Beyond the trestle was Carman, the last town along Little Toby Creek. (Elk County Historical Society.)

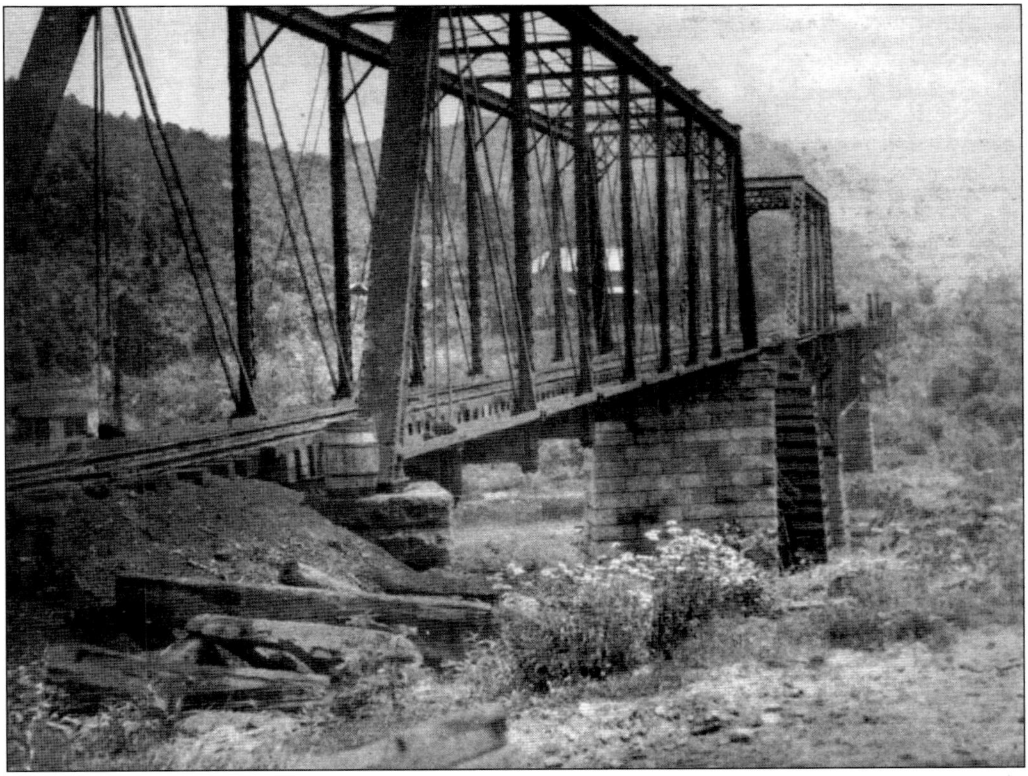

The Clarion River Railway connected with the Ridgway and Clearfield Railroad at Croyland, and the Buffalo, Rochester, and Pittsburgh Railway at Carman. It passed through Portland Mills, which had the large sawmill of the Portland Lumber Company, an Elk Tanning Company tannery, and a kindling wood factory. It spanned the Clarion River, passed through the tannery at Arroyo, and the lumber village of Irwintown along the way to Hallton.

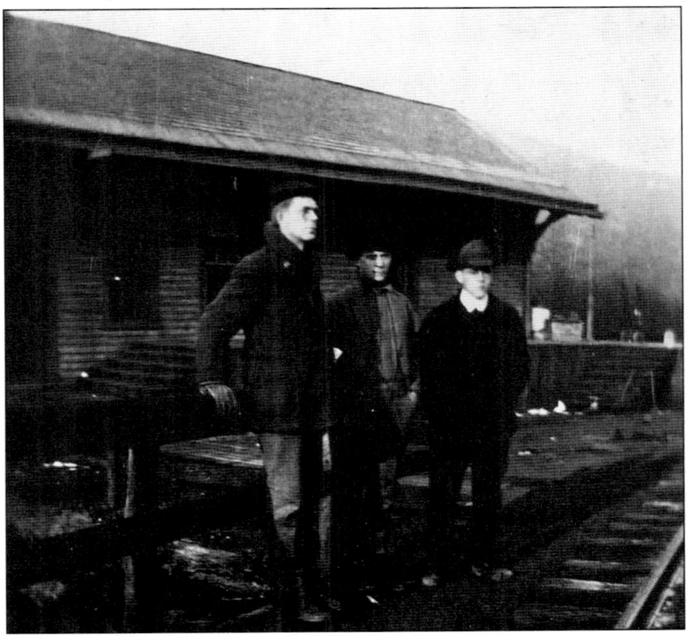

This small depot at Carman served the Buffalo, Rochester, and Pittsburgh Railway and the Clarion River Railway. The Baltimore and Ohio Railroad purchased the BR&P in 1930, which became the Clarion River Railway's only eastern connection. Freight could no longer be interchanged with the Pennsylvania Railroad at Croyland when the long bridge to the south of Carman was removed in 1939. (Elk County Historical Society.)

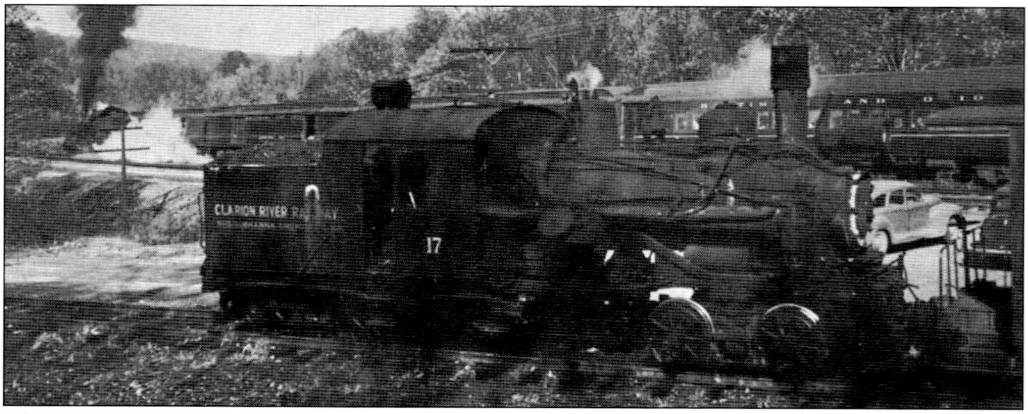

Clarion River Railway locomotive No. 17, a two-truck Heisler locomotive, waits for a Baltimore and Ohio Railroad passenger train to clear before picking up the freight from the B&O regular on October 27, 1947. It will soon make its trip to Portland Mills to pick up schoolchildren and to drop off the freight for the Clawson Chemical Company wood chemical plant at Hallton. (Thomas T. Taber III.)

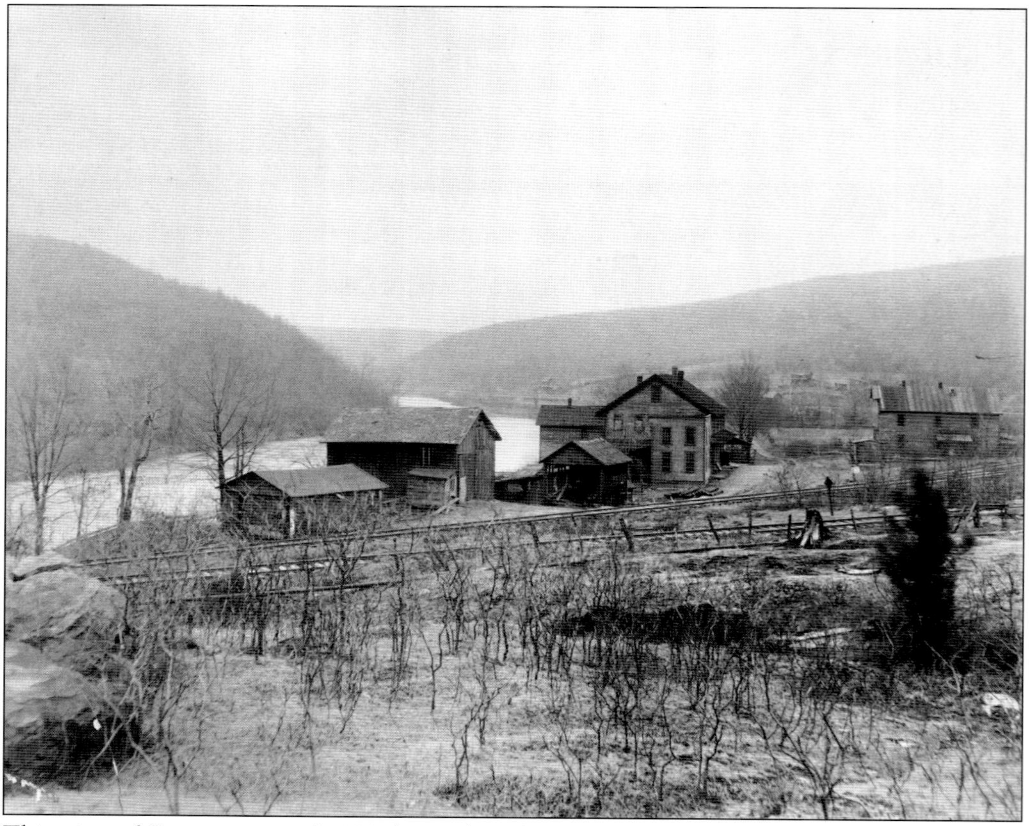
This view of Carman around 1920 shows the Clarion River Railway in the foreground and its connection with the Buffalo, Rochester, and Pittsburgh Railway to the south. The large building in the center is the Carman Hotel, and the old town store sat across the road. Carman had a sawmill and multiple other homes and farms but never reached a population over 100. (John Imhof.)

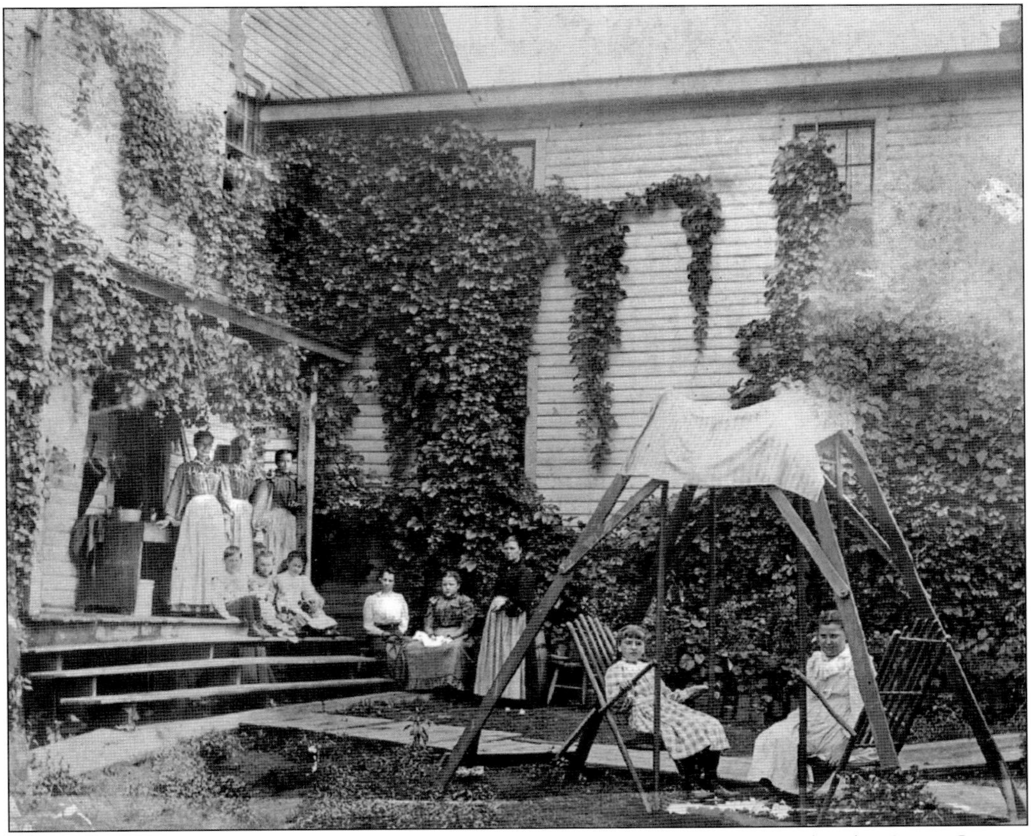

The Carman Hotel was begun in 1887 and was operated for many years by the Peter Gainor family, shown here with staff resting in the back. With the loss of the tanneries at Arroyo and Portland Mills in the 1920s, the Clawson Chemical Company plant at Hallton in 1948, and fires that destroyed the hotel and the store, Carman became a ghost town. (John Imhof.)

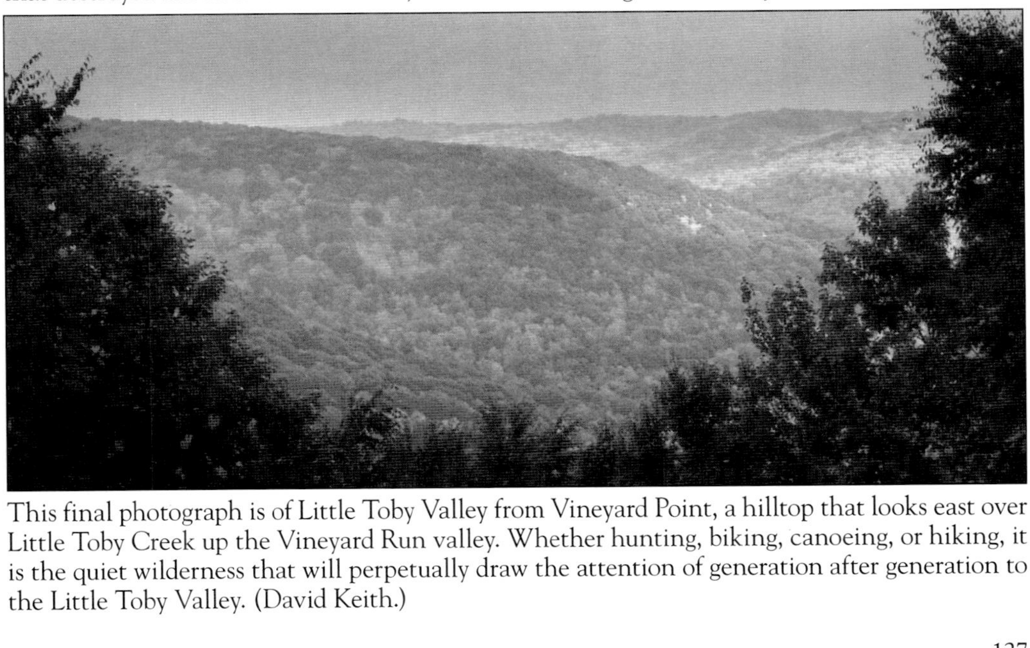

This final photograph is of Little Toby Valley from Vineyard Point, a hilltop that looks east over Little Toby Creek up the Vineyard Run valley. Whether hunting, biking, canoeing, or hiking, it is the quiet wilderness that will perpetually draw the attention of generation after generation to the Little Toby Valley. (David Keith.)

Find Your Place in History.

www.arcadiapublishing.com

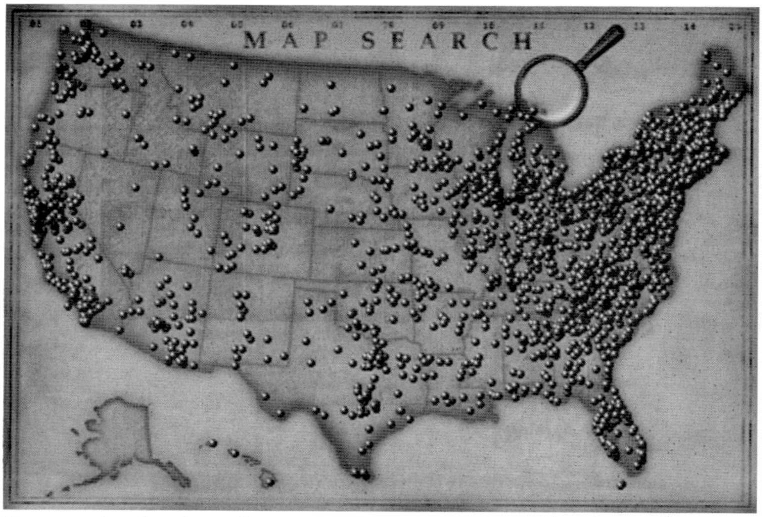

Discover books about the town where you grew up, the cities where your friends and families live, the town where your parents met, or even that retirement spot you've been dreaming about. Our Web site provides history lovers with exclusive deals, advanced notification about new titles, e-mail alerts of author events, and much more.

MADE IN THE USA

Arcadia Publishing, the leading local history publisher in the United States, is committed to making history accessible and meaningful through publishing books that celebrate and preserve the heritage of America's people and places. Consistent with our mission to preserve history on a local level, this book was printed in South Carolina on American-made paper and manufactured entirely in the United States.

This book carries the accredited Forest Stewardship Council (FSC) label and is printed on 100 percent FSC-certified paper. Products carrying the FSC label are independently certified to assure consumers that they come from forests that are managed to meet the social, economic, and ecological needs of present and future generations.

FSC
Mixed Sources
Product group from well-managed forests and other controlled sources

Cert no. SW-COC-001530
www.fsc.org